Sport in the Global Society

General Editor: J.A. Mangan

SPORT, MEDIA, CULTURE

SPORT IN THE GLOBAL SOCIETY
General Editor: J.A. Mangan

The interest in sports studies around the world is growing and will continue to do so. This unique series combines aspects of the expanding study of *sport in the global society*, providing comprehensiveness and comparison under one editorial umbrella. It is particularly timely, with studies in the cultural, economic, ethnographic, geographical, political, social, anthropological, sociological and aesthetic elements of sport proliferating in institutions of higher education.

Eric Hobsbawm once called sport one of the most significant practices of the late nineteenth century. Its significance was even more marked in the late twentieth century and will continue to grow in importance into the new millennium as the world develops into a 'global village' sharing the English language, technology and sport.

Other Titles in the Series

Football, Europe and the Press
Liz Crolley and David Hand

Sport and Memory in North America
Edited by Stephen G. Wieting

The Future of Football
Challenges for the Twenty-First Century
Edited by Jon Garland, Dominic Malcolm and Michael Rowe

Football Culture
Local Contests, Global Visions
Edited by Gerry P.T. Finn and Richard Giulianotti

France and the 1998 World Cup
The National Impact of a World Sporting Event
Edited by Hugh Dauncey and Geoff Hare

Scoring for Britain
International Football and International Politics, 1900–1939
Peter J. Beck

Shaping the Superman
Fascist Body as Political Icon –
Aryan Fascism
Edited by J.A. Mangan

Superman Supreme
Fascist Body as Political Icon –
Global Fascism
Edited by J.A. Mangan

Making the Rugby World
Race, Gender, Commerce
Edited by Timothy J.L Chandler and John Nauright

Rugby's Great Split
Class, Culture and the Origins of Rugby League Football
Tony Collins

Sport in Australasian Society
Past and Present
Edited by J.A. Mangan and John Nauright

Sporting Nationalisms
Identity, Ethnicity, Immigration and Assimilation
Edited by Mike Cronin and David Mayall

The Race Game
Sport and Politics in South Africa
Douglas Booth

Cricket and England
A Cultural and Social History of the Inter-war Years
Jack Williams

The Games Ethic and Imperialism
Aspects of the Diffusion of an Ideal
J.A. Mangan

Sport in Asian Society
Past and Present
Edited by J.A. Mangan and Fan Hong

SPORT, MEDIA, CULTURE

Global and Local Dimensions

Editors

ALINA BERNSTEIN
Tel Aviv University

NEIL BLAIN
University of Paisley

FRANK CASS
LONDON • PORTLAND, OR

First published in 2003 in Great Britain by
FRANK CASS PUBLISHERS
Crown House, 47 Chase Side, Southgate, London N14 5BP

and in the United States of America by
FRANK CASS PUBLISHERS
c/o ISBS, 5824 N.E. Hassalo Street
Portland, Oregon 97213-3644

Transferred to Digital Printing 2005

Copyright © 2003 Frank Cass Publishers

Website: www.frankcass.com

British Library Cataloguing in Publication Data

Sport, media, culture – (Sport in the global society)
1. Mass media and sports
I. Bernstein, Alina II. Blain, Neil, 1951–
306.4'83

ISBN 0-7146-5299-7 (cloth)
ISBN 0-7146-8261-6 (paper)
ISSN 1368-9789

Library of Congress Cataloging-in-Publication Data

Sport, media, culture: global and local dimensions / editors,
Alina Bernstein, Neil Blain.
    p. cm.
Includes bibliographical references and index.
    ISBN 0-7146-5299-7 (cloth) – ISBN 0-7146-8261-6 (pbk.)
    1. Mass media and sports – Cross-cultural studies. 2. Sports
– Social aspects – Cross-cultural studies. I. Bernstein,
Alina. II. Blain, Neil, 1951–
    GV742.S663 2003
    070.4'49796–dc21   2002151346

All rights reserved. No part of this publication may be reproduced, stored in or introduced into a retrieval system, or transmitted, in any form or by any means, electronic, mechanical, photocopying, recording or otherwise, without the prior written permission of the publisher of this book.

Contents

Series Editor's Foreword

Nietzsche once observed that there is no way of telling what yet may become part of history, adding that perhaps the past is still essentially undiscovered. In the index to J.M. Robert's recent *A History of Europe* there is no reference to 'media', the two references to sport are limited to 'pan-Hellenic games' and 'Roman games' respectively,[1] and while 'culture' is a little more generously considered with 11 references, there is only one reference dealing, highly selectively, with a single post-Second World War manifestation, namely 'international youth cultures in the 1960s and 1970s'.[2] In the postscript, 'Facing the Twenty-First Century', there is a fleeting and parsimonious mention of the 'influence of European games, arts and music the world round'![3] Clearly space is in short supply in a panoramic study of Europe from the earliest moments to the more recent moments, but the miserly consideration of modern sport in *A History of Europe* in the light of twentieth-century developments *inter alia* in the relationship between sport, media and culture, not to mention the evolution of these phenomena as individual manifestations, is surely a shortcoming.

Sport, Media, Culture: Global and Local Dimensions goes some way to repairing an analytical lesion in at least one major historical survey. Repair was required. The days when sport as an element of mainstream media attention was marginal are long gone. The populist celebrity cult with images of icons like David Beckham everywhere, the scandal of international match-fixing in cricket – that once most dignified of games (overlooking the self-serving behaviour of W.G. Grace, the brutal aggression of the odd Englishman in Australia and the occasional boorish 'pommy-bashing' of Australians in England) – the recent clumsy and careless financial mishaps of the world's first FA, earlier and recent political manoeuvres and machinations within FIFA, the odious publicity that trails in the wake of the IOC and, not least, the seismic eruption of Rupert Murdoch and others over the global sports terrain, have ensured the political, financial and cultural media 'headline' exposure of sport around the world. Shrewdly, one recent commentator on the relationship between sport, media and culture has as the subtitle to his book on the subject 'The Unruly Trinity';[4] the unruly invariably attract attention.

viii *Sport, Media, Culture*

Then there is the impact of new technologies on the relationship with far-reaching consequences for consumer involvement with the availability, processing and absorption of information in a plethora of new forms. Technological innovation is changing the relationship between public, sport, media and culture almost daily – for better or worse, depending on individual expectations, demands and responses.

As Alina Bernstein and Neil Blain state, therefore, with pinpoint accuracy – the relationship between media and sport in the modern global culture is a story that, to use an appropriate metaphor in this sporting context, will run and run. One admirable virtue of *Sport, Media, Culture* is that it provides a detailed consideration of their enmeshed relationship in Europe and beyond Europe which compensates for superficial considerations such as those of Roberts. It makes the sound argument that sport in the contemporary world – east, west, north and south – is a primary cultural force and the further argument that the growth of modern sport is most satisfactorily understood only when sport, media, culture, economics and ideology are all born in mind. This is a sensible assertion that adds width to more narrow analyses. Future, general surveys of the modern world will hardly be thought complete without a proper consideration of sport, culture and media with their varied, inescapable and powerful impact. 'The unruly trinity of sport, culture and the media is not, like its spiritual counterpart, three facets of the same, stable entity. Instead, it is a more dynamic metaphor of contested power and protean forms.'[5]

For this reason alone the plea in *Sport, Media, Culture* to bring together *in all their complexity*, sport, culture, economics, ideology and technology in any adequate attempt to comprehend the contemporary significance of sport in the 'global village' is well made.

J.A. Mangan
International Research Centre for Sport, Socialisation, Society
University of Strathclyde
October 2002

NOTES

1. See J.M. Roberts, *A History of Europe* (Oxford: Helicon, 1995), p.622.
2. Ibid., p.596.
3. Ibid., p.580.
4. D. Rowe, *Sport, Culture and the Media: The Unruly Trinity* (Buckingham: Open University Press, 1999).
5. Rowe, *Sport, Culture and the Media*, p.171.

Sport and the Media:
The Emergence of a Major Research Field

ALINA BERNSTEIN and NEIL BLAIN

In the United States, according to Kinkema and Harris, 'there are occasions when as many as ten sporting events are televised simultaneously'.[1] Many recent developments within mass sport have been guided by economic considerations that can easily be traced back to the media, and especially television. Sport for its part has also transformed the media.[2]

The relationship between media and sport has become of particular interest to media scholars over the last decade. However, as sport itself has been of interest in a variety of other disciplines, the study of the ways in which media and sport interact crosses boundaries and can be found in literature concerned with the sociology of sport, history of sport, gender studies, cultural studies, journalism, leisure studies and beyond. For scholars interested in the media in particular, sport is important as a popular content of the media, which can also shed light on a range of related issues central to media studies. Much of the writing on sport and the media addresses general issues within media studies, such as the vast field of representation and identity (some commentators see sport's most important contribution to society as symbolic) and globalization, as well as aspects of the political economy of the media (here the focus may well be institutional or economic, rather than concerned with symbolic processes).

'Theory' as a category is addressed explicitly at the end of this collection. Neil Blain suggests some approaches to theorizing the relationship between the symbolic functioning of sport and the domains of culture, and of media culture in particular. He argues that the symbolic development of sport is most satisfactorily comprehended when culture, sport, media, economics and ideology are all maintained as strong terms in the debate. This is an argument against compound constructions that subsume sport beneath the enveloping category of media ('media-sport' or 'mediasport'). The argument that emerges at the end of this volume is that sport's dispersal through various zones of culture and modes of reception reconstitutes it as a primary cultural force, even if the media drive some of its central cultural and social roles. The rest of this introduction puts the broad field of 'theory' on hold to concentrate on some individual topics (where appropriate, in the context of their own specific theoretical dimensions).

There is a textual emphasis in the study of mediated sport that is in keeping with an emphasis existing in media studies in general. However, two further sub-topics of media sport have also been explored, albeit to a lesser extent. These are the media production of sport and the matter of audiences for mediated sport. It is important to stress that the boundaries between these three domains (textual, production, reception) are often blurred and although they can be discussed separately, the fact that they interact with one another in practice has been recognized in much recent research into media sport.

In this collection, three contributions address formal concerns in the televization of sport. Nancy Rivenburgh looks at recent phenomena such as 'plausibly live' television reality and 'remote production'. Raymond Boyle and Richard Haynes examine further recent developments such as interactivity. Hans-Joerg Stiehler and Mirko Marr consider the television rhetoric of national soccer games. Hugh O'Donnell looks in detail at an example of that under-analyzed sport medium, radio, considering structural and discursive aspects of a football phone-in.

Three of these contributions also consider questions of representation and identity in sport. Overall, and despite the broad range of this collection, the sub-headings below are grouped around this very large domain of research; though the authors just mentioned, and Alina Bernstein's interview with Alex Gilady, also address economic and technological matters.

The categories explored here are necessarily selective. For example, we have not included a category on religious identity and media sport. In the context of countries such as Britain and France, analyses of Muslim identity and sport are still too few. This fact is partially redressed by Amir Saeed's contribution on Muhammad Ali and his Muslim fan base, which we refer to in more than one subsection below. We note that in writing about sport and the media, 'race' has figured particularly as an American theme. But while some of this race-based identity writing does indeed hold much relevance in the UK, France and elsewhere, the question of religion-based identity – especially Muslim identity – is at least as important where the development of British and French and some other European cultures are concerned. This is likewise bound to be of growing importance in North America and elsewhere. However, the current volume of writing associated with these themes determines the categories below.

STUDIES OF MEDIA AND SPORT: CENTRAL THEMES

The study of media and sport has developed mainly since 1980, flourishing in the 1990s. Over the past decade interest in sport in general and specifically its interaction with the media has grown immensely, as the long list of publications in this area testifies. There are many non-academic books in this area, including biographies and autobiographies of athletes like Michael Jordan[3] and broadcasters like Les Keiter,[4] and there are a variety of professional guides aimed at teaching the 'techniques, skills, and operations necessary for successful entry into the field of sportscasting'.[5]

There has also been a very rapidly growing quantity of academic writing. Many publications concerned with sport in general also include chapters focusing on mediated sport; a reflection on the fact that sport and the media have become associated to such an extent that it is often difficult to discuss sport in modern society without acknowledging its relationship with the media. Indeed, in recent years the study of media sport has become a central theme within the sociology of sport[6] and other books on sport generally also address the media.[7] For example, Schaffer and Smith suggest that the articles in their volume[8] 'blur the boundaries between sports and other forms of popular culture'[9] – they often engage with the media.

Toby Miller examines the way sport allows men and women (although mostly men) to consider their looks, vitality and their relationship to their gender in ways that would be taboo in any other context.[10] His discussion pays special attention to the way celebrity is constructed around the world and considers the role of the media in relation to the body and the nation.

Academic journals, often not especially focused on media matters, nonetheless feature articles about media and sport-related studies.[11] Recent media-focused books on sport suggest the range and

distribution of topics typical of the field, with production-orientated
work, textual analysis and audience-related research.[12] Much recent
research into mediated sport is concerned with the marketing and
commodification of sport; with media treatments of gender, race and
sport; with nationalism and globalization; and with violence, fandom
and audience experiences.

Multi-disciplinary approaches to mediated sport, such as Garry
Whannel's marshalling of media studies and sociological/cultural
studies perspectives, have been increasingly common.[13] Whannel
considers the ways in which masculinity and male identity are
represented through images of sport and sport stars. This historical
and case study-based book traces media narratives of sporting stars
from the pre-radio era to the present specialist television channels,
newspaper supplements and websites, exploring a range of masculine
types, from muscular Christians to 'New Lads'. In his contribution to
the present collection, Whannel argues that, in an era in which both
moralities and masculinities are perceived by many to be in crisis, sport
holds a central place in contemporary culture and sports stars become
the focal point of discourses of masculinity and morality.

Boyle and Haynes' recent book synthesizes a slightly different series
of subject approaches in an analytical account of how the media have
come to exercise considerable domination over how sport is organized,
performed and regarded.[14] The strand of media studies that
investigates the business dimension of the media is a prominent feature
of their work, which examines themes such as the function of sport as
a central media content provider and sport's relationships with
sponsorship. Their account is broadly based, marrying textual,
theoretical and political-economic dimensions.

In the present collection Boyle and Haynes juxtapose a number of
developments in the technology and delivery of sports content in the
media with considerations both of the commercial drives behind sport
and also the cultural importance of sport as 'a rich arena of myth,
image, narrative and a compulsive world of story-telling'. Their themes
articulate a growing concern that the values of business, especially
international conglomerate business, in both cases often closely
associated with the media development of sport, sit very uneasily
beside traditional sporting values; just as the globalizing world of
conglomerate sport presents challenges to its local dimensions.
Rivenburgh's analysis in this collection (further discussed below) of

recent transformations in the nature of media and business relationships with the Olympic Games, raises the possibility that the Olympics may have become subordinate to the larger advertising and entertainment industry.

Alina Bernstein's interview with Alex Gilady is a point of view from a media executive who has played the most central of roles in the international televization of sport. The concerns expressed by Boyle, Haynes and Rivenburgh are not his. On the assumption that it is good for academic writers to engage with views from the industry, the interview with Gilady presents an especially forceful view of the logic of a commercial, globalizing approach to television sport. Gilady puts a number of topics into an interesting alternative perspective. When asked, for example, about Britain's Channel Four's attempts to generate interest in American football, Gilady observes 'Leave it, that is a negligible sort of rating, all of Channel 4 is negligible'. When asked about minority sports on television, his judgement is that 'Most sports are not interesting ... The amount of sports that are attractive to both the advertisers and the viewers is very small, very small'.

It has been a significant feature of the growth of academic study of the media that despite often quite well-developed links between academics and media professionals there often remains a large gulf between the values expressed by each party. The interview with Alex Gilady is an important statement from a sports media entrepreneur, which represents the view from the world of market forces. If it jars with some other contributions in this volume, well and good, because the existence of dissonant values at the heart of the media-sport relationship is to an extent the concern of nearly every contribution here.

GENDER, MEDIA AND SPORT

The notion that in sport, physical and biological differences interact with social and cultural assumptions about gender has been central to many publications within the sociology of sport.[15] In recent years numerous publications have explored the role of the media in this context. Feminist writers, in particular, clearly agree that the media play a central ideological role, not only in 'reflecting', but also reinforcing, existing ideas about gender.

That 'gender' has chiefly meant a focus on women should come as no surprise. It is 'consistent with the lack of attention paid to other dominant groups'.[16] This is also true for the discussion of race (see below), which devotes relatively little attention to whites and whiteness. However, more recently, in the instance of gender, the study of men and masculinity has emerged although it is still clearly influenced by feminist thought (see below).

Women, Media and Sport

A feminist critique of sport emerged in the late 1970s and began to flourish during the early 1980s. Feminist studies of the time explored the sex differences in patterns of athletic socialization and whether sport as a social institution naturalizes men's power and privilege over women. They concluded that the marginalization and trivialization of female athletes served to reproduce the domination of men over women.[17] During the 1980s a dialogue between critical theorists in sport sociology and feminism resulted in recognition by some scholars that the concept of hegemony should be employed to analyze gender relations in sport.[18] A number of authors argued that perhaps more than any other social institution, sport perpetuates male superiority and female inferiority.

Interestingly, Dowling argues on the basis of research that women are as biologically capable as men of excelling in sports.[19] Over the last decades women have made many advances in organized, competitive, high performance spectator sport, particularly in Western societies and most clearly in the United States.[20] Feminist writers, however, argue that the media do not reflect this change and so inhibit sponsorship.

Existing work on women and mediated sport tends to focus on two main issues: first, the quantity of coverage; and, second, the media portrayal of women's sports and female athletes.[21] Recent edited books examining sport and the media tend to dedicate a substantial proportion of articles to these issues[22] and, as mentioned, related articles have appeared in academic sports journals, as well as journals with a feminist orientation.

Coverage

During the 1980s and most of the 1990s, research showed that the media persisted in covering mainly male athletes. A consistent finding is the under-reporting of female athletes and their sporting events throughout all mass media;[23] for example, in 1994 men were found to receive 93.8 per cent of coverage on US television.[24] Since the media are seen as helping to shape values,[25] this severe under-representation creates the impression that women athletes are of little importance in the sporting world. The claim that women tend to be 'symbolically annihilated'[26] is borne out by later studies, such as Koivula's exploration of televised sports in Sweden during 1995/96[27] and these findings likewise supported earlier studies offering similar indications.[28]

Yet some changes in the quantity of coverage of women's sports have been traced in major sporting events, particularly the Olympic Games: 'On its face, NBC's coverage of the 1996 Olympics seems balanced, with women receiving almost as much airtime as men.'[29] Among other findings Eastman and Billings also found that in the same summer Olympics, women's and men's events had virtually equal proportions of clock time and virtually identical numbers of medal events were covered.[30] However, in both examples, many qualifications emerge, for example over restrictions on the range of sports in which women seem ideologically acceptable.

Eastman and Billings argue that their results support the notion that NBC executives were concerned about the appearance of gender equity and that this concern certainly had an impact on some aspects of the telecast, namely those under their direct control, such as length of coverage and promos within prime time. They do however emphasize that, when it came to on-site reporters, the coverage was not balanced at all. Even in 1996 male athletes and men's sports continued to receive more salient coverage of all types than female athletes or women's events. Indeed, as both sets of researchers point out, the predominantly male identity of hosts, reporters and producers might be a primary cause of knowing or unknowing bias.

Women's tennis is one clear exception; a women's event to which television dedicates much airtime. In 1999, for instance, the American cable channel HBO devoted an unprecedented 70 per cent of its coverage to this sport.[31]

The Media Portrayal of Female Athletes in Women's Sports

Numbers (such as hours of coverage) are not the only important issue to consider in the context of women and mediated sport. Qualitative differences also occur although explanations as to how and why this happens vary.

Sabo and Curry Jansen argue that 'the skills and strengths of women

athletes are often devalued in comparison to cultural standards linked
to dominant standards of male athletic excellence, which emphasize the
cultural equivalents of hegemonic masculinity: power, self-control,
success, agency, and aggression'.[32] Furthermore, whereas male athletes
are 'valorized, lionized, and put on cultural pedestals'[33] female athletes
are infantilized by sport commentators who refer to them as 'girls' or
'young ladies' – male athletes are 'men'. Messner, Duncan and Jensen
found that commentators referred to female tennis players by their first
names 52.7 per cent of the time and to men only 7.8 per cent of the
time. While male athletes tended to be described in terms of strengths
and success, female athlete's physical strengths were often neutralized
by ambivalent language.[34]

Furthermore, while the male performance is often linked with
power metaphors (like war) the coverage of female athletes is often
framed within stereotypes that emphasize their appearance and
attractiveness rather than athletic skill. The media tend to focus on
female athletes as sexual beings rather than serious performers.[35] It is
argued that the sexualization of female athletes trivializes them and
robs them of athletic legitimacy. In their study of the 1996 Olympics,
Eastman and Billings found that although the presence of gender
stereotyping was not as overwhelming as expected, nonetheless 'as
traditional gender stereotyping suggests, the descriptors applied to
women athletes contained more commentary about physical
appearance than the descriptors applied to men athletes'[36] and 'what
can be labeled unfortunate stereotyping crept into the appearance
descriptors'[37] in the network's pre-produced profiles. Further studies
have focused on different practices through which the media construct
female athleticism as not only 'other than', but as 'lesser than' the
male's.[38]

More recently, however, Eastman and Billings noted that the
network's 'hosts and on-site reporters were careful to attribute
women's successes and failures to the same characteristics as men's
successes and failures'.[39] According to Jones, Murrell and Jackson, in
their study of the 1996 Olympic Games, for female athletes playing
'female-appropriate' sports, there was a trend toward print media
accounts that focused more on describing their performance than
personality or appearance.[40] Then again, Koivula's study is less
positive[41] and Jones, Murrell and Jackson's findings indicate that the
'beauty' and 'grace' of the female gymnasts were still the main point of

emphasis, despite the US taking gold in the event.[42] In his study of the representation of women in football-related stories during the course of the 1996 European Championships in the British popular press, Harris writes that the message that is still being portrayed to women and young girls is that sport is an essentially male activity in which women are afforded only subordinate and/or highly sexualized roles.[43]

Based on their analysis of television coverage of the first Women's National Basketball Association season in 1997, Stanley Wearden and Pamela Creedon's contribution to the present volume finds mixed messages in the account offered by television advertising. Although they detect some movement toward a greater number of non-stereotypical images of women in some product categories than in earlier studies, this finding is complicated by the fact that 'a new form of ghettoization' of women could be underway whereby strong or powerful women may be imaged in the context of sport, while in other areas of life women are expected to behave within the limits of traditional ideologies. While pilot work on commercials for the 2000 season seemed to indicate a slow progressive shift, the overall sense that emerges from their study is of a continuing restriction in the way that women are imaged in sport culture.

Some women are scarcely portrayed at all. Rinella Cere has had to engage in detective work to try to uncover the nature of the female Italian *ultrà* soccer fan for this collection. Her analysis has required her to probe both widely and deeply to try to elicit data on a sizeable phenomenon of considerable cultural and sociological interest. 'Women's *ultrà* support is practically invisible in the mass media, rarely are they discussed in the sports pages of the national newspapers or even in the three sport-dedicated dailies available in Italy'. This is equally true of both radio and television, despite the fact that women now increasingly present sport programmes in Italy. It is not only in the media, but also in some academic literature that Cere detects a process of suppression. Her account therefore not only raises questions about patterns of representation in sport, but also revisits a broader epistemological question in the social sciences about the values that preside over the construction of knowledge.

Men and Sport

It can still be argued that the hegemonic form of masculinity (which provides normative attributes against which other forms of masculinity are measured) still means to a great extent avoiding 'feminine behaviour' by focusing on success, being emotionally distant and taking risks.[44] It has been argued that the 'study of masculinity inevitably leads us back to issues of femininity and sexual orientations and the links between gender, and race, class and national identity, to the construction of individual subjectivities'.[45] Sport has been viewed by some as one of men's last 'chances' to escape from the growing ambiguity of masculinity in daily life.[46]

Burstyn notes the centrality of professional sports in popular culture in industrial countries, especially 'men's culture'.[47] Sport in her account is something around which men gather regularly to celebrate exaggerated forms of masculinity ('hypermasculinity'). Offering a critical history of the institutionalization of sport in schools and in male popular culture in the nineteenth and early twentieth centuries, Burstyn also addresses the developing interaction between (male) professional sports and the mass media.

Indeed, over recent years some scholars have addressed sport as a male preserve and a source of the production and reproduction of masculine identity. McKay, Messner and Sabo consider three central questions:[48]

- How can the study of masculinities in sport be integrated with critical feminist studies?
- How can researchers deal with the tendency in critical sport sociology to over-emphasize negative outcomes? And,
- How can the study of masculinity and gender best be consolidated with analyses of race and ethnicity, social class and sexual orientation?

Men, Masculinity, Media and Sport

Sabo and Curry Jansen observed a decade ago that although 'masculinity and sport have been culturally equated in the United States there is strangely very little research into this area'.[49] In the literature that does exist it has been noted that the sports media concentrate on success stories about men and, more specifically, on the theme of fighting back from adversity, like injury or drug addiction.[50] Indeed, 'the media do not ordinarily focus on men who fail to measure up in sports or life'.[51]

When male athletes fall from grace the coverage becomes a site for testing the challenges a fallen hero poses to the legitimacy of dominant cultural values. However, 'the net effect of the extended coverage is to rescue hegemonic masculinity by framing the transgressor as an anomaly, whether as a cheat, an impostor, a tragic victim of flawed judgment, or a compulsive personality'.[52] After the American basketball player Irwin 'Magic' Johnson announced that he was HIV positive, the media coverage depicted him as 'Tragic Magic', flawed in terms of personal strength, 'accommodating' his female groupies and sleeping with (one) too many of them.[53]

It is similarly argued that sports programming represents male athletes in relation to 'competition, strength and discipline'.[54] More specifically, they tend to be described by metaphors such as 'pounds, misfire, force, big guns, fire away, drawing first blood, or battles'.[55] Indeed, Duncan, Messner and Williams found that whereas commentators described male basketball players as 'attacking the hoop', female basketball players 'went to' the hoop![56]

When discussing 'masculinities' in the plural, it emerges that non-hegemonic forms of masculinity tend to be marginalized. In fact, 'alternative or counter-hegemonic masculinities are not ordinarily acknowledged or represented by sports media'.[57] A clear example supporting this argument is the very minimal coverage awarded to the Gay Olympics. Moreover, the media tends to ignore the fact that some male athletes are gay.

> Violence on-screen, like that in real life, is perpetrated overwhelmingly by males. Males constitute the majority of the audience for violent films, as well as violent sports such as [American] football and hockey. However, what is being 'sold' to the audience is not just violence, but rather a glamorized form of violent masculinity.[58]

The concept of the male sports hero as a role model was brought into severe doubt in both the cases of Mike Tyson and O.J. Simpson. In the case of Tyson, Rowe notes that 'the economic structure and cultural complexion of professional sport interact in a manner that produces problematic forms of [especially masculine] sports celebrity'.[59] The case of Simpson again brought the problem of gender violence to the forefront of America's social agenda and also called the concept of sports hero into question.[60] Burstyn argues that the television coverage of professional men's sports offers an arena in which male athletes become public heroes, contributing to 'hypermasculine' variants of identity.[61]

Muhammad Ali, whose celebrity and symbolic operation are analyzed in this volume by Amir Saeed, embodies both a considerably more complex set of values and has in general – though, as will be seen, not always – enjoyed much more sympathetic treatment from the media than Tyson. Ali's significance for this collection lies in his high visibility within a globalizing trend affecting collective identity, specifically in relation to international discourses of race and religion. But 'Ali-ologists', as Saeed observes, rightly tend to see him as an inclusive figure. His symbolic operation has ranged very widely, not only within American culture and counter-culture generally but, as Saeed's account makes clear, across boundaries of religions, nations and cultures. Largely because of Ali's developed symbolic functioning, his mythic connection with the kind of masculinity represented by a Tyson or a Foreman has always been constrained: he has transcended this category effortlessly (he was sometimes constructed in the media as 'threatened' by the 'brutality' of boxing opponents).

Stanley Matthews, a strikingly different but symbolically potent sportsman, part of whose myth emerges from a clash between the values of the media age and an earlier era of sport, has been metaphorically important largely within national boundaries. But like Ali, Matthews embodies a complex range of values. Garry Whannel analyzes the attribution – some of it self-attribution – to Matthews of a particular form of working-class masculinity that, by definition, is seen as sufficiently lost in the past to merit nostalgia. As with Ali, it is difficult to separate the elements within the Matthews myth. Just as it is necessary to discuss the fact that Ali is a Muslim in association with the fact that he is a black American, Matthews' masculinity is hard to detach from his working-class identity or the presumed personal character of Staffordshire and the Potteries. In Whannel's account the construction, not least by the media, of the version of Matthews by which he is remembered, is thoroughly revealed.

NATIONAL IDENTITY AND THE MEDIA

The question of the role that the media might assume in the construction of collectivities, with specific focus on nations, has been addressed by several writers.[62] Dayan and Katz point out the importance of what they refer to as 'festive television', including 'epic contests' of politics and sports, most notably the Olympics, in the construction of national dimensions of identity.[63] They argue that national identity is a sense of membership, similarity, equality and familiarity, though they perceive these media events as portraying 'an idealized version of society, reminding society of what it aspires to rather than what it is'.[64] Other writing concentrates just as much on the adversarial mutual constructions of national identity in World Cup football.[65]

In their account of the media in Britain, Scannell and Cardiff refer to the nation as an abstract collectivity, which is 'too big to be grasped by individuals'.[66] The sense of belonging, the 'we-feeling' of the community, has to be continually engendered by opportunities for identification, for which the media are potent agents, sport providing important symbolic material for the facilitation of such emotions.[67]

The significance of sport's contribution to the development and reinforcement of national identity has been underlined by many writers.[68] If 'national identity' is a popular focus, 'nationalism' and 'nationality' are also sometimes accompanying, if not always specified, categories.[69]

'Athletes and teams become our symbolic warriors defending the honor of our schools, towns or nation.'[70] Sport is one legitimate arena in which national flags can be raised and other patriotic rituals exercised.[71] Norbert Elias notes that 'sport continues to constitute an area of social activity in which overt emotional engagement remains publicly acceptable'.[72] He further observes that 'a level of national sentiment' can be found in the sports section of a newspaper which is hard to imagine elsewhere. Anthony Smith points out that 'other types of collective identity – class, gender, race, religion – may overlap or combine with national identity but they rarely succeed in undermining its hold'.[73] It is worth observing that a few scholars extend this argument so much as to suggest that sport is in fact a substitute for war.[74]

International professional sport provides a compelling means by which 'the nation can be represented as positive and dynamic'.[75] This 'heady cocktail of sport and national chauvinism'[76] is not seductive to all sections of the population and in certain domains, such as the English tabloids, it can be unprepossessing.[77] Actually winning a major international competition provides a great opportunity for the nation to celebrate, though the role of such victories varies from nation to nation. O'Donnell and Blain point out that the French chastised themselves after winning the World Cup for lacking the right kind of national character to celebrate it.[78] Increasing attention has been conferred upon the role of national teams and their importance for national prestige, especially as the media celebrate nationalism and national identity when it comes to the coverage of sporting competitions.[79] Blain *et al.* concluded that 'the most universal form of expression we have found is the notion of the nation as one sentient being'.[80]

'Sports have frequently been used to promote political socialization within countries and to establish prestige and power in international relationships'.[81] The Olympic Games have been the focus of much of the writing in this context and indeed, the link between collective identity and sport has been traced by some to the Greek Olympic Games. Since that time, athletes and teams have served as important sources of collective identity.[82] Much more recently, one of the first acts of Latvia, Lithuania and Estonia as separate nations was to establish Olympic committees.[83] Hosting the Olympics is a particularly potent sign of national success; the 2000 Olympics conferred upon Sydney (and, more widely, Australia) a confirmation of grand assessments of progress.[84]

Despite their potential for producing discourses and imagery of internationalism,[85] large sports events like the Olympics also serve as occasions for national 'flag-waving'.[86] Tomlinson proposes that large-scale international sporting events embody fundamental tensions seen in bodies such as the International Olympic Committee (IOC),[87] seeking to represent their events as catalysts to international understanding, but at the same time producing platforms for 'the public fanning of nationalist sentiments'.[88] Tomlinson suggests a colourful metaphor: it is 'as if nations wanted to reach out to each other for a handshake, while simultaneously puffing out their chests in self-satisfaction'.[89]

Media coverage of international sports gatherings sometimes promotes them as a form of war.[90] Despite the Olympic Opening Ceremony's showcasing of rituals and icons meant to symbolize peace, friendship and international community, its structure and design also promote a nationalistic perspective.[91] Erikson actually views this as a stylized introduction to a metaphorical war between nation-states,[92] while Moragas Spa *et al.* believe that, 'at the very least, participation in the Olympics is seen as a presentation of national membership, ability and identity in a global arena as expressed through athletic teams'.[93]

Images of Nations

Studies show that there is an extremely thin line between generalizations and 'crude national stereotypes'.[94] Moreover, 'stereotyping can make an easy transition into out-and-out racism'.[95] Blain *et al.* report the findings of a number of large-scale studies[96] of the images of nations through sports coverage in the European media.[97] In their studies of the press coverage of Italia '90 and the press and television coverage of Wimbledon 1991, Blain *et al.* found many examples of stereotypical images of nations and athletes who participated in these competitions. Furthermore, their interpretation of these findings holds that the behaviour of both the participants and their fans read like 'an index of the nature of national characteristics'.[98] They found that although the most extreme cases of stereotypical portrayal of 'other' nations could be found in the English popular press, other national media have their own versions of this tendency, a clear example being of the coverage of the German team in the 1990 Football World Cup.[99] Throughout Europe the team was found to be presented as the personification of 'discipline, dedication to work and reliability'.[100] They were presented as a 'machine team' and often in metaphors suggesting military character. The media were baffled if German players displayed 'flair' (a Latin quality) and concocted elaborate explanations of such inconsistencies.

As well national teams, individual athletes are often portrayed as representing their nation. Nowadays, top performers in the same teams may often compete against each other for star status and to enhance their earning power.[101] In the Olympic Games it might seem obvious that individual athletes 'play for their country', but even in clearly individual competitions such as Wimbledon national identity exerts an important role in the coverage, although it is less evident than in national-team sports.[102]

The national dimension in the sport-media relationship is discussed by several contributors to this collection, including Hugh O'Donnell (see below) and Garry Whannel, and it is present in the contributions by Nancy Rivenburgh and Rinella Cere, while the complexities of religious-national identities are addressed by Amir Saeed.

The contribution most emphatically focused on the national dimension is Hans-Joerg Stiehler and Mirko Marr's innovative account of media responses to the failures of the German national soccer team. Employing methods from the field of social psychology and basing their approach particularly upon attribution research, Stiehler and Marr pursue the thesis that in certain circumstances sport coverage exhibits 'pseudo-scientific', or what they prefer to call 'para-rational', characteristics, for which the focus on one's own national side tends to cause problems, compromising the desired appearance of 'objectivity'. They discuss data from World and European championships in 1994, 1996 and 1998 (adding some data from 2000) in order to analyze the institutionalization of communication about sport in television and examine the logic of media interpretations of sport results. Stiehler and Marr produce detailed data on both formal aspects of television coverage and the pattern of attributions that emerges amidst the desire to produce a coherent and simultaneously gratifying account of the national team's performance – not an easy task in the light of the German side's performances in some tournaments over the last decade. Underlying the media constructions is a shared sense of what the German national side is supposed to be good at (strength, discipline, team spirit) and a shared surprise at the under-performance of what is normally, inside and outside Germany, seen as a 'tournament team', supposedly stronger with every round.

Though Stiehler and Marr's analysis represents a groundbreaking approach to understanding sports culture, the domain of the national in writing about sport and the media is frequently addressed. We lack the space here to try and explore the relatively undeveloped field of social class and collective identity in sport, though some references have been made above (for example) to research on the English tabloids, which does foreground class. However, the contributions to this collection by O'Donnell and Whannel redress the balance by emphasizing the enduring class basis upon which sport in the UK requires (like the society and culture generally) to be understood, though both are careful to give due emphasis to a range of demographic factors.

O'Donnell's investigation of the themes and customs emerging from a popular Scottish commercial radio football programme – an address to a neglected area in literature on the sport media – uncovers a nexus of values associating class identity with masculinity and propriety, just as Whannel discovers in responses to the death of Matthews. O'Donnell notes a broad range of demographic characteristics in the cultural context and discourses of the programme, including religion, nationality, age and urban and rural provenances. His account ranges widely from the popular role of this and similar programmes to arguments about their political and democratic significance and the discussion is embedded in sociolinguistics, drawing a variety of international comparisons.

At the other end of the spectrum from this determinedly local media programme are the Olympics, as presented in this collection by Nancy Rivenburgh's study of 'media events'. It is the global reach of the Games on television that makes them so attractive to television conglomerates, sponsors and advertisers. Rivenburgh predicts that 'international mega-events', which she observes are phenomena that reach into other areas of provision well beyond sport, will in future multiply in the competition to achieve the status of 'global media event'. Citing coverage of the O.J. Simpson trial and world reactions to the deaths of Diana, Princess of Wales and John F. Kennedy Jr., Rivenburgh points out that 'the increased linkage and co-operation among international news organizations, coupled with a greater worldwide awareness of international celebrities and political actors, allow for media events to more easily emerge out of news coverage'.

RACE, SPORT AND THE MEDIA

The term 'race' is problematic, not least as 'there is little or no biological evidence to support the use of the term at all'.[103] In fact, it can be argued that 'there is no such thing as "race"', however 'there is racism'.[104] Put differently, 'race' is far from an innocent term; it carries much ideological weight.

The issue of race in relation to sport has been dealt with in academic writing since the 1960s, but has been most evident in the literature (mainly American) of recent years.[105] Several researchers deal with aspects of this issue, including higher education and the plight of black male athletes[106] and the cultural diversity on campus.[107] A special issue of the *Journal of Sport and Social Issues* has also focused on race and sport.[108]

It is important to emphasize that much of the discussion of race in the media studies literature that originates from Britain and the US refers to media images of black people, so much so that the term 'race' is often assumed to have restricted reference. Existing studies in the media field generally tend to look at the representation of black people in television texts, mainly 'in drama and light entertainment. There is very little information available on the coverage of black people in news, current affairs and documentaries'.[109] Much of this work has called attention to the ways in which black people in the media have remained largely invisible, marginalized to the point of insignificance, or have been limited to specific stereotypes.[110]

When considering the media's role in relation to race and sport, Sabo and Curry Jansen point out that:

> Media images of black male athletes are a curious confluence of athletic, racial, and gender stereotypes. The intermeshing of racial stereotypes with images of hegemonic masculinity, in effect, reflects and *reinforces* timeworn racist notions about the sexuality and masculinity of black men. It would therefore appear that sport media are complicit in ... the larger institutional and cultural processes that reproduce and exonerate white men's domination over black men.[111]

In 1992, Whannel noted that in Britain, 'the world of sport as seen on TV is a world in which ... blacks are not quite full-status Britons';[112] in the decade since, this has arguably become less of a concern. As with the discussion of the representation of gender and national identity, what transpires is that 'issues around media representation are fundamentally about power and status in society'.[113]

Commentators have noted the existence of a perception that blacks are good at sport because it requires physical rather than intellectual qualities.[114] Furthermore, when it comes to boxing in particular, the image of black boxers may be constructed in terms of 'brute animalism'.[115] Davis and Harris present an interesting discussion of the classic stereotypes of African-American athletes, including their stereotyping as 'deviant' compared with the stereotypes of African-American athletes who appeal to European-Americans, in L.A. Wenner's book *MediaSport*.[116] This is associated with black male sexuality being represented – at least in the US context – as dangerous.[117]

The Italia '90 Football World Cup provided the media with an opportunity to describe a successful African team. In subsequent years it became clear that the success of the Cameroon team was the beginning of the emergence of African football, which climaxed with the Nigerian team winning the football gold medal in Atlanta 1996. In 1990, the relative success of the Cameroon team was completely unexpected by the media, as indeed was the victory of the Nigerian team six years on. 'In terms of their football, there was, initially, a noticeable tendency to describe the Cameroon players by reference to European or South American stars, present or past.'[118] Thus, in accordance with this portrayal, the Cameroon player Omam Biyik was described as 'a black van Basten' and 'an African Pele'.[119]

However, this approach became one that highlighted the differences between African and European football and this was where the main stereotypes revealed themselves. The Cameroon footballers were described as 'joyful, uninhibited, enthusiastic'[120] and, like the Brazilians before them, they were also credited with bringing 'magic' to the game. Many newspapers regarded their play as 'temperamental', 'inventive', 'creative' and above all 'joyful'.[121] In extreme cases, the Cameroon style of play was presented as 'irrational', 'as befits children below the age of reason'.[122] Indeed, Cameroon were described as football's version of the 'savage infant'. Not surprisingly then, when Cameroon was eventually eliminated from the tournament, the coverage attributed this to the very same characteristics that made them attractive in the first place – 'their ingenuousness, their lack of professionalism and polish, even their lack of cynicism, in short, a style of football which had not yet grown up'.[123]

Large-scale research conducted by Sabo, Curry Jansen, Tate, Duncan and Leggett for the Amateur Athletic Foundation of Los Angeles analyzed seven televised international sports events occurring between 1988 and 1993:[124]

- The 1988 Olympic Winter Games;
- 1990 Goodwill Games;
- 1991 Pan American Games;
- 1992 Olympic Winter Games;
- 1992 Barcelona Olympic Games;
- 1993 World University Games; and
- 1993 World Track and Field Championships.

These seven events were broadcast on different television networks. Sabo *et al.* analyzed sport competitions, personal profiles and opening and closing ceremonies for their treatment of race, ethnicity and nationality and studied the racial/ethnic composition of broadcast images by commentators and interviewers. The results of this extensive study showed, on the one hand, that 'producers of televised international athletic events generally are attuned to issues of racial representation and cultural diversity' – a fact they attribute to some extent to growing awareness of related issues in the USA. However, while previously-documented patterns of media representation of black athletes were being addressed, they did find the treatment of 'Asian' athletes was 'biased'.

We should note that 'Asian' is a problematic term internationally. As Saeed *et al.* note:

> the term 'Asian' in the United States is usually associated with those of Far Eastern origin, for example with Chinese or Japanese heritage and not readily with South-Asian provenance [the Indian sub-continent]: this suggests an immediate difficulty with the term 'black' if applied to American Asians, a difficulty produced by specific social and cultural circumstances.[125]

In addition, the authors note that 'black' in some British usages incorporates 'Asian' Britons despite evidence of its limited use as a self-descriptor by British Pakistani Muslims and others.

In the American context, as has been noted, 'black' tends to have specific African-American reference. There were many interesting findings in the 1995 American research by Sabo *et al.*[126] In the vast majority of cases there were no overt narrative references to race although ethnicity was occasionally mentioned by commentators, especially when it was connected with some history of ethnic conflict. No evidence was found that commentators constructed negative representations of black athletes, rather black athletes were least likely to receive negative comments. Qualitative analyses of the personal interview segments showed that race, ethnicity, or nation did not appear to determine the types of stories or metaphors that producers and commentators used to portray athletes. Although commentators avoided making overt references to race in the case of black athletes, they seemed less constrained with Asian athletes and commentators often seemed to make a conscious effort to place Hispanic athletes in a favourable light. However, despite the high visibility of racial and ethnic minorities as athletes, whites held the greatest presence in the broadcasting booth.

It was observed in the opening section of this introduction that the 'race' focus of some American research has not been augmented elsewhere by enough research on the question of Muslim reception of sport culture, particularly in the European context. Saeed's examination of the Ali myth in this collection, as was noted above, addresses this under-investigated domain both autobiographically – in his consideration of Ali's role in his own Glasgow Muslim background – and also internationally (though Saeed also considers the question of boxing and 'race'). He poses a question that well conveys the complexities of racial and ethnic identities in the globalized world: 'How can a Pakistani family living in Scotland have such strong feelings for an African-American who specialized in a sport that had no real following within South-Asian communities until Ali's arrival?'

GLOBALIZATION, SPORT AND THE MEDIA

One of the central aspects assessed in the literature regarding globalization is the degree to which it is characterized by processes and tendencies that take place beyond the nation-state.[127] Some theorists acknowledge the evidence that although the state might seem redundant functionally, 'culturally and psychologically it remains of critical significance in structuring the political and social organization of humankind'.[128] We have already noted the centrality of national identity in the operation of sport as a symbolic system.

Given the multiple causal logics of globalization,[129] the media, though only one force among others at work, are central to any understanding of the process.[130] The spread of modern sport is considered to provide an interesting example of globalization.[131] In fact, sport sociologists entered the globalization debate during the 1980s, in other words from the very beginning of the concept's fashionableness among the social sciences in general. The discussion of global sport, which originates mainly from North America,[132] takes different forms and the various contributors explore many dimensions of the process.[133] As with the theorizing of globalization in general, this results in a range of literature, which is sometimes 'confusing, often contradictory, and always partial'.[134] Writers addressing the impact of global processes on sport may either emphasize globalization or processes such as Americanization, modernization and post-modernization, as well as cultural imperialism and cultural hegemony.[135] Wishing to clarify the issue of global sport, Harvey *et al.* developed a model of globalization that incorporates political, economic, social and cultural dimensions.[136] Their 'web-model' provides a theoretical framework to enable analyses of the influence of globalization of sport on national sport policies, taking into account the tensions between the local and the global.[137] One such example is the tension surrounding international sporting events that have become outlets for nationalism and where national comparisons inevitably occur.[138] Blain and O'Donnell have provided extensive theorization of the manner in which the local-global debate in sport belongs within post-modernism theory.[139]

For some writers sport falls more convincingly into the concepts of Americanization and cultural imperialism.[140] Much of the debate expressed in the literature on sport engages the issue of globalization versus Americanization. 'Arguments about the imperialist Americanization of sport have not been quite so straightforward as those for film and television because the product is not always so clearly American'.[141] This is illustrated by basketball, popular around the globe (although not everywhere), but not played in its American version in most countries. However, basketball is an example of American marketing headed by the National Basketball Association (NBA)[142] that led to world-wide interest in American basketball, the peak of which was the entry of the American Dream Team to the 1992 Barcelona Olympic Games.

The hypothesis of 'Americanization' in the sport context is problematic when considering that truly international sports like football (soccer) and international events like the Olympics and the football World Cup are not American,[143] but another aspect of Americanization has emerged in the literature, relating to 'corporate sport'.[144] This entails the notion that sport has become less important in itself than in its capacity as a vehicle for attracting massive audiences and, even more than that, that sport has come to express ideas about 'competition, excellence, corporate efficiency, and what it is necessary to do to win – ideas that have their origins in the United States'.[145] In this sense the American style of sport has become the international example for corporate sport around the world; offering 'show-biz' elements, the ability to attract sponsors and, not least, displaying telegenic quality. Donnelly concludes that 'Americanization as cultural imperialism has at least some explanatory power'.[146] Rowe also advocates that for global sport, Americanization and cultural imperialism make persuasive partners,[147] as do others.[148]

Globalization, Television and the Olympic Games

From their inception, Pierre de Coubertin intended the modern Olympic Games to take place on a global scale.[149] Over the years the Games were transformed into 'the most prominent regular global event of our times',[150] most of the transformation taking place in the last 20 years (during which time the soccer World Cup may have taken on greater salience for some television viewers). The current global status of the Olympics has been attributed to its media coverage, especially that of television and, more specifically, American television.[151] The most important factor has been the massive sums of money that have become readily available to the Olympic movement from American networks battling over exclusive broadcasting rights.

The IOC is an example of a non-governmental international body that influences and affects the making and changing of sport policies in different countries[152] and the Olympic Games have had a major role in the merger of professional and corporatized sport. This was underlined by rumours that the former IOC President, Juan Antonio Samaranch, had threatened to withdraw baseball as an Olympic sport unless American major league players were permitted to participate in the 2000 Sydney Olympics.[153]

We cannot address here a very large literature on the question of whether 'globalization' implies any degree of homogenization of cultural identities, though we might summarize very roughly by saying that while once the emphasis was on growing cultural similarity, now it is not. In the context of sport and in a comparative study of television coverage of the Opening Ceremony of the Barcelona Olympics by 28 broadcasters around the world, Moragas Spa *et al.* found varying local perspectives of the event. These local perspectives 'serve as an important reminder that local circumstances can greatly colour the experience of a global event like the Olympic games'.[154] The researchers proclaim their most interesting finding to be the fact that while the Opening Ceremony, and by extension the Olympics as a whole, certainly has a global character, it is the local dimensions that sustain the broadcasters' and audience's interest, that is, special attention to specific performers, largely to a nation's own performing athletes. This is in accordance with much audience research in media studies and with other evidence, such as the study of news.[155]

The sense of complexity and ambiguity that surfaces from the existing literature on the topic of globalization may result from the fact that this process is understood as being 'essentially dialectical',[156] in the sense that it embraces contradictory dynamics. Robertson has phrased this succinctly as 'the twofold process of the particularization of the universal and the universalization of the particular'.[157] In a media-saturated society, this process has become both rapid and self-aware, so that, for example, during the 1998 soccer World Cup, French newspaper journalists, invoking the character of other fans and their countries, offered their readers a variety of explanations as to why French fans were not ardent enough as spectators, including that France and the French were not underdeveloped enough (unlike the Paraguayans), not new enough (unlike the Croatians) and did not drink enough (unlike the Scots).[158]

As noted, several of the contributions in this collection deal with aspects of globalization. Bernstein's interview with Alex Gilady, Boyle and Haynes' analysis of the technology and economics of media sport and Saeed's account of Ali are all bulletins from globalized society as, perhaps most of all, is Nancy Rivenburgh's account of the Olympics. It is hoped that the international dimensions of the research in this volume do some justice to the scale of the analytical challenge that the sport-media relationship poses in a world marked – in its more affluent and settled sectors, at least – by more and more connection across a variety of boundaries, accompanied by a growing sense of struggle between the local and the global.

NOTES

1. K.M. Kinkema and J.C. Harris, 'MediaSport Studies: Key Research and Emerging Issues', in L.A. Wenner (ed.), *MediaSport* (London: Routledge, 1998), p.27.

2. See G. Whannel, *Fields of Vision: Television, Sport and Cultural Transformation* (London: Routledge, 1992); R. Boyle and R. Haynes, *Power Play: Sport, the Media, and Popular Culture* (London: Addison Wesley, 2000); R. Brookes, *Representing Sport* (London: Arnold, 2002).

3. D.L. Andrews, *Michael Jordan, INC* (New York: State University of New York Press, 2001).

4. L. Keiter and D. Christianson, *Fifty Years behind the Microphone: The Les Keiter Story* (Honolulu: University of Hawaii Press, 1991).

5. J.R. Hitchcock, *Sportscasting* (Burlington, MA: Butterworth-Heinemann, 1991).

6. A. Yiannakis and M.J. Melnick (eds.), *Contemporary Issues in Sociology of Sport* (Champaign, IL: Human Kinetics, 2001).

7. K. Toohey and A.J. Veal, *The Olympic Games: A Social Science Perspective* (Wallingford and New York: CABI, 2000).

8. K. Schaffer and S. Smith (eds.), *The Olympics at the Millennium: Power, Politics and the Games* (Piscataway, NJ: Rutgers University Press, 2000).

9. Ibid., p.15.

10. T. Miller, *Sportsex* (Philadelphia, PA: Temple University Press, 2001).

11. Such as *Journal of Sport and Social Issues* and *International Review for the Sociology of Sport*.

12. Wenner (ed.), *MediaSport*; Brookes, *Representing Sport*.

13. G. Whannel, *Media Sport Stars: Masculinities and Moralities* (London: Routledge, 2002).

14. Boyle and Haynes, *Power Play*.

15. See, for example, R.E. Lapchick (ed.), *Sport in Society: Equal Opportunity or Business as Usual?* (London: Sage, 1996), Part II.

16. J. Katz, 'Advertising and the Construction of Violent White Masculinity', in G. Dines and J.M. Humez (eds.), *Gender, Race and Class in Media* (London: Sage, 1995), pp.133–41.

17. D. Sabo and S. Curry Jansen, 'Images of Men in Sport Media: The Social Reproduction of Gender Order', in S. Craig (ed.), *Men, Masculinity, and the Media* (London: Sage, 1992), pp.169–84.

18. L. Bryson, 'Challenges to Male Hegemony in Sport', in M.A. Messner and D. Sabo (eds.), *Sport, Men, and the Gender Order: Critical Feminist Perspectives* (Champaign, IL: Human Kinetics, 1990), pp.173–84; M.A. Hall, 'How Should We Theorize Gender in the Context of Sport?', in Messner and Sabo (eds.), *Sport, Men, and the Gender Order*, pp.223–40; M.A. Messner, 'Sports and Male Domination: The Female Athlete as Contested Ideological Terrain', *Sociology of Sport Journal*, 5, 3 (1988), 197–211.

19. C. Dowling, *The Frailty Myth: Women Approaching Physical Equality* (New York: Random House, 2000).

20. Following Title IX – an amendment to the Civil Rights Act guaranteeing equal funding for girls and boys sports which became law in 1972.

21. P.J. Creedon (ed.), *Women, Media and Sport: Challenging Gender Values* (Thousand Oaks, CA: Sage, 1994) – still the most comprehensive work on this topic.

22. See Wenner (ed.), *MediaSport*; Brookes, *Representing Sport*.

23. See discussion in M.J. Kane and S.L. Greendrofer, 'The Media's Role in Accommodating and Resisting Stereotyped Images of Women in Sport', in P.J. Creedon (ed.), *Women, Media and Sport*, pp.28–44.

24. See M.C. Duncan and M.A. Messner, 'The Media Image of Sport and Gender', in Wenner (ed.), *MediaSport*, pp.170–85 – who also cite an Australian survey showing even less attention to female athletes.

25. Kane and Greendrofer, 'The Media's Role'.

26. G. Tuchman, A. Kaplan Daniels and J. Benet (eds.), *Hearth and Home: Images of Women in the Mass Media* (New York: Oxford University Press, 1978).

27. N. Koivula, 'Gender Stereotyping in Televised Media Sport Coverage', *Sex Roles*, 41, 7/8 (1999), 589–603.

28. Kane and Greendrofer, 'The Media's Role', p.35. See also R. Jones, A.J. Murrell and J. Jackson, 'Pretty Versus Powerful in the Sports Pages', *Journal of Sport and Social Issues*, 23, 2 (1999), 183–92; and Duncan and Messner, 'The Media Image of Sport and Gender'.

29. C.A. Tuggle and A. Owen, 'A Descriptive Analysis of NBC's Coverage of the Centennial Olympics: The "Games of the Women"?', *Journal of Sport and Social Issues*, 23, 2 (1999), 171–82.

30. S.T. Eastman and A.C. Billings, 'Gender Parity in the Olympics: Hyping Women Athletes, Favoring Men Athletes', *Journal of Sport and Social Issues*, 23, 2 (1999), 140–70.

31. D. Mackay, 'One for the ladies', *Observer*, 4 July 1999.

32. Sabo and Curry Jansen, 'Images of Men in Sport Media', p.176.

33. Ibid., p.174.

34. M.A. Messner, M.C. Duncan and K. Jensen, 'Separating the Men from the Girls: The Gendering of Televised Sports', Paper presented at the meeting of the North American Society for the Sociology of Sport, Denver, CO, 1990.

35. Kane and Greendrofer, 'The Media's Role'.

36. Eastman and Billings, 'Gender Parity in the Olympics', p.163.
37. Ibid., p.165.
38. See Kane and Greendorfer, 'The Media's Role'; B. Shifflett and R. Revelle, 'Gender Equity in Sports Media Coverage: A Review of the NCAA News', in Lapchick (ed.), *Sport in Society*, pp.237–43; Duncan and Messner, 'The Media Image of Sport and Gender'.
39. Eastman and Billings, 'Gender Parity in the Olympics', p.165.
40. Jones *et al.*, 'Pretty Versus Powerful in the Sports Pages'.
41. Koivula, 'Gender Stereotyping in Televised Media Sport Coverage'.
42. Jones *et al.*, 'Pretty Versus Powerful in the Sports Pages'.
43. J. Harris, 'Lie Back and Think of England: The Women of Euro 96', *Journal of Sport and Social Issues*, 23, 1 (1999), 96–110.
44. M. Kimmel (ed.), *Changing Men: New Directions in Research on Men and Masculinity* (Newbury Park, CA: Sage, 1987).
45. M.D. Kibby, 'Real Men: Representations of Masculinity in the Eighties Cinema', Ph.D. Thesis submitted to the University of Western Sydney, Nepean (1997).
46. M. Nelson Burton, *The Stronger Women Get, The More Men Love Football: Sexism and the American Culture of Sport* (New York: Avon Books, 1994).
47. V. Burstyn, *The Rites of Men: Manhood, Politics, and the Culture of Sport* (Toronto: University of Toronto Press, 1999).
48. J. McKay, M.A. Messner and D.F. Sabo (eds.), *Masculinities, Gender Relations, and Sport* (Thousand Oaks, CA: Sage, 2000).
49. Sabo and Curry Jansen, 'Images of Men in Sport Media', p.169.
50. See M.C. Duncan, M.A. Messner and L. Williams, *Gender Stereotyping in Televised Sports* (Los Angeles, CA: Amateur Athletic Association Los Angeles, 1990); Duncan and Messner, 'The Media Image of Sport and Gender'.
51. Sabo and Curry Jansen, 'Images of Men in Sport Media', p.178.
52. Ibid., p.178. See, for example, M.J. Sloop, 'Mike Tyson and the Perils of Discursive Constraints: Boxing, Race, and the Assumption of Guilt', in A. Baker and T. Boyd (eds.), *Out of Bounds: Sports, Media, and the Politics of Identity* (Bloomington, IN: Indiana University Press, 1997), pp.102–22.
53. D. Rowe, 'Accommodating Bodies: Celebrity, Sexuality, and "Tragic Magic"', *Journal of Sport and Social Issues*, 18, 1 (1994), 6–26.
54. R. Hanke, 'Redesigning Men: Hegemonic Masculinity in Transition', in S. Craig (ed.), *Men, Masculinity, and the Media* (Thousand Oaks, CA: Sage, 1992), pp.185–98.
55. Sabo and Curry Jansen, 'Images of Men in Sport Media', p.175.
56. Duncan *et al.*, *Gender Stereotyping in Televised Sports*.
57. Sabo and Curry Jansen, 'Images of Men in Sport Media', p.177.
58. Katz, 'Advertising and the Construction of Violent White Masculinity'.
59. D. Rowe, *Popular Cultures: Rock Music, Sport and the Politics of Pleasure* (London: Sage, 1995), p.116.
60. See Lapchick, *Sport in Society*.
61. Burstyn, *The Rites of Men*.
62. P. Schlesinger, 'Wishful Thinking: Cultural Politics, Media, and Collective Identities in Europe', in P. Rutten and M. Hamers-Regimbal (eds.), *Internationalization in Mass Communication and Cultural Identity* (Nijmegen: ITS, 1995), pp.29–41; J. Tomlinson, *Cultural Imperialism: A Critical Introduction* (London: Pinter, 1991); H. Van den Bulck and L. Van Poecke, 'National Language, Identity Formation and Broadcasting: Flanders, The Netherlands and German-speaking Switzerland', *European Journal of Communication*, 11, 2 (1996), 217–33; M. de Moragas Spa, N.K. Rivenburgh and J.F. Larson, *Television in the Olympics* (London: John Libbey, 1995).
63. D. Dayan and E. Katz, *Media Events: The Live Broadcasting of History* (London: Harvard University Press, 1992).

64. Ibid., p.17.
65. N. Blain, R. Boyle and H. O'Donnell, *Sport and National Identity in the European Media* (Leicester: Leicester University Press, 1993); H. O'Donnell and N. Blain, 'Performing the Carmagnole: Negotiating French National Identity During France '98', *Journal of European Area Studies*, 7, 2 (1999), 211–25.
66. P. Scannell and D. Cardiff, *A Social History of British Broadcasting* (Oxford: Basil Blackwell, 1991), p.319.
67. Ibid., p.319.
68. See, for example, M. Billig, *Banal Nationalism* (London: Sage, 1995); Boyle and Haynes, *Power Play*; M. Roche (ed.), *Sport, Popular Culture and Identity* (Aachen: Meyer and Meyer, 1998). For specific cases of Catalan Nationalism, Spanish Identity and the Barcelona Olympic Games, see J. Hargreaves, *Freedom for Catalonia? Catalan Nationalism, Spanish Identity and the Barcelona Olympic Games* (Cambridge: Cambridge University Press, 2000); H. O'Donnell and N. Blain, 'La Dimension Nacional en Barcelona 92: Las Identidades Catalana y Escocesa en Los Medios de Communicacion, *Journal of the Association for Contemporary Iberian Studies*, 6, 1 (1993), 42–53.
69. Blain *et al.*, *Sport and National Identity in the European Media*; Hargreaves, *Freedom for Catalonia?*
70. P.J. Creedon, 'Women, Media and Sport', in idem (ed.), *Women, Media and Sport*, pp.3–27.
71. Billig, *Banal Nationalism*.
72. N. Elias and E. Dunning, *Quest for Excitement: Sport and Leisure in the Civilizing Process* (Oxford: Blackwell, 1993), p.354.
73. A. Smith, *National Identity* (London: Penguin, 1991), p.143.
74. For a discussion of this in relation to the Olympic Games, see G. Whannel, 'The Television Spectacular', in A. Tomlinson and G. Whannel (eds.), *Five Ring Circus: Money, Power and Politics at the Olympic Games* (London: Pluto Press, 1984), pp.30–43.
75. Rowe, *Popular Cultures*, p.136.
76. Ibid., p.136.
77. N. Blain and H. O'Donnell, 'Living Without the *Sun*: European Sports Journalism and its Readers During Euro '96', in Roche (ed.), *Sport, Popular Culture and Identity*, pp.37–56.
78. O'Donnell and Blain, 'Performing the Carmagnole', 211–25.
79. Whannel, *Fields of Vision*, p.182.
80. Blain *et al.*, *Sport and National Identity in the European Media*, p.80.
81. J. Lever, 'Sports and Society', in E. Barnouw (ed.), *International Encyclopedia of Communication* (New York: Oxford University Press, 1989), Vol.1–4, pp.158–61.
82. C.R. Hill, *Olympic Politics: Athens to Atlanta, 1896–1996* (Manchester: Manchester University Press, 2nd Edn. 1996).
83. Whannel, *Fields of Vision*.
84. Rowe, *Popular Cultures*.
85. D. Whitson and D. Macintosh, 'The Global Circus: International Sport, Tourism, and the Marketing of Cities', *Journal of Sport and Social Issues*, 20, 3 (1996), 278–95.
86. Billig, *Banal Nationalism*.
87. A. Tomlinson, 'Going Global: The FIFA Story', in A. Tomlinson and G. Whannel (eds.), *Off the Ball: The football World Cup* (London: Pluto Press, 1986), pp.83–98.
88. Whitson and Macintosh, 'The Global Circus', 278.
89. Tomlinson, 'Going Global', p.83.
90. Billig, *Banal Nationalism*.
91. Moragas Spa *et al.*, *Television in the Olympics*.
92. T.H. Erikson, *Ethnicity and Nationalism: Antropological Perspectives* (London: Pluto Press, 1993).
93. Moragas Spa *et al.*, *Television in the Olympics*, p.144.
94. Whannel, *Fields of Vision*, p.30.

95. Ibid.
96. Blain *et al.*, *Sport and National Identity in the European Media*.
97. For further studies, see S. Wagg, *Giving the Game Away* (Leicester: Continuum International, 1995); R. Boyle and R. Haynes, 'The Grand Old Game: Football, Media and Identity in Scotland', *Media, Culture and Society*, 18 (1996), 549–64; Blain and O'Donnell, 'Living Without the *Sun*'; O'Donnell and Blain, 'Performing the Carmagnole'.
98. Blain *et al.*, *Sport and National Identity in the European Media*, p.57; Wagg, *Giving the Game Away*.
99. Blain *et al.*, *Sport and National Identity in the European Media*; S. Wagg, 'Playing the Past: The Media and the England Football Team', in J. Williams and S. Wagg (eds.), *British Football and Social Change* (Leicester: Leicester University Press, 1991); Blain and O'Donnell, 'Living Without the *Sun*'.
100. Blain *et al.*, *Sport and National Identity in the European Media*, p.69.
101. Whannel, *Fields of Vision*.
102. See N. Blain and H. O'Donnell, 'The Stars and the Flags: Individuality, Collective Identities and the National Dimension in Italia '90 and Wimbledon '91 and '92', in R. Giulianotti and J. Williams (eds.), *Game Without Frontiers: Football, Identity and Modernity* (London: Arena, 1994), pp.245–65.
103. D. McQueen, *Television: A Media Student's Guide* (London: Arnold, 1998), p.155.
104. T. O'Sullivan, J. Hartley, D. Saunders, M. Montgomery and J. Fiske, *Key Concepts in Communication and Cultural Studies* (London: Routledge, 2nd Edn. 1994), p.257.
105. See, for example, Lapchick (ed.), *Sport in Society*.
106. D. Siegel, 'Higher Education and the Plight of the Black Male Athlete', in Lapchick (ed.), *Sport in Society*, pp.19–34.
107. D.F. Anderson, 'Cultural Diversity on Campus: A Look at Intercollegiate Football Coaches', in Lapchick (ed.), *Sport in Society*, pp.35–41.
108. *Journal of Sport and Social Issues*, 18, 3 (1994).
109. T. Daniels, 'Television Studies and Race', in C. Geraghty and D. Lusted (eds.), *The Television Studies Book* (London: Arnold, 1998), pp.131–40.
110. See, for example, J. Tulloch, 'Television and Black Britons', in A. Goodwin and G. Whannel (eds.), *Understanding Television* (London: Routledge, 1990), pp.141–52.
111. Sabo and Curry Jansen, 'Images of Men in Sport Media', p.182.
112. Whannel, *Fields of Vision*, p.206.
113. Boyle and Haynes, *Power Play*, p.112, and 'The Race Game: Media Sport, Race and Ethnicity', pp.111–26; see also Brookes, *Representing Sport*.
114. L.R. Davis and O. Harris, 'Race and Ethnicity in US Sports Media', in Wenner (ed.), *MediaSport*, pp.154–69.
115. See Sloop, 'Mike Tyson and the Perils of Discursive Constraints'.
116. Davis and Harris, 'Race and Ethnicity in US Sports Media', pp.154–69.
117. See Sloop, 'Mike Tyson and the Perils of Discursive Constraints'.
118. Blain *et al.*, *Sport and National Identity in the European Media*, p.71.
119. Ibid.
120. Ibid.
121. Ibid., p.72.
122. Ibid.
123. Ibid., p.76.
124. D. Sabo, S. Curry Jansen, D. Tate, M.C. Duncan and S. Leggett, *The Portrayal of Race, Ethnicity and Nationality in Televised International Athletic Events* (Amateur Athletic Foundation of Los Angeles, Nov. 1995).
125. A. Saeed, N. Blain and D. Forbes, 'New Ethnic and National Questions in Scotland: Post-British Identities Among Glasgow Pakistani Teenagers', *Ethnic and Racial Studies*, 22, 5 (1999), 821–44.

126. Sabo *et al.*, *The Portrayal of Race, Ethnicity and Nationality*.

127. J. Harvey, G. Rail and L. Thibault, 'Globalization and Sport: Sketching a Theoretical Model for Empirical Analyses', *Journal of Sport and Social Issues*, 20, 3 (1996), 258–77. See also M. Featherstone (ed.), *Global Culture: Nationalism, Globalization and Modernity* (London: Sage and Theory, Culture and Society, 1994); J. Friedman, *Cultural Identity and Global Processes* (London: Sage and Theory, Culture and Society, 1994); R. Robertson, *Globalization: Social Theory and Global Culture* (London: Sage and Theory, Culture and Society, 1992).

128. A. McGrew, 'A Global Society', in S. Hall, D. Held and A. McGrew (eds.), *Modernity and its Futures* (Cambridge: Polity Press, 1992), pp.61–116.

129. Ibid.; Robertson, *Globalization*.

130. S. Braman and A. Sreberny-Mohammadi (eds.), *Globalization, Communication and Transnational Civil Society* (Mount Waverly, VA: Hampton Press, 1996).

131. J. Horne, '"Sakka" in Japan', *Media, Culture and Society*, 18 (1996), 527–47; J. Maguire, 'Globalization, Sport Development, and the Media/Sport Production Complex', *Sport Science Review*, 2, 1 (1993), 29–47; T. Miller, D. Rowe, J. McKay and G.A. Lawrence, *Globalization and Sport: Playing the World* (London: Sage, 2001); D. Rowe, 'The Global Love-Match: Sport and Television', *Media, Culture and Society*, 18, 4 (1996), 565–82; Whannel, *Fields of Vision*.

132. Harvey *et al.*, 'Globalization and Sport'.

133. L.A. Wenner, 'One More "-ism" for the Road: Dirt, Globalism, and Institutional Analysis', *Journal of Sport and Social Issues*, 20, 3 (1996), 235–8.

134. Harvey *et al.*, 'Globalization and Sport', 258.

135. Ibid., 259. For further discussion, see P. Donnelly, 'The Local and the Global: Globalization in the Sociology of Sport', *Journal of Sport and Social Issues*, 20, 3 (1996), 239–57; J. Maguire, *Global Sport: Identities, Societies, Civilizations* (Cambridge: Polity Press, 1999); Rowe, 'The Global Love-Match'.

136. Harvey *et al.*, 'Globalization and Sport'.

137. See also Whitson and Macintosh, 'The Global Circus'.

138. Donnelly, 'The Local and the Global'. See also Boyle and Haynes, 'The Grand Old Game'; Hargreaves, *Freedom for Catalonia?*

139. N. Blain and H. O'Donnell, 'Current Trends in Media Sport, and the Politics of Local Identities: A "Postmodern' Debate"?', *Culture, Sport, Society*, 3, 2 (2000), 1–22.

140. Maguire, *Global Sport*.

141. Donnelly, 'The Local and the Global', 245.

142. Rowe, 'The Global Love-Match'.

143. J. Sugden and A. Tomlinson, *FIFA and the Contest for World Football: Who Rules the People's Game?* (Cambridge: Polity, 1998).

144. J. McKay, G. Lawrence, T. Miller and D. Rowe, 'Globalization and Australian Sport', *Sport Science Review*, 2, 1 (1993), 10–28. See also, Rowe, 'The Global Love-Match'.

145. Donnelly, 'The Local and the Global', 246.

146. Ibid., 248.

147. Rowe, 'The Global Love-Match'.

148. Whannel, *Fields of Vision*.

149. Whitson and Macintosh, 'The Global Circus'.

150. Whannel, *Fields of Vision*, p.173.

151. Hill, *Olympic Politics*; A. Tomlinson, 'Olympic Spectacle: Opening Ceremonies and Some Paradoxes of Globalization', *Media, Culture and Society*, 18 (1996), 583–602; Whannel, *Fields of Vision*.

152. Donnelly, 'The Local and the Global'.

153. Ibid.

154. Moragas Spa *et al.*, *Television in the Olympics*, p.11. See also, A. Bernstein '"Things You Can

See From There You Can't See From Here": Globalization, Media and the Olympics', *Journal of Sport and Social Issues*, 24, 4 (2000).

155. See, for example, A. Cohen, M.R. Levy, I. Roeh and M. Gurevitch, *Global Newsrooms Local Audiences: A Study of the Eurovision News Exchange* (London: John Libbey, Acamedia Research Monograph 12, 1996).
156. McGrew, 'A Global Society', p.74.
157. Robertson, *Globalization*, pp.177–8.
158. O'Donnell and Blain, 'Performing the Carmagnole'.

2

The Olympic Games:
Twenty-First Century Challenges
as a Global Media Event

NANCY K. RIVENBURGH

The age of television introduced us to the media event. Media events are a unique media genre that results when television's visual and narrative power taps into public fascination with a story that transcends daily experience.

In their book, *Media Events: The Live Broadcasting of History*, Daniel Dayan and Elihu Katz summarize over a decade of their writings on the importance of media events as a social, political and technological phenomenon.[1] They refer to media events as the 'high holidays of mass communication'. They give examples of both national and global media events: the wedding of Prince Charles and Lady Diana, man's first landing on the moon, the Reagan-Gorbachev summit, the funeral of John F. Kennedy, Jr., the Live Aid concert, the fall of the Berlin Wall and, of course, the Olympic Games.

What do these events from the spheres of sport, science and politics have in common that they compose a unique genre of media experience? In Dayan and Katz's view, the hallmark of media events is their rarity and therefore their ability to interrupt our daily lives. Media events are live and unfolding. Both broadcasters and audiences adjust their schedules in order to attend to a media event.[2]

Despite being live, media events are also announced and advertised in advance, further distinguishing them from regular news coverage. Media events are organized in a location outside of the media (for example, in a city rather than a studio) and by public or other organizations that stand for consensual values. This may be governments, but may also result from the mobilization of private citizens as in the case of the Live Aid concert. This is important, in Dayan and Katz's view, because it means that television acts as the narrator rather than the creator of the event.

As narrator, television presents media events with reverence, hailing them as historic and 'invok[ing] deeply rooted narrative forms that are associated with heroics'.[3] It is a narrative based on continuity – of institutions, of values, of one hero to the next – that takes place within a shared set of rules. In this sense, media events tend to promote dominant or idealized values.[4] While they may emerge from conflict or even death, they do so to celebrate reconciliation as in Sadat's famous trip to Egypt, a restoration of order as with the Kennedy funeral, or a new era as with the moon landing or the fall of the Berlin Wall. The narration of these events purposefully transcends the problems and imperfections that surround them. As a result, media events have the ability to integrate and unify people, even to dissolve social divisions – however momentarily. They create a 'spirit' or a 'mood' that can allow new things to happen and new definitions to emerge.[5]

Finally, and of most interest to media and researchers alike, media events have unprecedented audiences – in both size and composition. They *compel* people to watch.

> When successful, people tell each other that viewing is mandatory, that they must put all else aside. When successful, they electrify very large audiences – an entire nation, sometimes the whole world. They are rare realizations of the technological dream of the electronic media – to reach everybody, directly, and simultaneously.[6]

For the greater part of the twentieth century the Olympic Games have indeed met the essential requirements, as put forth by Dayan and Katz, to be considered a quintessential global media event. With more than 120 communication satellites beaming television signals to every inhabited continent and the number of television sets now in use exceeding 1.2 billion there is little doubt that the audience size and composition of the present Olympic Games is at a peak. While global audience size for the Olympics is routinely overstated in the popular press,[7] the 2000 Sydney Olympics was still broadcast to 220 countries and territories, making it the most watched television sports event in history.[8]

But what does the future hold for the Olympics as a media event? Or, more broadly, what are the future prospects for media events as a unique broadcast genre? Some scholars suggest that global media events represent a twentieth-century convergence of satellite communication technology and an unprecedented intensification of world-wide social relations.[9] The thrill of seeing, in one's home, elite athletes from around the world gather together at the Olympic Games was indeed a novelty for most of that century.

This essay argues that the changing dynamics of media, audiences and world affairs present a challenge to the Olympics Games as a media event. While presently at a peak in audience size, in competition for broadcast rights and in hosting desirability, when one compares Dayan and Katz's essential characteristics of a media event to current trends in sport and Olympic broadcasting and to more broad-based changes in our political and social world, it becomes apparent that the Olympic Movement faces serious challenges if the Games are to remain a premier global media event.

THE OLYMPIC GAMES BROADCAST: LESS UNIQUE AND MONOPOLISTIC

Enter the 500-Channel Universe

With digitalization and increased channel capacities the world over, Olympic Games broadcasts have serious competition. Paradoxically, the absolute number of hours of an Olympic Games broadcast is large (and in some cases growing) in many countries, but at the same time it represents an increasingly smaller percentage of the available programming viewers can choose from. There is evidence, in more channel-saturated countries, that audiences no longer seem as compelled to watch the Olympics when faced with an array of programming choices. In Germany, where audiences could potentially watch 520 hours of 1996 Olympic coverage, the Games telecast garnered an audience rating high of only 9.8 per cent.[10] Despite trends such as multi-channel programming for Olympic events, the Games simply does not loom as large as it used to in countries' expanding channel environments. Even Dayan and Katz, in more recent writing about media events, have dropped from their list of defining elements that media events are 'monopolistic' (that is, that either all channels focus on it or it can be watched at all times).[11]

More International Sports Events

Daniel Bell has meticulously documented the growth in international multi-sport events over this past century.[12] Long before the 'X' Games hit television screens, there had been a steady increase in multi-sport championship events. Figure 1 shows the number of international multi-sport events that have taken place each decade since 1900. Of particular interest is the growth over the past two decades. Beginning with the 1980s (234 events), one can see at least a 215 per cent increase in number of events (to 502) in the 1990s. While many events are regional or specialized in nature – such as the Euro Games or the International Senior Games – and only a few attract global media attention at this time, they do serve to make the Olympic 'concept' less unique in the world of sports.

Perhaps more threatening to the Olympics is the growing global reach and mega-event publicity given to single sports championship competitions. World Cup soccer already has a rival grip on global audiences. The rugby union's 'Super 12' competition commenced in 1996.[13] There are indications that in the next 25–50 years sports such as baseball and basketball will join tennis, gymnastics and figure skating in spawning divisions that lead to a greater number of compelling World Series, World Cup, or World Championship events packaged and heavily promoted for world-wide audiences.[14] The half-time show of Super Bowl 2000, with its theme of global unity – children carrying doves of peace in a pastiche of the Barcelona, Albertville and Lillehammer Olympic Opening Ceremonies – was clearly designed with a global audience in mind.

FIGURE 1
INTERNATIONAL MULTI-SPORT COMPETITIONS

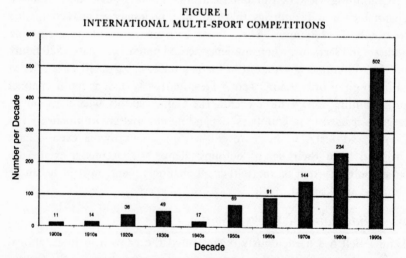

Source: D. Bell, *Encyclopedia of International Games* (Jefferson, SC: McFarland, 2002).

As Wenner, Boyle and Haynes and others convincingly argue, sport is essential to the globalizing structure of media organizations.[15] Sport is a relatively cheap method for filling hours of television time and moves easily across cultural and linguistic borders. Rupert Murdoch called sports the 'cornerstone of our [News Corporation] worldwide broadcasting'.[16] This strategic vision of using sport programming to reach new international audiences is being aggressively shared by a growing number of media organizations – Eurosport, Sky, ESPN, Fox and Japan Sports Channel to name a few.[17] Whitson summarizes the situation by saying that:

> it is clear in the late 1990s that most of the major professional sports and television conglomerates that now have investments in them are exploring how to reach global audiences. All the major professional sports seek to demonstrate to transnational advertisers that they can attract global audiences.[18]

As such, we have seen the competition to secure the rights for sport seasons and finales intensify to unprecedented levels of financial investment on the part of media outlets.[19]

The result will be a greater number of heavily promoted, world championship level sports and multi-sport competitions on the media calendar, rendering the Olympics Games – while still unique in its inclusion of all the nations of the world – less prominent in terms of elite sports competition.

More Mega-Events

It is not only in sport that an increasing number of international mega-events are being staged. Woodstock 99 and other concert extravaganzas merely add to the number of events that are promoted by various media organizations as premier, special and 'must see' global events. Not all mega-events succeed in capturing national or global attention, but the point is that there are more attempts to be the next global 'media event'. In addition, the increased linkage and co-operation among international news organizations, coupled with a greater world-wide awareness of international celebrities and political actors, allows for media events to emerge more easily out of news coverage. This was the case with the O.J. Simpson trial, the death and funeral of Diana, Princess of Wales, and the John F. Kennedy, Jr. aeroplane crash.

INCREASED MEDIA INTERVENTION

Real correctly points out that the 1971 International Olympic Committee (IOC) takeover of television rights fee monies and the 1984 shift to corporate sponsorship have combined to allow the Olympics to be hosted without financial loss, but also to increase the influence of television and sponsors in the organization of Olympic events.[20] As broadcast rights fees have grown, so have the demands of television broadcasters for an optimally-staged event that will enable them to recoup their large investments in the Games. As Real states:

> Olympic schedules and sites have been unmistakably influenced by television. Consider how television and sponsorship have come to shape the selection of the host city, the array of stadiums and sites, the style of the opening and closing ceremonies, the dates of the games, the timing of the final events, [the rules of Olympic sports] – and time zones.[21]

Boehm logically observes that as media organizations pay more for rights in all sports they want more control.[22] So, rather than acting as Dayan and Katz's humble narrator and observer of an historic and seminal event, television increasingly inserts itself as a central actor, organizer and manipulator of the event in an increasingly overt manner, altering the sports events and adding studio produced features and network personalities as central foci. Real goes on to say that, 'contemporary television's ability to selectively cover events and tailor coverage to each rich country's tastes has tended to fragment the unifying international potential of Olympic pageantry and unity'.[23]

A 'Plausibly Live' Television Reality

For example, led in recent years by new strategies of American broadcasters, there is less concern with broadcasting the Olympic Games live. Since Barcelona, NBC officials have insisted that people do not really care if the events are live as long as they tell a dramatic story. The US network introduced what it calls a 'plausibly live' approach to Olympic broadcasting. This refers to the mixing of live and tape-delayed segments to present the sports competitions 'as if' they were live, yet not taking pains to inform the audience of the manipulations.[24] This trend hit its extreme during NBC's broadcast of the 2000 Sydney Games where, in part because of the 15-hour time difference between Sydney and the US east coast, virtually the entire broadcast was a tape-delayed construction. (NBC made a 'commitment' to telling viewers of the time delay for the first three days of competition.[25]) Yet this strategy may have been taken too far, as NBC received unexpectedly low ratings (in fact, its worst in 32 years) for the Sydney Games. So how did NBC manage to miscalculate the success of a tape-delayed Olympics? Dayan and Katz would say that tape-delay removes from the television viewer the special role of 'expectant witness' watching live history unfold – a key ingredient in their definition of a media event. Now NBC has asked the 2004 Athens Olympic Organizers to consider changing the start times for some competitions so that more events can be live in US prime time.

The 'plausibly live' technique also gives studio producers a chance to re-package a taped competition in order to heighten its excitement. To do this, for example, NBC uses the venue announcers' original live play-by-play commentary for authenticity in the broadcast, edits this in order to increase the pace (and create time for commercial breaks) and then adapts the lead-ins and promotional teasers to the known outcome of the event. US media critics reprimanded NBC for its 'plausibly live' construction of the final vault of US gymnast Kerri Strug at the Atlanta 1996 Games. Grimacing with an injured leg, she executed a heroic final jump that, according to NBC's framing, won the United States the team gold medal. 'Not true!' cried the critics. The event had been won on the prior jump.[26] Puijk details a similar example occurring in CBS' coverage of Dan Jansen's final career attempt at a gold medal in 1,000m speed skating at the 1994 Lillehammer Games. With the positive outcome known before the evening's delayed broadcast, CBS produced promotional teasers and added some voice-over commentary to highlight the 'Will He or Won't He?' drama of Jansen's gold medal attempt.[27]

It is no coincidence that the above examples are US networks for at this point in time they seem the most comfortable manipulating the time and space of Olympic broadcasts. Other international broadcasters are using similar techniques with more frequency (as was already evidenced in the Barcelona broadcasts), but as yet with less bravado than NBC in Atlanta and Sydney or CBS at the Nagano Games.

This trend toward re-packaging the Games telecast has not only given the Olympics the same overly produced 'look' of other sports events but, in the eyes of some, has also diminished their contribution to sport. Frank Deford writes:

Original modern events, such as the World Series and Super Bowl, and various European and Asian team championships have superseded the Olympics in passion, as truly *pure* competitions. As sport, it is the Olympics that have ended up more sideshow; the most important Olympic competition now is between cities fighting to host future games [emphasis in original].[28]

Remote Production

There were 180 video circuits in Barcelona and more than 500 in Atlanta. As technological advances allow for increased bandwidth, international broadcasters are basing more of their Olympic production activities at home in order to reduce the high expenses of on-site construction and staff.[29] With each successive Olympics, more of the final telecast for each country is being put together outside the host city's International Broadcast Centre. For example, the rights-holding Canadian broadcaster sent fewer people to Atlanta in 1996 (closer geographically) than to Barcelona in 1992 because it could do more of the broadcast production in its home studio. This clever use of technology – which saves broadcasters tens of thousands of dollars – also begins to move the perceived organizational centre of the Olympics to the home nation studio rather than the host city, giving less of a sense of the Games as being 'outside of the media'. These trends of media intervention run contrary to Dayan and Katz's requirement that television must act as humble observer and narrator of a media event and not as its architect.

History that's No Longer Free

In a different type of intervention, some broadcasters also want to compel audiences to pay. While the US pay-per-view (PPV) television trial for the 1992 Barcelona Games was unsuccessful for a variety of reasons, observers believe that PPV will become the norm for sports broadcasting.[30] FIFA, soccer's global governing body, sold the world-wide television rights for the 2002 and 2006 World Cup broadcasts to a partnership between pay-TV's Leo Kirch and the Swiss company Sporis. They paid $2.2 billion in a deal struck in 1996 – $1 billion for 2002 and $1.2 billion for 2006.[31] FIFA claims currently that certain key games – such as the opener, semi-finals and finals – will be reserved for free television (and some countries, such as France, have laws to that effect).

PPV sports have been a growing reality throughout Europe since the mid-1990s with Telepiu in Italy offering future digital subscribers 'season tickets' to games of their choice. Despite uproar from audiences and politicians alike, the trend seems set and it is only a matter of time before it is tried on the Olympics once again. The result will not only serve to further commodify an event that is supposed to reach the largest possible audience, but will likely discriminate against smaller sports without celebrity athletes or teams. Both these results seem to conflict with the spirit of the Olympic Games.[32]

THE TARNISHED VENEER OF THE OLYMPIC MOVEMENT

Draped in Commercial Messages

The Olympic Games is the only major sporting event in the world where there is no advertising in the stadia or on the athletes. Telecasts of the sports and ceremonial events themselves are supposed to be 'clean'; that is, images of Olympic events are not to be broadcast with any kind of commercial association. However, it is likely that most audiences are unaware of this.

In the aftermath of her finest Olympic performance, figure skater Nancy Kerrigan announced, 'I'm going to Disney World!'.[33] On another national broadcast, a superimposed bank logo floated on the screen next to the torch entering the Olympic stadium. In another, 'side-by-sides' showed images of the Opening Ceremony boxed in the corner of the screen during a commercial break.[34] While these examples are all violations of the Olympic Charter and rights-holder contracts, they are increasingly commonplace in Olympic telecasts world-wide.

One of the most serious threats to the unique posture traditionally held by the Olympic Games is the encroachment of advertising messages. In countries with commercial broadcast systems, it is becoming harder to distinguish the format and commercial decor embedded in an Olympic telecast from other sports extravaganzas. Even Dick Ebersol, Chairman of NBC Sports and NBC Olympics, admits that broadcasters are doing 'too little to set it [the Olympics broadcast] apart'.[35] As Drozdiak pointed out, 'The transformation of the Olympics into a global commercial spectacle has become so complete that its fate as well as its fortunes are now determined by corporations'.[36] Many others join in Drozdiak's sentiment and see the Olympic Games entering into the mega-sports entertainment business from which there can be no return.[37] The following statements reflect the tenor of these criticisms:

> In recent decades the postmodern Olympics have become a virtual circus of commodity values and fetishes. Corporate logos and sponsorship abound, Olympic memorabilia multiply, merchandising and marketing pre-occupy officials, shoe sponsors become powerful decision makers, promotions begin months before the Games and suffuse their media presentation, and Olympic leaders and the public learn to accept this commodification as if it were part of the (post)modern Olympic creed.[38]

> A sporting event? Or merely a branch of the advertising and entertainment industry? In the centenary of their reinvention by Baron Pierre de Coubertin, the Olympic Games look more like a celebration of the marketing muscle of Coca-Cola, Kodak and BMW than a display of human prowess and courage ... the Olympics has changed almost beyond recognition in its first modern century.[39]

While no fan itself of excessive commercialism, the IOC necessarily views this situation from a different perspective. As Richard W. Pound of the IOC Executive Board stated, 'Take away sponsorship and commercialism from sport today and what is left? A large, sophisticated finely-tuned engine developed over a period of 100 years – with no fuel.'[40] The IOC correctly argues that the turn to corporate sponsorship programmes saved the Olympic Games from demise in the 1970s (when only Los Angeles and Teheran were willing to bid for the 1984 Games). In fairness, some of the problem lies outside of IOC control. Violations of Olympic rules on advertising, such as those noted above, are commonplace and extremely hard for the IOC to police. In addition, there are no rules limiting how often a network may interrupt an Olympic broadcast for commercial breaks. One study of Barcelona Olympic broadcasts found that 18 of 28 international broadcasters departed from the Opening Ceremony for commercial breaks to miss an average 11 per cent of the official ceremony. The extreme cases were the North American broadcasters CTV of Canada and NBC of the United States who dedicated more than 21 per cent (40 minutes) and 40 per cent (62 minutes) respectively to advertising breaks during the Opening Ceremony.[41]

Ambush marketing is also a persistent and growing problem for IOC officials.[42] This is when companies place advertising with Olympic themes near the Olympic venues and within the Olympic broadcast in order to give the appearance of being an Olympic sponsor, but stop short of using the trademarked Olympic symbols that are reserved for official sponsor use. This further cluttering of television screens with Olympic–commercial associations is well beyond what the IOC deems 'acceptable'. It also upsets the legitimate sponsors who contribute 40 per cent of Olympics Games revenue.

Technological advances may further compound the commercial clutter surrounding the Games. One futurist at the National Digital Television Center in West Los Angeles sees television of the future as having no commercial breaks, giving up the battle of the remote with audiences. Instead, programming will be filled with brand images inserted through digital manipulations known as virtual advertising and virtual product placement.[43] Many networks are already inserting virtual logos, banners and products into sports venues.[44]

Finally, while the new two-year cycle of the winter and summer Games is viewed by the IOC as a boon to raising sponsorship dollars, for many observers it also detracts from the special (or as Dayan and Katz would say, 'rare') nature of the Olympics.

Vote-Buying Scandal

'From their inception, the Olympics have rarely, if ever, lived up to the lofty ambition of serving as an oasis of peace, fair play, and friendship in a troubled world.'[45] Recent years have seen the tarnish on the Olympic Movement darken further. The Salt Lake City vote-buying scandal implicated, at one point, one-quarter of the entire membership (24 members) of the IOC for accepting at least $1 million in cash, gifts and other benefits from the Salt Lake bid committee. This created a new crisis for the Olympic Movement and incited a series of US Congressional hearings and proposed US legislation to strip the IOC of its tax-exempt status, which would redirect television rights fees from the IOC to the US Olympic Committee.[46] The scandal, which resulted in the suspension of six IOC members and the resignation of three others, put Salt Lake City fundraising efforts behind schedule as at least one major $30 million sponsor, Johnson & Johnson, backed out.[47] In a harsh critique of the situation, Drozdiak stated:

The IOC will continue to endure crises of confidence as long as it persists in living on a diet of myth and hypocrisy. The latest challenge in the checkered history of the Olympics only proves it is time to remove the Games from their pedestal of false nobility and recognize them as a mirror of our faded times.[48]

Drugs that Won't Go Away

Others envisage even more severe challenges for the image of the Olympics. Building on the Salt Lake City scandal one article stated:

a little graft in Utah pales beside what a growing number of coaches, trainers, officials and athletes call the real scandal in sports. The greatest threat to the image, integrity and even the continued existence of elite-level international competitions ... is the use of illicit, performance-enhancing drugs.[49]

The ugly practice of doping in sports came to light during the 1960 Rome Games when a Danish cyclist died from an amphetamine overdose.[50] Nowadays some believe that doping is in fact the biggest single threat to the future of the Games. With the human body nearly at the limits of its physical performance capacity, evidenced by the smaller increments by which new world records are set, the pressure for drug use is ever strong – despite the risk of scandal and disqualification.[51]

Broadcasters and Olympics Ideals

It is, of course, media coverage of the Games that brings to light issues of scandal and drug use that may affect perceptions of the Olympic Movement. However, these same media profit from the success of the Olympics as a media event. In light of that, broadcasters do remarkably little to promote the Olympic Movement in their telecasts. As data from the Barcelona and Atlanta Olympics have shown, both print and television commentators around the globe rarely mention Olympic values beyond their direct association with the specific rituals of the Opening Ceremony. In a study of 28 international broadcasts of the Barcelona Olympic Opening Ceremony, in general, only one to three per cent of broadcast commentary referenced Olympic values or ideals in any way. The most prominent Olympic value mentioned across broadcasts was 'participation'. Few other mentions were made of the philosophies or values of the Olympic Movement, despite the Opening

Ceremony's role as the primary ceremonial event of the Games.[52] Yet, Dayan and Katz argue that, 'The issue [of television's central role in the success of a media event] ... is not one of truth, but of loyalty' to the significance of that event.[53]

In Seattle, a 1998 poll showed that the majority of citizens opposed pursuing a bid to host the 2012 Olympics. The top three reasons given were cost, traffic and too many people.[54] These are all reflective of existing local-level problems facing the city, so perhaps the poll results were understandable. What was more disheartening, however, were the top three reasons people gave for supporting a Seattle Olympic bid: a desire for prestige, a chance to see high-level sports locally and money. Is the purpose of the Olympic Games already fading? Where were concerns with promoting intercultural friendships or engaging in peaceful exchange as a deterrent to international conflict?

In a report entitled 'Worldwide Consumer Perceptions of the Olympic Games', McCann-Erickson World Group confirmed that the perceptions of the Olympics are indeed shifting. In a survey of consumers in 46 countries:

> McCann discovered that the Olympics has two conflicting images: one symbolizes the high-minded, universal ideals associated with the brand over a long time; the other represents contemporary troubles like drug and political scandals and related media coverage, which is often negative.[55]

Dayan and Katz emphasize that, 'If a ceremonial event is to succeed, the audience must agree to its elevated definition. Audiences must be willing to take a ceremonial role'. The media event must 'evoke the enthralled response of a willing audience'.[56]

THE SIZE OF THE OLYMPICS AS A VARIABLE IN ITS SUCCESS

The growing size of the Olympics has made a city's ability to host the Games a significant variable in their success. The Olympics have become a near impossible logistical challenge, considering the technological, security, transportation and general hosting requirements of more than 11,000 athletes and officials, 20,000 media personnel and thousands of additional volunteers, protesters and spectators – including world dignitaries. As Verveer states, 'To understand the organizational complexity of [the Olympic Games], one must realize that it corresponds to the simultaneous holding of around 30 world championships in a single city'.[57]

While successful in terms of broadcast ratings and host city profit, the 1996 Atlanta Games were not characterized as a success by international media, in part because of logistical and safety problems that were too great to be ignored.[58] The 1996 Games were negatively foreshadowed by the crash of TWA 800 and then plagued by serious computer problems, traffic mishaps, complaints from athletes and journalists, a bomb scare in the International Broadcast Centre (IBC) and a pipe bomb explosion near hundreds of people gathered in Centennial Park. Even avid Olympic supporters began murmuring that the logistical limits of hosting a safe and smooth running Games had been reached. Four years later, fans of the Olympic Movement sighed in relief as Sydney hosted an organizational and sporting success. However, with the terrorist tragedy of 11 September 2001 concerns regarding the safety, logistics and costs of hosting such a large event have returned to the forefront. Security costs at the Salt Lake City 2002 winter Olympics, a considerably smaller event than a summer Olympics, were just over $300 million – about three times the security costs for Atlanta 2000. This new cost reality is causing a re-evaluation by some cities about the viability of making a bid to host future Olympics.[59]

AUDIENCE FRAGMENTATION

Audience-produced Sports

Dayan and Katz's picture of the media event experience is one of a large and rapt audience simultaneously watching history unfold. NBC Sports and NBC Olympics Chairman Dick Ebersol explained that the prime value of the Olympics is that it is the only thing guaranteed to put the whole family together in front of the television.[60] However, the changing world of television sports and communications technology is one where audience members (even within a household) will be allowed – and encouraged – to create 'personal viewing experiences'. Interactive television already enables sports fans to choose their own picture angles. People will eventually be able to view sports, 24-hours a day, on palm-size televisions with mini-satellite dishes. Digital systems allowing for a 500-channel environment offer video on demand via cable – perfect for selecting out one's own private collection of Olympic sports experiences.[61] According to Lowry, 'packaged' media will experience more and more problems because people will become more sophisticated about taking the package apart.[62]

The internet, of course, further complicates and fragments the sports spectator experience. A few years from now, compression technology will make it far easier to send high-quality video and audio across the internet, which could mean a greater draw for sports fans and advertising revenue. While one scenario sees the internet adding to the competition for viewers, a more realistic one is that traditional media will more actively seek partnerships with internet companies. In a hypothetical scenario, NBC could broadcast Olympic women's gymnastics and cable network MSNBC could handle a men's basketball game between Croatia and Germany, while an internet affiliate offers in-depth coverage of the men's marathon and several other events – all at the same time.[63]

There are already an increasing number of viewers surfing the internet while watching television. A study conducted by Showtime Networks estimated that roughly 18 per cent of American households have their televisions and computers on at the same time.[64] There were a total of 186 million hits on the official Atlanta '96 website and 634 million hits the Nagano '98 site.[65] In 1996 IBM collaborated with NBC to create the 'web's first cybercast' of the 1996 Super Bowl including direct coverage, press conferences and news. During the 2001 baseball World Series, audiences could express their approval – or disapproval – of team managers' decisions to pull players as the game was happening. Today's interactive computer technology is merging the role of the sports spectator and the participant, effectively allowing sports to be tailored to the schedules and desires of individual viewers. As a result of such changes, the form and experience of what constitutes a media event may alter significantly in the twenty-first century.

A CHANGING WORLD

Another type of challenge to the long-term future of the Olympics as a media event is highlighted in the research of political scientists who show that as citizens lose confidence in their government's ability to solve social and economic problems, the nature of politics is redefined and relocated to the local and civic sphere. This trend, accompanied by processes of globalization that give more economic relevance to transnational entities, has been linked to a general decline – documented in Western democracies – in the strength of identity people hold with the nation-state. Other more local, and more translocal, identities are emerging as central motivators in people's lives, yet the Olympics as media event is organized around nation-state groupings and thrives on nationalism.[66] These groupings may well lose their hold as the new century progresses.

In addition, intercultural awareness and exchange are simply more a part of everyday life. The Olympics Games no longer offer people a *rare* opportunity to experience other cultural groups in an arena of peace. Changing school curricula, consumer products, businesses, non-profit organizations exchanges, tourism and global migration have made the world, while not necessarily a better place, at least more intercultural in flavour.

A Generational Divide

Perhaps one of the more important findings contained in the aforementioned McCann-Erickson report was that adults over 40 had a significantly different view of the Olympics than those of younger generations. For older adults, the Olympic Games still maintain a 'transcendent' aura when compared to other sports events. This audience segment grew up watching the Olympics within the context of post-war and Cold War international relations, a time when every Olympic Games (from Berlin 1936 to Seoul 1988) was cast in a heavy shadow of international politics. It might be speculated that those viewers sought out the Olympics in order to experience, however momentarily, the vision of peaceful interchange (or of national superiority) symbolized by the Olympics. According to Riggs *et al.*, the first of several relatively 'non-political' Games occurred in Barcelona 1992.[67] Therefore for a younger, post-Cold War generation, the co-operative, yet competitive spirit of the Games may not be as symbolically linked to broader ideals of world peace or world order.

In fact, according to the McCann-Erickson report and other internal research sponsored by the IOC, young audiences tend to view the Olympics as 'getting worse rather than better' and just another big event equivalent to the MTV awards. As such, the Olympics are simply not considered the required viewing experience they were for past generations.[68] Beyond the inclusion of newer 'X' generation sports such as snowboarding into the Olympic competition, what will it take to draw younger adults and children into the Olympic spirit?

CONCLUSION

According to Dayan and Katz, a fundamental allure of media events is that they resonate with human mythology and a fascination with the transcendent or the 'bigger than life'. This is true for any time period. In 1995 the best-selling *Time* magazine covers were not the cover stories that featured the conflict in Bosnia, the US Social Security crisis, or even a celebrity, but those with headlines such as, 'How Did the Universe Begin?', 'Is the Bible Fact or Fiction?', and 'Mysteries of the Deep'.[69] In the same spirit, Dayan and Katz argue:

> From casual, tired, consumer-oriented pleasure seekers we are transformed into expectant witnesses of a historic moment. But television cannot do this alone. Its call to prayer – if it is to succeed – must be echoed in the worlds of national leaders, by our friends, by the newspapers, by the schools that declare a recess, by employers who allow us to view on company time, by the flickering lights in all the neighbors' windows.[70]

The purpose of this overview of trends and issues in Olympic broadcasting is not to forecast the demise of the Olympic Games, but rather to emphasize the challenges the Olympic Movement faces to preserve its unique nature as a global media event invoking the unity, inspiration and commitment described above. If the Olympic Games are to remain a media event – a unique and transcendent experience that compels, not convinces, viewers to watch – some serious attention needs to be given to adapting the Games and its broadcasting in ways that maintain those essential characteristics outlined by Dayan and Katz.

Is this an impossible challenge? Real suggests that the 'well-articulated Olympic ideal' born of a nineteenth-century modernist viewpoint simply cannot sustain itself in this post-modern era characterized by a lack of 'grand narratives'. He goes on to say that the '(post)modern Olympic Games in all their commercialism are not aberrations but logical expressions of the age in which they [now] exist'.[71] If Real is correct, and many of the current trends in Olympic broadcasting seem to support this, then the Olympic Games as a global media event is destined to remain a phenomenon largely associated with this past century.

Whether we are ready to accept that conclusion or not, Puijk suggests that Dayan and Katz's definition of a media event may also face a challenge.[72] We have already seen subtle changes in their original definition in response to changes in the television channel environment (for example, dropping the need for media events to be monopolistic). Now we are evolving into an even more fragmented, networked, personalized and interactive communication world. How should we define a media event in a post-television world? For the concept to survive this century, we must re-think not just *what* will compel people to focus on the same event, with the same intensity and reverence that Dayan and Katz suggest are integral to the media event experience, but also *how* will people experience it and refine the definition accordingly.

When the Pathfinder landed on Mars in July 1997 a then record 45 million people (80 million hits per day) visited the Jet Propulsion website to get their first glimpse of Mars. By most news media polls this was the biggest event of 1997, largely fuelled by the internet 'broadcast'. Perhaps this provides a clue to the nature of the global media event of the twenty-first century. In the Mars landing example, profit-motivated media manipulations, excessive advertising breaks and scandals were once again stripped away and individuals – now irrespective of nationality, ideology or age – were transformed into expectant witnesses of a live, unfolding, rare and networked media experience.

NOTES

The author wishes to thank Neil Blain, Alina Bernstein and the anonymous reviewers for their help and support.

1. D. Dayan and E. Katz, *Media Events: The Live Broadcasting of History* (Cambridge, MA: Harvard University Press, 1992). See also, E. Katz, 'Media Events: The Sense of Occasion', *Studies in Visual Anthropology*, 6 (1980), 84–9; E. Katz and D. Dayan, 'Media Events: On the Experience of Not Being There', *Religion*, 15 (1985), 305–14.
2. D. Dayan and E. Katz, 'Political Ceremony and Instant History', in A. Smith (ed.), *Television: An International History* (Oxford: Oxford University Press, 1995), pp.169–88.
3. Ibid., p.179.
4. This promotion of dominant values is also a primary source of criticism of media events.
5. Dayan and Katz, *Media Events*, pp.147–87.
6. Dayan and Katz, 'Political Ceremony and Instant History', p.170.
7. M. de Moragas Spà, N. Rivenburgh and J. Larson, *Television in the Olympics* (London: John Libbey, 1995), pp.209–21.
8. P. Verveer, 'Telecommunications and the Olympic Games', *IEEE Communications Magazine* (July 2001), 69–70.
9. R. Negrine, *Political Communication in the Age of Global Electronic Media: The Communication of Politics* (London: Sage, 1996), pp.167–88.
10. International Olympic Committee (IOC), *Olympic Marketing Fact File 1998* (Lausanne: IOC, 1998).
11. Cf. Dayan and Katz, *Media Events*, p.5, and Dayan and Katz, 'Political Ceremony and Instant History', 179.
12. D. Bell, *Encyclopedia of International Games* (Jefferson, SC: McFarland, 2002).
13. D. Rowe, 'The Global Love-match: Sport and Television', *Media, Culture and Society*, 18 (1996), 565–82.

14. Brown *et al.*, 'The Games of the Future, Sport by Sport', *USA Today* (19 May 1999), 9C.
15. L.A. Wenner (ed.), *MediaSport* (New York: Routledge, 1998), pp.73–87; R. Boyle and R. Haynes, 'Sport in the New Media Age: The Battle for Control', Paper presented at the 1999 International Association of Mass Communication Research (IAMCR) Conference, Leipzig, Germany, 28 July 1999.
16. R.V. Bellamy, Jr., 'The Evolving Television Sports Marketplace', in Wenner (ed.), *MediaSport*, p.77.
17. D. Guterson, 'Moneyball! On the Relentless Promotion of Pro Sports', *Harper's Magazine* (Sept. 1994), 37–46.
18. D. Whitson, 'Circuits of Promotion: Media, Marketing and the Globalization of Sport', in Wenner (ed.), *MediaSport*, p.68.
19. As examples, ABC, Fox, CBS and ESPN came up with $17.6 billion for rights to National Football League games over the next eight years. NBC is spending $3.55 billion for the 2000–8 summer and winter Olympics. See E. Boehm, 'Jocks Itchy Over Costly Cup', *Variety*, 371, 5 (1998), 1–2; J. Steinbreder, 'Big Spender', *Sky* (July 1996), 37–42.
20. M. Real, 'Is Television Corrupting the Olympics?', *Television Quarterly* (Fall 1999), 100–9.
21. Ibid., 105.
22. Boehm, 'Jocks Itchy Over Costly Cup', 1–2. In sports outside the Olympics, media are also buying the teams in order to gain more control. For example, in 1998 Fox acquired the Los Angeles Dodgers for over $300 million after previously acquiring ownership of Madison Square Garden, the New York Knicks, the New York Rangers and eight strategic regional sports channels. See 'The Man With the Game Plan', *Broadcasting & Cable*, 128, 26 (22 June 1998), 40–41. Boyle and Haynes, 'Sport in the New Media Age', write of similar situations in Italy, France and the United Kingdom.
23. Real, 'Is Television Corrupting the Olympics?', 108.
24. R. Williams, 'Telling Tales on Tape', *Sportvision* (Jan. 1997), 34; R. Blount, 'High Ratings Don't Vindicate NBC's Slick Coverage of Games', *Star Tribune* (5 Aug. 1996), 3S.
25. 'NBC Expects Profit on Taped Games', *Associated Press Wire Service* (28 June 2000).
26. K. Mayberry, M. Proctor and R. Srb, 'The Agony of Deceit: Ladies' Night at the NBC Olympics – Television Coverage of the 1996 Olympics', *Humanist*, 56, 6 (21 Nov. 1996), 4; B. Jenkins, 'All-Time Videotaped Olympics', *San Francisco Chronicle* (27 July 1996), D12; 'A "Plausible" Olympics', *Seattle Times* (2 Aug. 1996), B4.
27. R. Puijk, 'Sports as Media Events', Paper presented at the IAMCR Annual Conference, Leipzig, Germany, July 1999. In another example, for the diving competition NBC selectively edited out competitors in the final round to increase the pace and drama of the event. The resulting production was so seamless that audiences had no notion that some finalists were missing from the broadcast.
28. F. Deford, 'Let The Games Begin', *National Geographic* (July 1996), 49.
29. T. Harper, 'And the Bandwidth Played On', *Sky* (July 1996), 44, 46–50.
30. In contrast to the situation in Europe, the large size of the US television audience allows broadcasters to charge more money for advertising, offsetting the need for pay-per-view revenues.
31. Boehm, 'Jocks Itchy Over Costly Cup', 1–2.
32. C. Barrie, 'Pity the New Digital Underclass', *Guardian* (6 Nov. 1998), 21.
33. Guterson, 'Moneyball!', 45.
34. Moragas *et al.*, *Television in the Olympics*, p.199.
35. D. Ebersol, 'I was Old Enough to be in Grenoble in 1968 and I Want to be Here in the Future', *Television in the Olympic Games: The New Era* (Lausanne: International Symposium Proceedings, Olympic Museum, 1998), pp.69–71.
36. W. Drozdiak, 'Torching the Olympic Myth', *Washington Post* (14 Feb. 1999), B01.
37. Brown *et al.*, 'The Games of the Future', 9C.
38. M. Real, 'MediaSport: Technology and the Commodification of Postmodern Sport', in Wenner (ed.), *MediaSport*, p.21.
39. 'The Zillion Dollar Games', *Economist* (20 July 1996), 13.
40. IOC, *Olympic Marketing Fact File 1998*, p.7.
41. Moragas *et al.*, *Television in the Olympics*, p.194.

42. IOC, *Olympic Marketing Fact File 1998*, p.22.
43. B. Lowry, 'Pop Culture / Get Ready for the 21st Century', *Los Angeles Times Magazine* (13 June 1999), 25.
44. 'Virtual Advertising', *Economist* (15 Jan. 2000), 68.
45. Drozdiak, 'Torching the Olympic Myth', B01.
46. 'Samaranch: Political Interference Threatens Olympics', *Washington Post* (27 April 1999), D02.
47. 'Sponsors Keep IOC Honest', *Atlanta Constitution* (21 April 1999), A10.
48. Drozdiak, 'Torching the Olympic Myth', B01.
49. S. Begley and M. Brant, 'The Real Scandal', *Newsweek* (15 Feb. 1999), 48–54.
50. 'Samaranch', D02.
51. 'The Zillion Dollar Games', 13.
52. Moragas *et al.*, *Television in the Olympics*, pp.123–41.
53. Dayan and Katz, *Media Events*, p.78.
54. E. Almond and S. Brynes, 'Poll Reveals That City Voters Oppose Having Games Here', *Seattle Times* (6 Oct. 1998), A1, 13.
55. P.W. Lauro, 'Poll Points Out Image Problems for the Olympics', *New York Times* (11 Jan. 2001), http://nytimes.com/2001/01/11/business/11ADCO.html (18 Jan. 2001).
56. Dayan and Katz, 'Political Ceremony and Instant History', pp.178–9.
57. Verveer, 'Telecommunications and the Olympic Games', 69.
58. N. Rivenburgh, 'Journalists Take Aim at Atlanta: Understanding the Dynamics of International Media Coverage of the 1996 Olympic Games', Paper presented at l'Institut Nacional d'Educacó Fisica de Catalunya (INEFC), Barcelona, Spain, 5 Dec. 1997.
59. T. Dahlberg, 'Olympic Budget nearly $2 million', *Associated Press Wire Service* (10 Dec. 2001); 'Sources: Greece Seeks Loan to Pay for 2004 Athens Summer Olympics', *Associated Press Wire Service* (18 April 2002).
60. R. Harvey, 'Sites Unseen, NBC Locks in Olympics Through 2008', *Los Angeles Times* (13 Dec. 1995), C-1.
61. H. Wolinsky, 'Cable Moguls Tout Digital Technology', *Chicago Sun-Times* (16 June 1999), 66.
62. Lowry, 'Pop Culture', 25.
63. J. Swartz, 'Cyber Sports Coverage Puts Fans in the Thick of It: Quokka's Technology Called the Next Big Thing on Net', *San Francisco Chronicle* (7 Dec. 1998), B3.
64. Lowry, 'Pop Culture', 25.
65. José Luis Iribarren, Program Director Internet Strategy, IBM, cited in M. de Moragas Spà, 'The Olympic Movement and the Information Society: New Internet Challenge and Opportunities', Paper presented at the International Symposium on Television in the Olympic Games, Lausanne, Switzerland, Oct. 1998.
66. See, for example, J. Hargreaves, 'Olympism and Nationalism: Some Preliminary Considerations', in R.C. Jackson and T.L. McPhail, *The Olympic Movement and the Mass Media: Past, Present and Future Issues* (Calgary: Hurford Enterprises, 1989), pp.143–52.
67. K. Riggs, S. Eastman and T. Golobic, 'Manufactured Conflict in the 1992 Olympics: The Discourse of Television Politics', *Critical Studies in Mass Communication*, 10 (1993), 253–72.
68. Lauro, 'Poll Points Out Image Problems for the Olympics'; A. Shipley, 'Extreme Winter Games: Olympics Targeting a Younger Audience', *Washington Post* (25 Nov. 2001), A01.
69. *Columbia Journalism Review* (July/Aug. 1998), 32.
70. Dayan and Katz, *Media Events*, p.120.
71. Real, 'MediaSport', p.18.
72. Puijk, 'Sports as Media Events'.

3

What's in a Name?
Muhammad Ali and the Politics of
Cultural Identity

AMIR SAEED

Muhammad Ali has recently re-emerged into the media spotlight, lighting the Olympic flame in Atlanta and the subject of Hollywood films *When We Were Kings* and *Ali*. Considering his last fight was a devastating and embarrassing defeat in December 1981 the endurance of his appeal is all the more remarkable. His legacy cannot be confined neatly into any one category; to label him as simply a boxer or athlete not only represents an injustice to him, but also displays an ignorance of what he represented to the world. As the cover of *I'm A Little Special* notes, 'Fighter, celebrity, draft dodger, activist, poet, victim, inspiration, champion – pick a year and choose a label. Muhammad Ali has been them all.'[1]

Marqusee notes that Ali's personality and career could not be confined to one nation;[2] he inspired people from all around the globe, even people whose primary interests were not that of sport or boxing. Ali's was and is a 'global constituency who belonged not to America but to the world'[3]. It appears that writers trying to assess the impact of Muhammad Ali, or 'Ali-ologists' as Early describes them,[4] characterize Ali as an inclusive rather than exclusive figure. Considering Ali's allegiance to the separatist Nation of Islam (NoI) in America, these conclusions add to the complexity of Ali and his ongoing legacy.

A PERSONAL REFLECTION

From a personal point of view, Ali's fights were received with great anticipation in my family household. My mother (not even a sport fan, never mind a boxing fan) would cook special South Asian dishes, the house would be filled with an air of excitement and my brothers would enthuse about Ali's greatness. The fight itself would be watched, commentated and enjoyed in admiration. Any small act of 'defiance' or 'playful misdemeanour' by Ali was lapped up with great applause and recognition. Quite simply Ali belonged to *us* and we would observe with a mixture of awe and envy, especially at how white people *respected* Ali the Muslim.

This concluding sentence is in part what this essay attempts to explore. How can a Pakistani family living in Scotland have such strong feelings for an African American who specialized in a sport that had no real following within South-Asian communities until he arrived? In order to examine these issues, the essay explores key events in Ali's history, tracking the emergence of an apolitical boxing contender as a symbol of a divided America. These historical considerations are further debated in relation to questions of ethnic minority cultural identity; namely the use of ethnic and religious labels.

BOXING AND 'RACE'

Marqusee notes that one of the defining principles of modern sport is the concept of the level playing field.[5] In short, for sport to be seen as a truly egalitarian competition all the participants must operate within the same rules and boundaries. Failure to do this diminishes the quality of contest and an air of suspicion or uncertainty may surround the outcome.

> The logic of the level playing field gives sport an egalitarian premise. This is undoubtedly one of the reasons for its enduring appeal to the masses, and especially the most dispossessed among them. The major cliché about race in sport is that sport offers black people opportunities denied to them in other spheres.[6]

Cashmore quotes Henderson noting that 'sport was the only arena in which blacks were able to assert themselves'.[7] He further observes that in many ways sport is regarded as a reflection of social life,[8] however he does stress that black sporting success does not equate with reduced prejudice in wider society. Furthermore, access to the 'level playing field' is anything but equal. As a consequence of this, the early black boxing pioneers were more than just fighters; they automatically became symbols of their communities.

The history of heavyweight boxing is just one example of this. Historically white boxers refused to fight their black counterparts. When

Jack Johnson became heavyweight champion in 1908 (he won the title in Sydney, Australia because no American city would stage the bout) his victory was received with the worst racial violence of that decade as white Americans avenged his triumph. In many respects Jack Johnson was 'the white man's nightmare come alive'.[9] He appeared invincible and more importantly, arrogant, in the ring. Furthermore his personal lifestyle appeared to flaunt his wealth and sneer at the white establishment. His preference for white women further aggravated white society. Johnson was the most famous black person at the time and even the black community was divided in their reception of his lifestyle. In many ways Johnson's defilement by the white media echoed the treatment that Ali received over 60 years later. Ironically, after seeing a play of Jack Johnson, Ali himself remarked, 'So that's Jack Johnson ... That was a bad nigger! ... This play is about me. Take out the interracial love stuff and Jack Johnson is the original *me*'.[10]

Johnson was eventually forced into exile by the white establishment and it was 25 years before another black fighter was allowed a shot at the heavyweight championship. Joe Louis' professional career was handled by a team of sponsors and managers who set in motion a slick, efficient public relations exercise to make Joe Louis acceptable to white America. To further endear himself to the American public (that is, white America) Louis enlisted in the Army and fought promotional bouts for various Army departments (all in racially segregated units). His reward for this public show of patriotism was to be hounded by the federal government for taxes on these 'promotional bouts', which left him emotionally and financially broken.

In many respects Jack Johnson and Joe Louis were to become the benchmarks for the black fighters who followed them although of course these benchmarks were created and sustained by the white media, who failed to attempt to comprehend either the complexities of the men or how they were received in black communities.

> There seemed to be only these two stereotypes for black sportsmen in America: the 'bad nigger' and the 'Uncle Tom'. Both Johnson and Louis, of course, were subjected to critical scrutiny never lavished on white champions, and both were defined by white perceptions.[11]

By 1960 these racial stereotypes of the black fighter had been in some ways 'played by' Sonny Liston and Floyd Patterson. Liston was an ex-convict who was believed to be backed by the Mob, whilst Patterson was courted by the white liberal establishment. In reality both were complex figures who received support and criticism from different sections of the black community.[12] By 1963 Liston had become heavyweight champion having twice defeated Patterson. Many fans and reporters grudgingly believed him to be unassailable and his mere presence was said to intimidate opponents even before they stepped into the ring, 'The press now declared him [Liston] "invincible" – but they still thought someone else should be champion'.[13]

'WORTHY OF ALL PRAISE': FROM CASSIUS CLAY TO MUHAMMAD ALI

In some respects that 'someone else' may have been Cassius Clay. When the 18-year-old Clay returned from the Rome Olympics in 1960 he was received as an 'All-American Hero'. While many fight fans were unsure about his unorthodox style and considered his clowning a disguise to hide his lack of boxing skill, they nevertheless welcomed him into the boxing world.

When asked by a Russian reporter about the condition of blacks in the US, Clay responded that 'qualified people were working on those problems' and retorted that, 'To me, the USA is still the best country in the world, counting yours'.[14] In many ways he was the personification of American patriotism and typified this on his return to his home town in Louisville, which celebrated his triumph over his cold war adversaries:

> To make America the Greatest is my goal
> So I beat the Russian and the Pole
> And for the USA won the medal of Gold.[15]

Clay was proud to be American and loved his Christian name, 'Don't you think it's a beautiful name? Makes you think of the Coliseum and those Roman Gladiators'.[16]

Quickly turning professional, Clay endeared himself to the American nation. Mainstream publications like *Life* and *Time* awarded him with glowing articles praising him for re-inventing boxing with his repartee, boastfulness and endearing personality:

> Cassius Clay is Hercules, struggling through the twelve labours. He is Jason chasing the Golden Fleece ... When he scowls, strong men shudder, and when he smiles, women swoon. The mysteries of

the universe are his tinker toys. He rattles the thunder and looses the lightning.[17]

The reference to (possible) inter-racial intimate affection, coupled with the references to Greek mythological metaphors, illustrates how popular Clay had made himself to the white American public. Despite America not being used to *arrogant* blacks and, especially, not tolerating acts of self-centred conceit from them, white America appeared to accept Clay for his endearing personality.

It could be suggested that the main reason for this was not the witnessing of increased tolerance on the part of the US establishment, but rather that Cassius Clay was not regarded as a social threat. Indeed it could be argued that in a perverse sort of way Clay was the twin embodiment of another racist stereotype of blacks, that of the happy-go-lucky but ultimately dumb Negro and the muscle-bound but brainless athlete. Certainly his clowning-around covered some subtle political thinking:

> Where do you think I'd be next week, if I didn't know how to shout and holler and make the public take notice? I'd be poor and I'd probably be down in my home town, washing windows or running an elevator and saying 'yes suh' and 'no suh' and knowing my place. Instead I'm one of the highest paid athletes in the world. Think about that. A southern coloured has made one million dollars.[18]

Ebony magazine noted that while Clay was the darling of the white liberal establishment his pride in his ethnic background was conveniently overlooked in favour of his alleged patriotism:

> Cassius Marcellus Clay – and this fact has evaded the sports-writing fraternity – is a blast furnace of racial pride. His is a pride that would never mask itself with skin lighteners and processed hair, a pride scorched with memories of a million little burns.[19]

Certainly in the early years after the 1960 Olympics Cassius Clay's political thoughts were, it always seemed, pro-American. Compare the previous statements with that of Paul Robeson, another black entertainer/athlete who was ostracized in ways that mirrored Ali's later fall from white grace: 'Shall negro sharecroppers from Mississippi be sent down to shoot brown skinned peasants in Vietnam – to serve the interests of those who oppose Negro liberation at home and colonial freedom abroad?'[20]

BROTHER MALCOLM AND THE NATION OF ISLAM

However, Clay's seemingly apolitical stance disguised a growing interest in civil rights and, in particular, a fascination with a small but growing organization called the Nation of Islam (NoI), also known as the Black Muslims.

The NoI was founded during the Great Depression and rapidly grew into the biggest African-American nationalist organization since Marcus Garvey's Universal Negro Improvement Association (UNIA). Gardell notes that the NoI combined pseudo-Islamic doctrines with Black Nationalist thought:

> The Nation was from the very beginning exclusively black and formulated emphatic political demands. The United States was depicted as the modern day Babylon soon to be destroyed by the wrath of God, whereupon the blacks would ascend to their predestined position as world rulers.[21]

The NoI, unlike other black organizations, tried to recruit members from prisons and poor inner cities. The migration of southern blacks to northern cities also provided a vast source of potential recruits. The NoI grew modestly until the 1950s, but the release of another ex-prison convert quickly changed that.

Born Malcolm Little and son of UNIA activists, Gardell describes Malcolm X's life as the alternative American dream:

> Malcolm's life was to become the symbol of the black version of the American dream. When Malcolm was six years old, his father was murdered by white racists. Louise Little [Malcolm's mother] was unable to provide for her family and had a nervous breakdown when state welfare workers wanted to place her children in foster homes. She was sent to an asylum, the children were scattered, and Malcolm grew up in different homes in Michigan. A talented student, but discouraged from higher education because of the colour of his skin, Malcolm embarked upon another career. Leaving for Boston and then Harlem, Malcolm became a street hustler and a burglar, which in 1946

brought him a ten-year prison sentence. While incarcerated, Malcolm was reached by the message of the NOI, and his life took yet another turn.[22]

Upon his release from prison Malcolm X rose quickly in the NoI hierarchy and toured the United States extensively, establishing 27 mosques in different cities. He became renowned for his rhetorical skill and oral mastery and appeared in various shows and lecture theatres.

Cassius Clay first met Malcolm X in 1962. Clay was already interested in the NoI and had wanted to write his high school dissertation project about them back in 1958. Whether intentionally or not, these views were on the whole kept hidden from the public domain, not by Clay's insistence, but rather it seems by the ignorance of the mainstream media.

In 1964 Cassius Clay was scheduled to fight Sonny Liston for the WBA/WBC Heavyweight Title. Clay was the 7/1 underdog and nobody gave him a chance against the awesome Sonny Liston. In some respects Liston lived the life of the 'bad nigger'. He was arrested over 100 times, jailed twice and was also a former Mafia 'heavy'. In boxing terms the classic scenario of 'good guy' (Clay) against 'bad guy' (Liston) was in place.

Despite his public boastfulness, Clay was himself in doubt about his ability to beat a world champion like Liston until Malcolm X convinced him of his own ability. Malcolm X, who was in the process of leaving the NoI and becoming an orthodox Sunni Muslim, told Clay that it was his destiny to win.

As Marqusee notes, Malcolm X saw in Clay a symbolic power similar to that which *Ebony* had glimpsed and convinced Clay that he could harness this power in the ring. Malcolm X is quoted as suggesting:

> This fight is the truth, I told Cassius. It's the Cross and the Crescent fighting in the prize ring – for the first time. It's a modern crusade ... Do you think Allah has brought about all this, intending for you to leave the ring as anything but the champion?[23]

Malcolm X's presence also brought Clay his first negative publicity and the fight was almost cancelled. The support and empathy normally shown to an underdog was somewhat limited once the public heard of Clay's association with Malcolm X. In some respects the 'good guy/bad guy' scenario was declared null and void.

On 25 February 1964 Cassius Clay became the world champion, beating Sonny Liston by a technical knock-out when Liston failed to get up for the eighth round. Marqusee suggests that Malcolm X saw in Clay what the white sports journalists refused to acknowledge: an independent intelligent boxer who played by his own rules and not the stereotypes laid down by white society.[24]

THE EMERGENCE OF MUHAMMAD ALI

At the press conference the next day the media ignored Clay's boxing ability and wanted to know whether or not he was a member of the NoI. The vilification had begun, but Clay stood defiant:

> I believe in Allah and in peace, I don't try to move into white neighbourhoods. I don't want to marry a white woman. I'm not a Christian anymore. I know where I am going and I know the truth and I don't have to be what you want me to be, I'm free to be what I want.[25]

In a perverse manner Clay was actually complying with white racist sentiment about integration, inter-racial marrying and so on, however he was doing so on his own terms. Marqusee summarizes the position thus:

> For the first time here was a black American sports hero who would not allow himself to be defined according to white racist stereotypes. He was seizing back his persona. Johnson and Louis, Patterson and Liston had been endowed with their public identities by the white press; Clay was going to create his own identity and shove it down their throats.[26]

Elijah Muhammad, leader of the NoI, was at first cautious of publicly backing Clay, but realising the potential publicity the World Heavyweight Champion would bring, the NoI quickly named him *Muhammad Ali*. In some respects the change straight to an Arabic name was quick, considering that Clay had not received an 'X' from the NoI. However the rift between Malcolm X and Elijah Muhammad was widening and the NoI could not afford to lose their most valuable recruit.

Cassius Clay was no longer. Muhammad Ali was here and the new heavyweight champion of the world. When asked what his new name meant, Ali replied in the literal sense, 'Muhammad means *worthy of all praises*, Ali means the *most high*'.[27] However this was more than just a change of name. Countless entertainers before and after Ali changed names, 'But this was different. This was a black man signalling by his name change, not a desire to ingratiate himself with mainstream America, but a comprehensive rejection of it'.[28] The mainstream media refused to call Ali by his proper name and the response by the predominately white media was swift and disparaging. Jimmy Cannon wrote in the *New York Journal*:

> The fight racket, since its rotten beginnings, has been the red-light district of sports. But this is the first time it has been turned into an instrument of mass hate. It has maimed the bodies of numerous men and ruined their minds but now, as one of Elijah Muhammad's missionaries, Clay is using it as a weapon of wickedness.[29]

Almost immediately the WBA stripped Ali of his title because of his conversion to Islam.[30] In *Soul on Ice*, Eldridge Cleaver gave a black perspective on the outpouring of all this negative publicity:

> Ali is the first 'free' black champion ever to confront white America ... In the context of boxing, he is a genuine revolutionary ... To the mind of 'white' white America and 'white' black America, the heavyweight crown has fallen into enemy hands. Ali is conceived as 'occupying' the heavyweight kingdom in the name of a dark, alien power.[31]

The media billed Ali's first title defence against Floyd Patterson as 'Islam vs. Christianity'. Furthermore, Patterson argued that the Black Muslims were a threat to the USA and had no place in boxing. He stressed that the heavyweight champion should be a good Christian and that therefore he felt it his duty to bring the title 'back to America'. Finally, Patterson fuelled the animosity by calling Ali 'Clay'.

The fight itself was no contest. Ali toyed with Patterson, prolonging the agony for 12 rounds and taunting him with insults. Ali called Patterson 'Uncle Tom' and shouted 'Come on White America'. *Life* magazine called the fight 'a sickening spectacle'.[32]

Ali grew more assertive in his new role as NoI figurehead. He toured Africa and Asia where his popularity was such that he met with heads of state, such as Abdel Nasser of Egypt. From 1964 to 1966 it appeared the sports press were more interested in Ali's political and religious views than they were in his fighting ability.

However, worse was to follow. In 1966 Ali was re-classified as eligible for draft and called up in 1967. He refused, citing his religious and political objections to the war. The reaction was instant. Within hours the WBC stripped Ali of his title. The *Los Angeles Times* proclaimed 'Clay is a black Benedict Arnold', while the *New York Times* argued 'Clay could have been the most popular of all champions but he attached himself to a hate organisation'.[33] Congressman Frank Clark stated: 'The heavyweight champion of the world turns my stomach. To back off from the commitment of serving his country is as unthinkable as surrendering to Adolf Hitler or Mussolini'.

In a few short years Ali went from being the epitome of American patriotism to what many writers have called a symbol of a divided America. He was called a traitor and a fascist for standing up to what he believed were racist doctrines governing his every move and portrayed as the instigator and troublemaker for not bowing to public pressure.

Marqusee notes that many draft boards were all white[34] and that in the southern states they had a tendency to enlist young blacks, especially those that were vocally active. Furthermore Ali was virtually alone in his outspoken criticism of the US involvement in Vietnam where he would have been undoubtedly stationed. In 1965/66 Americans overwhelmingly supported the war in Vietnam and public support for Ali was minimal. Even respected black leaders like Martin Luther King had not yet openly spoken against the war. In some respects Ali was ahead of these 'leaders' and more in tune with the ghettos where the price of the war was felt the sharpest. Ali later wrote:

> It was as though I had touched an electric switch that let loose the pent-up hatred and bitterness that a section of white America had long wanted to unleash on me for all my cockiness and boasting, for declaring myself 'The Greatest' without waiting for their kind of approval.[35]

Ring magazine refused to name a boxer of the year because Ali (the most obvious candidate) was not considered a role model for young America. Despite being stripped of his title, refused a boxing licence, having his passport confiscated and being threatened with jail, Ali remained defiant. His famous pre-bout poems now had a political edge to them:

Keep asking me, no matter how long
On the war in Vietnam, I sing this song
I ain't got no quarrel with the Vietcong.[36]

The African-American cultural critic James Baldwin echoed Ali's famous 'no Viet-cong ever called me nigger' quote:

> A racist society can't but fight a racist war – this is the bitter truth. The assumptions acted on at home are the assumptions acted on abroad, and every American Negro knows this, for he, after the American Indian, was the first 'Vietcong' victim.[37]

Ali's growing assertiveness paralleled similar developments in the civil rights movement. Younger blacks, such as H 'Rap' Brown and Stokely Carmichael, started to feature more strongly in the civil rights movement. These people represented a more militant viewpoint and reflected a growing interest and pride in expressing their blackness. Influenced strongly by the political philosophies of Malcolm X and the growing independence movements in ex-colonial countries, these different movements heralded the rise of the black consciousness movement popularly called the Black Power movement.[38] This led to symbolic acts of defiance from other black sports stars including the formation of the Olympic Project for Human Rights (OPHR), which demanded that Muhammad Ali be restored as world boxing champion and that South Africa and Rhodesia be from international competition.

Harry Edwards, a former basketball star and professor of sociology at Cornell University, was the organizer of the OPHR and articulated the grievances of black athletes in relation to wider socio-economic inequality and racism in society:

> The Star Spangled Banner, the US national anthem would be the focal point of the expected victory stand protests ... for the black man in America ... the national anthem has not progressed far beyond what it was before Francis Scott Key put his words to it – an old English drinking song. For in America, a black man would have to be either drunk, insane or both, not to recognise the hollowness in the anthem's phrases.[39]

Symbolic pressure was applied to the Olympic Games when Tommie Smith and John Carlos, who won gold and bronze medals respectively in the 200 metres, received their awards. As they stood on the podium the two athletes raised clenched fists:

I wore a black right-hand glove and Carlos wore the left-hand glove of the same pair. My raised right hand stood for the power in black America. Carlos's raised left hand stood for the unity of black America. Together they formed an arch of unity and power. The black scarf around my neck stood for black pride. The black socks with no shoes stood for black poverty in racist America. The totality of our effort was the regaining of black dignity.[40]

Black assertiveness had been growing out of the civil rights movements along with a radical student movement, both of which challenged the *status quo*. Even respected leaders like Martin Luther King spoke out about the consequences of continuing a war overseas whilst poverty was still rife in black America. On 16 March 1968 a US Army lieutenant ordered his troops to slaughter 500 unarmed Vietnamese villagers (including 200 children) at My Lai. Ali's lone stance against an unjust war now started to find growing support and European cities saw demonstrations against US involvement in Vietnam. By spring 1968 the majority of blacks were opposed to the war. Black soldiers in Vietnam who had been outraged at Ali's refusal to join the Army increasingly saw him along with Malcolm X and the recently formed Black Panther Party as their role models.[41]

Ali was 25-years-old when he was stripped of his title and it took nearly three years of concerted pressure from his lawyers (with little support from the Nation of Islam who suspended Ali in 1969, echoing the suspension of Malcolm X in 1963) to have his conviction reversed. It was discovered that the FBI had illegally wiretapped Ali's phone. It was later alleged that the FBI had also used illegal methods to disrupt the Nation of Islam, Martin Luther King's student support base, the Student Non-Violent Co-ordinating Committee (SNCC), the Black Panther Party and various other black organizations.[42] These illegal methods led to the imprisonment of key black activists – such as Bobby Seale of the Black Panther Party – and the self-imposed exile of others – Stokely Carmichael eventually emigrated to Ghana and Eldridge Cleaver to Algeria. The FBI is also said to have had active involvement in the deaths of a number of key black activists; most notoriously Fred Hampton, head of the Chicago Black Panther Party.[43] Considering the fervour with which the establishment attacked prominent black activists, in some respects it is surprising that Ali was not imprisoned or even killed although Bingham and Wallace suggest that he did fleetingly contemplate exile.[44]

In 1971 Ali was allowed to return to the ring and in 1974 he regained the heavyweight championship of the world, beating George Foreman in Zaire. By the end of 1974 Ali the former 'draft dodger' had been invited back to the White House by President Gerald Ford.

'BLACK' AND 'MUSLIM' IMAGINED AND REAL COMMUNITIES

In many respects Ali's conversion to Islam and his refusal to be drafted can be seen as the impetus behind the process that transformed him from being just a heavyweight boxing champion to a *world champion*. His stance was an inspiration for many black activists in America and this black civil rights movement was the catalyst for other human rights movements in America and around the globe. For example, Van Deburg notes:

> Black Power energized and educated black Americans, introducing many to the concept of political pluralism. It spurred new interest in African liberation struggles and the plight of the powerless world-wide. Newly sensitised to the political nature of oppression, Black Power converts set out to remedy the situation by forming numerous political action caucuses and grass roots community associations. These, in turn, served as often-utilized models for the various ethnic, gender and class consciousness movements of the seventies and eighties.[45]

Whilst it would be clearly wrong to suggest that Ali was alone in influencing the process of social protest in the 1960s, his defiance certainly influenced and helped empower groups who related to similar experiences not just of racism but prejudice and exclusion due to political and religious beliefs. Marqusee recalls watching the 1974 clash with George Foreman:

> the fight meant a great deal to many people on the left. One friend of mine, an Asian community activist with no interest in boxing, came into central London to watch the fight at a cinema because Ali, to him, embodied a political concept of blackness.[46]

Marqusee notes that many of the recently arrived non-white immigrants into Britain looked to black America for role models.[47] For these communities, especially South-Asian communities, the concept of Black Power that Ali clearly embodied was never just about blackness or pan-Africanism.

Sivanandan argues that 'Black Power' was a rallying-cry for non-white and Third World activists:

> It was the catalyst which showed up the essential unity of the struggles against white power and privilege – whether in the US itself, in Britain, in Southern Africa, or in former colonies of the Caribbean. Through it, black became a political colour with which other Third World activists and radicals could identify – the Dalit Panthers from among the untouchables of India took their name from the Black Panthers of the US ... Black Power is a political metaphor ... but also, in the terse, explosive precision of its language, a resounding call to arms.[48]

Similarly, Hall notes that:

> Black was created as a political category in a certain historical moment. It was created as a consequence of certain symbolic and ideological struggles ... in that very struggle is a change of consciousness, a change of self-recognition, a new process of identification, the emergence into visibility of a new subject.[49]

In certain respects Ali embodied that new black consciousness. Marqusee notes that for many British-Asians, Ali, a battling Muslim, was a source of inspiration and solace in the racist climate of the time.[50] This led to the younger generation of immigrants in the 1960s and 1970s adopting a black politics that was more assertive and demanding. In some respects younger generations were not willing to 'bow down to the white master' and adopted an ideology of asserting their rights and being more vocal and visible in their demands to achieve equality in society.

Recently there has been a contentious debate surrounding the use of this term 'black' in relation to those of South-Asian origin in Britain.[51] Some authors regard the term as inaccurate, especially in relation to subsequent generations, whilst others believe it is useful in creating a pan-identity with which to challenge (white) racism. Modood has spoken critically of the assumption that:

> the descendants of immigrants would lose all their 'difference' except colour and would therefore be thought of as a relatively undifferentiated 'black' mass both by themselves and by the white British, and that the only area of conflict would be socio-economic, or more broadly of inclusion/exclusion into white British society.[52]

Research on racism and discrimination in Scotland has used the term 'black' to embrace all of Scotland's ethnic minorities. Community groups such as the Edinburgh Lothian Black Forum employ the term in a similar spirit and this, it could be argued, is a usage employing 'historical' contexts reminiscent of 1960s America. That is, non-white groups in Scotland employ a political concept of blackness rather than a culturally specific label. Certainly recent work notes that 'black' identity is one self-descriptor which Scottish-Asian groups such as Scottish-Pakistanis still deploy.[53]

With the Scottish instance and personal experiences in mind, but also as a general observation, it might be argued that such debates need to take more account of the specific social, cultural and political circumstances that help to develop identity categories. In the United States the term 'Asian' is usually associated with those of Far Eastern origin, for example with Chinese or Japanese heritage,[54] and not readily with the Indian sub-continent. This suggests an immediate difficulty with the term 'black' if applied to American Asians, a difficulty produced by specific social and cultural circumstances. Marqusee argues that the young non-whites who were rallying around the term 'black' were in some respects creating a community and sense of belonging that superseded boundaries:

> Younger blacks ... Demanded the right to live and work in Britain on their own terms, while at the same time identifying themselves as part of a world community of the oppressed, through its linkage of self-discovery and self-assertion with a call to solidarity beyond national boundaries.[55]

In some respects it could be argued that Black Power created a global 'imagined community'.[56] By relating to this community, young blacks in the 1960s were in some ways displaying solidarity and gaining strength from images of black assertion embodied by Ali. This is similar to the concept of the 'ummah' – the global Islamic community that supersedes nationality: explained briefly, there are two tiers to Muslim identity, one related to faith and one related to country, but faith overrides any other component of identity.

In this way, the boundaries defining Muslim identity may also be strengthened; the young Muslims are likely to feel that although within British society they are members of a relatively small and weak minority, their religious beliefs and practice traverse the globe and history and are thus components of what is a vast and [potentially at least] powerful force.[57]

Participants may be drawing strength from an Islamic identity that can provide solidarity with other Muslims, as well as an avenue of escape from being constantly identified in negative terms. The logic of this process implies a positive (re)conceptualization of Islamic identity transcending local, negative attributions.

Thus in certain respects the concept of the 'ummah' and conceptualizations of political blackness draw upon similar feelings of exclusion and empowerment. Another reason Ali was so popular in a global context was his appeal to countries that did not previously follow boxing, but were either Muslim states or newly independent nations. Ali himself was aware of his popularity in Islamic countries:

> I can't name a country where they don't know me. If another fighter's going to be that big, he's going to have to be a Muslim, or else he won't get to nations like Indonesia, Lebanon, Iran, Saudi Arabia, Pakistan, Syria, Egypt and Turkey – those are countries that don't usually follow boxing.[58]

When Ali joined the NoI it was a separatist, black supremacist organization that contained elements of Islamic doctrine along with what can only be described as folklore. This folklore foretold the ultimate destruction of the white race. Malcolm X's autobiography, as told to Alex Haley, hints that the Islamic world was wary of the organization. However the organization was radically altered by the death of Elijah Muhammad in 1975. Elijah's son, Wallace Muhammad, re-named the organization *Al-Islam*. He de-emphasized racial issues and moved the movement closer to orthodox Islam – closer to the teachings of Malcolm X than his father. In Remnick's recent biography Ali notes that his biggest regret in his life was his hasty rejection of Malcolm X in 1964. Muhammad Ali welcomed these changes.

Such is Ali's influence in the Islamic world that he has regularly toured Middle Eastern countries and assisted in the release of American hostages from Iraq prior to the Gulf War.[59] His willingness to identify with Muslims world-wide, regardless of ethnicity, may have further endeared him to Muslim minority communities in Western secular societies.

The concept of community or 'ummah' features strongly in Muslim personal identities; my parents would always emphasize that Ali was a practising Muslim who embodied the notion of the 'ummah'. For my brothers and sisters, whilst religion was important, Ali's stance against white racism superseded his religious identity. For my brothers and I, Ali's defiance and willingness to confront racism mirrored our attitude that we would assert or demand recognition rather than have to 'turn the other cheek'. The fact that the younger male members of our household respected Ali for his 'confrontational' manner could be understood by reasoning that we were more likely (than our female siblings) to be victims of physical or verbal racist abuse or attacks. It could be argued that by being victims of such abuse we adopted a harsher attitude in understanding our position in society and developed a more militant response when confronted by racism. Thus our family appropriated Ali's multiple identities in distinct, but in some respects similar, ways.

CONCLUSION: THE POLITICS OF IDENTITY AND BELONGING

Hoberman notes that recent black sporting success has much to do with racist stereotypes of blacks as being intellectually inferior, but physically gifted:

> Stereotypes of black athletic superiority are now firmly established as the most recent version of racial folklore that has spread across the face of the earth over the past two centuries, and a corresponding belief in white athletic inferiority pervades popular thinking about racial differences. Such ideas about the 'natural' physical talents of dark skinned peoples, and the media-generated images that sustain them, probably do more than anything else in our public life to encourage the ideas that blacks and whites are biologically different in meaningful ways ... The world of sport has thus become an image factory that disseminates and even intensifies our racial preoccupations.[60]

He further notes that black athletic success has contributed to the argument that race problems do not exist in American society. De Mott claims that the American mass media have engaged in relentless promotion of 'feel good images' of black-white sameness that denies the deep conflicts between ethnic groups in America.[61] 'This propaganda of racial bonhomie is also a *de facto* policy of the American sports industry and is elaborated most effectively and ingeniously in advertisements.'[62]

In certain respects it could be argued that Ali has now been incorporated into the establishment. It could be argued that one of the reasons for this is to show how America has changed, that it now respects 'black militants'. Certainly Ali's pride in his ethnic and religious background has not diminished. Thus Hobermans' argument that real black-white relationships in America are glossed over in favour of a racial harmony, expressed most clearly through its promotion of black sports stars, seems justifiable. Marqusee notes that the rewards in sport have increased dramatically, intensifying the gulf between what he terms the black masses and black sport stars.[63] The consequent effect is that on societal face value there are more wealthy black individuals in prominent places, suggesting a decrease in economic racial inequality. Furthermore the ever-increasing numbers of black singers and actors, and the emergence of black subcultures such as hip-hop into the white mainstream, suggest ever increasing cultural/social integration and to some extent the fulfilment of Martin Luther King's 'dream'.

However, Marqusee suggests that corporate-backed black stars such as Michael Jordan and Tiger Woods are tolerated because of their lack of political activity and thought.[64] Jim Brown, a former American football player and member of the OPHR which demonstrated in the 1968 Olympics, is more scathing: 'Take a look at black superstars today ... Watch them twist their mouths and make money and pretend, yet do virtually nothing but pay tokenism to black freedom.'[65] Bingham and Wallace quote Jack Todd who links Michael Jordan's association with Nike to Ali's refusal to go to Vietnam: 'A decade after the end of the Vietnam War, Jordan willingly became a world-wide spokesman for a U.S. corporation that exploited the children of the Asian boys Ali refused to fight.'[66]

It is possible to compare the contemporary condition of blacks in America with the conditions of blacks in the 1930s. Van Deburg cites statistics from the 1990s that explode the myth of racial progress in America:[67]

- 40 per cent of all black children lived in households with incomes below the poverty-line;
- Black infant mortality was three times higher than the national rate for whites; and
- Blacks were six to seven times more likely to be victims of homicide.

Recent years have also witnessed a growing interest in Muslim communities in the UK, the US and throughout the world. Beginning with national issues such as the Rushdie affair and international matters such as the Gulf War, a series of events have brought Muslims into the media spotlight and adversely affected the Muslim population in the UK, the US and elsewhere. Ahmed argues that media language has been fashioned in such a way as to cause many to talk about a 'criminal culture'.[68]

The Muslim population in America, estimated at 8 million, has been placed under media scrutiny. The Gulf War, US involvement in Sudan and Afghanistan and the 11 September 2001 attacks on the World Trade Centre all placed American Muslims under a negative spotlight. These events have sparked into active operation latent stereotypes of Islam and the 'Orient' so that Muslim communities have come to represent a threatening 'enemy within'. Yet somehow Ali, probably the most famous Muslim in the world, is elevated beyond this prejudice.

Both of Ali's symbols of defiance against America, his black consciousness and his Islamic faith, might be seen as potential 'threats' to the Western world. While Ali undoubtedly suffered personal grievance as a result of his adherence to these identities in the 1960s, his personal allegiances now seem to be overlooked. It is not that this oversight appears to bear witness to decreased religious or racial intolerance, indeed the evidence suggests the contrary. Hoberman's argument that black sport stars are given positions of prominence that dispel racial strife appears plausible in the case of Ali.

It could be argued that in many respects Ali and his image have been appropriated by different sections of society for their own purposes. Parts of the establishment that once attacked Ali for his political stance (for example, the media, or prominent politicians) now view his experience as an example of triumph over adversity. Ali's symbolic legacy appears to be a site of constant negotiation, as *I'm A Little Special* noted at the start of this essay.

One possible reason why Ali has appealed to many white people in Britain is that 'Islam' and 'Muslims' are equated with the British–South Asian population and British Pakistanis in particular. In short, Islam has become racialized to mean 'Asian' in the British context. Thus people who dislike Muslims in Britain may in fact be displaying an animosity towards British Asians and British Pakistanis. Modood notes that British Pakistanis suffer from double racism based upon colour (of skin) and culture (Islamic religious background).[69] Many white people who have a racialized view of Islam may not regard Ali, by his physical appearance and national background, as a 'typical Muslim'.

Despite his insistence on stressing his pride in his ethnic and religious identities, while simultaneously and paradoxically belonging to an organization that preached black supremacy, Ali's attractiveness to people of a variety of different political, religious and social spectrums all around the world has not been diluted. Marqusee summarized why Ali's legacy appealed to him thus:

> America wants to forget what it did to the people of Vietnam, and has yet to pay a penny in war reparations. Yet America also wants to embrace Muhammad Ali and even convert him into a symbol of national identity. Perhaps I've lived abroad too long, but for me what makes Ali a role model is precisely his rejection of American national identity in favour of a broader, transnational sense of selfhood and social responsibility. Ali's career is a standing reminder to us all that national affiliation – in sports, in politics, in life – is not natural or God-given; it is constructed and can therefore, as Ali demonstrated, be deconstructed.[70]

Ali's appeal has always inclusive and global. This may explain why a Scottish-Pakistani family with little or no previous interest in boxing sought solace in Ali's defiant stance against racism and American imperialism.

NOTES

1. G. Early (ed.), *I'm a Little Special: A Muhammad Ali Reader* (London: Yellow Jersey Press, 1999).
2. M. Marqusee, *Redemption Song: Muhammad Ali and the Spirit of the Sixties* (New York: Verso, 1999).
3. Ibid., p.4.
4. Early, *I'm a Little Special*, p.xv.
5. Marqusee, *Redemption Song*, p.4.
6. Ibid., pp.4–5.
7. E. Cashmore, *Black Sportsmen* (London: Routledge and Kegan Paul, 1982), p.17.
8. Ibid., pp.16–19.
9. M. Marqusee, 'Sport and Stereotype: From Role Model to Muhammad Ali', *Race and Class*, 36, 4 (1995).
10. H.L. Bingham and M. Wallace, *Muhammad Ali's Greatest Fight: Cassius Clay vs. The United States of America* (New York: M. Evans, 2000).
11. Marqusee, *Redemption Song*, p.29.
12. D. Remnick, *King of the World: Muhammad Ali and the Rise of an American Hero* (New York: Random House, 1998).

13. Marqusee, 'Sport and Stereotype', 9.
14. Marqusee, *Redemption Song*, p.47.
15. Ibid., p.48.
16. Ibid.
17. Bingham and Wallace, *Muhammad Ali's Greatest Fight*, p.53.
18. Marqusee, 'Sport and Stereotype', 11.
19. Bingham and Wallace, *Muhammad Ali's Greatest Fight*, p.53.
20. Ibid., p.18.
21. M. Gardell, *Countdown to Armageddon: Louis Farrakhan and the Nation of Islam* (London: Hurst, 1996).
22. Ibid., p.65.
23. Marqusee, 'Sport and Stereotype', 12.
24. Ibid., pp.14–17.
25. Marqusee, 'Sport and Stereotype', 15.
26. Marqusee, *Redemption Song*, p.29.
27. Early, *I'm a Little Special*, p.146.
28. Marqusee, 'Sport and Stereotype', 15.
29. Bingham and Wallace, *Muhammad Ali's Greatest Fight*, p.73.
30. Ibid., p.92.
31. E. Cleaver, *Soul on Ice* (New York: Dell, 1970), p.91.
32. Bingham and Wallace, *Muhammad Ali's Greatest Fight*, p.109.
33. Ibid., pp.124–6.
34. Marqusee, *Redemption Song*, p.29.
35. Bingham and Wallace, *Muhammad Ali's Greatest Fight*, p.126.
36. Ibid., p.124.
37. Marqusee, *Redemption Song*, p.224.
38. W.L. Van Deburg, *New Day in Babylon: The Black Power Movement and American Culture, 1965–1975* (Chicago, IL: University of Chicago Press, 1992).
39. Bingham and Wallace, *Muhammad Ali's Greatest Fight*, p.199.
40. Marqusee, *Redemption Song*, p.204.
41. Van Deburg, *New Day in Babylon*, pp.129–44.
42. Ibid., pp.292–309.
43. C.E. Jones (ed.), *The Black Panther Party Reconsidered* (Baltimore, MD: Black Classic Press, 1998), pp.391–416.
44. Van Deburg, *New Day in Babylon*, pp.206–7.
45. Ibid., p.306.
46. Marqusee, 'Sport and Stereotype', 24.
47. Marqusee, *Redemption Song*, pp.201–5.
48. Ibid., p.203.
49. S. Hall, 'The Local and the Global: Globalization and Ethnicity', in A.D. King (ed.), *Culture, Globalization and the World System* (New York: Bingham Press, 1997).
50. Marqusee, *Redemption Song*, pp.201–5.
51. T. Modood, 'Political Blackness and British Asians', *Sociology*, 28, 3 (1994).
52. T. Modood, *Changing Ethnic Identities* (London: PSI, 1994), pp.5–6.
53. A. Saeed, N. Blain and D. Forbes, 'New Ethnic and National Questions in Scotland: Post-British Identities among Glasgow-Pakistani Teenagers', *Ethnic and Racial Studies*, 22, 5 (1999).
54. R. Schaefer, *Racial and Ethnic Groups* (Illinois: Scott Foreman/Little Press, 1990).
55. Marqusee, *Redemption Song*, p.203.
56. B. Anderson, *Imagined Communities: Reflections on the Origins and the Spread of Nationalism* (London: Verso, 1983).
57. J. Jacobsen, 'Religion and Ethnicity: Dual and Alternatives Sources of Identity', *Nations and Nationalism*, 3, 2 (1997).
58. Early, *I'm a Little Special*, p.158.
59. Bingham and Wallace, *Muhammad Ali's Greatest Fight*, pp.252–63.
60. J. Hobberman, *Darwin's Athletes: How Sport has Damaged Black America and Preserved the Myth of Race* (New York: Mariner Books, 1997), p.xxii.

61. Ibid., p.xxiv.
62. Ibid., p.xxii.
63. Marqusee, *Redemption Song*, p.295.
64. Marqusee, 'Sport and Stereotype', 27.
65. Ibid., 28.
66. Bingham and Wallace, *Muhammad Ali's Greatest Fight*, p.258.
67. Van Deburg, *New Day in Babylon*, pp.293–308.
68. A. Ahmed, *Living Islam* (London: BBC Books, 1999).
69. T. Modood, *Not Easy Being British* (London: Trentham, 1992).
70. Marqusee, *Redemption Song*, p.297.

4

From Pig's Bladders to Ferraris: Media Discourses of Masculinity and Morality in Obituaries of Stanley Matthews

GARRY WHANNEL

Are we too naïve if we expect to ever return to the days when sport was played with chivalry and respect, where the authority of its laws was sacrosanct, and its famous exponents noted for their skill rather than their rebelliousness? Are professional sportsmen so overpaid and amateurs so influenced by the behaviour of these stars that past standards cannot be recovered?[1]

It's all right to have two or three or four kids in a team, but when the time comes for responsibility you need men. In our team we were men of character. What does being a man mean? To play calmly, to talk, to not feel the weight of responsibility, to do what you're told. That's character.[2]

The first of these two quotations contrasts a professional and corrupt present with an amateur and noble past. It is fairly typical of romanticized nostalgia for a 'pure' past of athletic endeavour for its own sake. It is rooted in the ideologies of fair play that had their formative period in the English public schools of the mid-nineteenth century and were made concrete in the practices and cultural power of the sport governing bodies formed by the late Victorian male bourgeoisie. In such utterances, it is the intrusion of money, through professionalism, that in turn has fostered violence, cheating, lack of respect for rules and use of performance-enhancing drugs and so destroyed the Corinthian ideals of amateurism. In structure, this discursive element contrasts a golden past with a corrupted present.

The second quotation contrasts the irresponsibility of boys with the calmness of men. Being a man here means having 'character', being able to exert leadership whilst also, paradoxically, respecting and obeying higher authority. It is the ideology of the subaltern class within a social hierarchy, exerting a moral and intellectual leadership on the troops, but always within the framework of and, under the authority of, a senior officer class. It is the condensation of these two discursive elements onto each other – the idea that a responsible and dutiful masculinity is situated in the past – that is a key feature of the discursive presentation of the crises of morality and masculinity in the context of representations of contemporary sport.

The irony underpinning the second quotation is that Rattin is best known in England for his sending off in the England–Argentina quarter-final in the 1966 World Cup. In an ill-tempered match, with England committing the most fouls, Rattin was constructed in the English press as the villain of the piece after he clashed with referee Kreitlin. The impression that Rattin was threatening was strengthened by the manner in which the giant muscular Argentine towered over the small balding German referee. Rattin was sent off but refused to go, insisting instead on an interpreter. England manager Ramsey subsequently intervened at the end to prevent the English players swapping shirts with the Argentinians and referred to the Argentines as 'animals', a remark reported in the media around the world. The incident contributed in no small measure to an interpretative frame through which the English press represented Latin football. The silky skills of the Brazilians were constantly juxtaposed with Argentinian brutality. However, in the Argentine, a recent book suggests it is widely felt that referees were biased and that, for commercial reasons, England's path to the final was made as easy as possible.[3]

Since 1966, the transformation of sport by television has been at its most dramatic in the case of football. The popular appeal of football, combined with the global reach of televised games, has produced an astonishing growth in the revenue that flows into football from television rights payments, advertising and sponsorship. The World Cup has grown in popularity to the extent that it now challenges the Olympic Games as the major sporting event. The expansion of the sporting media, with sport-based satellite channels, sport supplements in newspapers and specialist sport magazines, has placed sport imagery in the cultural mainstream. At times of major competition, football imagery in advertising, in product-linked promotions, in replica kit shops and in give-away competitions is everywhere. The media-rich environment and the enhanced speed of circulation of imagery and intensive intertextuality and self-referentiality in post-modern culture have fostered a football-ization of culture whereby even those who hate the importance bestowed on the sport feel compelled to write about it.[4]

Anthony King's account of post-modernism in relation to the representation of sport emphasizes a shift in values from thrift to profligacy.[5] Drawing on Jameson and Mandel, King argues that the third stage of capitalism:

> is characterised by huge multi-national corporations, whose existence depends on the emergence and expansion of the consumer market. The emergence of this consumer market has necessitated a shift in the focus of capitalism from production to consumption, which in turn has required a complete overhauling of the value system. The values of thrift, discipline and reason, which Weber so famously associated with the Protestant spirit, and which he argued were essential for the emergence and continuity of capitalism have become unsuitable to the third, consumer, stage of capitalism. For this economic system to survive, individuals must not repress their desires and discipline themselves for work, but must satisfy those desires by indulgence in the consumer market. Thrift is similarly outmoded as expenditure is essential to the growth of the economy.[6]

This contrast of thrift and profligacy can be exemplified by comparing representations of Stanley Matthews and David Beckham. David Beckham has all the attributes of a 'golden boy' – football talent, good looks, highly publicized romance with another media star (Victoria Adams, Posh Spice from the Spice Girls). He plays for a team (Manchester United) that attracts both massive support and considerable loathing because they have become a symbol of the dominance of football by the richest clubs. In the summer of 1998, a widely publicized photograph of him on holiday with Victoria wearing a garment described as 'a sarong', was presented in the tabloid press in terms of deviance from the conventions of masculinity, with hints of his supposed 'emasculization'. Shortly after this episode, Beckham's sending-off in England's key match in the World Cup provided a point of condensation for discourses of morality and fair play in sport, in which national pride became national shame. Yet after a season spent shrugging off the abuse, winning Premiership, FA Cup and European Champions Cup medals, fathering a child and marrying Victoria, the story in the popular press became a narrative of redemption and triumph.[7] The wedding itself was the climax of a media blitz, vortextual in character,[8] in which football, pop music and fashion glamour, conspicuous consumption and romantic narrative were all filtered through the lens of *OK!* magazine.

King's highlighting of a post-modern shift from the work ethic to conspicuous consumption can be explored by a schematic comparison of the images of David Beckham and Stanley Matthews. While there are similarities between the two – both highly celebrated, English, key players for their team, both mythologized and neither especially articulate – it is the differences that are the more striking:

Matthews	Beckham
ordinary	superstar
working class	new 'classlessness'
thrift	extravagance
sobriety	profligacy
paternal authority	makes own rules
modest	markets own image
shuns limelight	seeks limelight
dedicated	indisciplined
family invisible	family highly visible

One of the most striking features in the image of Beckham is the way in which the division between public and private has been eroded. The romance with Victoria Adams, the wedding, the tattoos and the parading of the baby have all taken place in the full glow of public exposure. Indeed, the Beckhams would appear precisely to have exploited their marketability by transforming their private lives into a set of marketing opportunities, utilizing the commodification of domesticity that magazines like *Hello!* and *OK!* have had so much success with. In commodifying his own lifestyle, David Beckham has become a figure defined partly by commodity. He rarely speaks or gives interviews and so his image, freed from the embedding anchorage of utterance, has the character of a floating signifier. It is in this sense that the image (if not the person) can be thought of as rather 'classless'. Beckham himself is from a working-class background and while in many senses he remains clearly working class his image, in the ways in which it breaks with some of the conventions of working-class masculinity, is a more complex affair.[9]

By contrast, the image of Stanley Matthews is deeply embedded in a regionally located cloth-capped working-class nostalgia, characterized by a suspicion of public attention and a separation of public and private spheres. Matthews, although aware of and exposed to media pressure, deeply resented it. In *The Stanley Matthews Story* he says of the build-up to the 1951 Cup Final:

> My telephone never stopped ringing. Not only were the sports writers on the line, but all kinds of people asking if it was true that I was considering retiring. I was hopping mad. What right had these people to invade the privacy of my own home, to make my life almost unbearable?

In autumn 1951, Stanley Matthews switched on the 300,000 lights for Blackpool's Festival Year Illuminations. It is easy to imagine his embarrassment as:

> Eight thousand people jammed against the Town Hall steps to watch as he pulled the switch. He had a surprise. Above his head an illuminated set-piece came to life. Picked out in lights, it showed Stanley scoring a goal, the goalkeeper sprawling beaten as the ball entered the net. The winking lights repeated the scene again and again.[10]

MYTHOLOGY AND (AUTO)BIOGRAPHY

The key moment in the mythologizing of Matthews was his eventual success in winning an FA Cup Winners Medal in 1953. A year later another British sporting mythology was produced when Roger Bannister became the first man to run a mile in less than four minutes. The Matthews final was the first to be televised; film of Bannister's race appeared on the first *Sportsview*. Both stars had the climax of their careers at the very dawn of television sport, yet their fame was fundamentally pre-televisual. It preceded the era in which we came to expect interviews with stars immediately after the moment of triumph and it preceded by some years the tabloidization of the press and the erosion of distinctions between the public and the private. The coverage of sport stars in the 1950s was characteristically respectful and full of praise.

Although there are several titles that cite Matthews as their author, all involved a ghost writer who was probably largely responsible for the text. Star biographies and autobiographies, while rarely being high in literary value, provide useful evidence of the ways in which narrative is constructed and mythology consolidated. Indeed, although not engaged in the production of image as commodity on quite the scale of Beckham and Posh Spice in the era of *Hello!* and *OK!*, Matthews has always been involved in the production of his own image and one suspects that he is not simply the innocent observer of his own mythology. The advantage of the ghost writer mode of production is of course that image construction appears to take place at arm's length from its subject. In *Sport Stars of Today* Stanley is described as, 'the best known and best-loved footballer of them all. The Wizard of Dribble, modest too – the man who hates flattery and reminds you, "There are ten other players in a team, you know".'[11] His characteristics are enumerated in a manner that highlights their noble qualities. He 'looks like a wise old eagle ... strong lines from thin cheeks lead past a mouth notable for a dominant top lip and teeth free from dentistry, to a slightly pointed chin'.[12]

Anthony Davis refers to Matthews as inspiring young people the world over, 'His modesty, simplicity and sportsmanship have won him the inalienable affection of millions'.[13] The lives of sport stars in this period were often narrated as moral fables in which good embedded traditional values are emphasized:

> His father Jack Matthews ... expounded a rough and ready code of honour and physical fitness. He saw to it in a blunt Staffordshire accent that his only son Stan kept his body right and his thoughts straight ... Stanley went in awe of his father, a strict disciplinarian, a stand-no-nonsense man – but a good man and a man who tried always to do what he believed was best for his family.[14]

The salt of the earth image presented here is not simply embedded in 'traditional' values, such as the family, discipline and thrift, but is also localized. Staffordshire and the Potteries were written firmly into the Matthews mythology and when he returned to Stoke City from Blackpool (an event prefigured in fiction in Arnold Bennett's *The Card*, which features the return of footballer Callear to the 'Five Towns' of the Potteries) he was celebrated as a prodigal son.

Matthews himself describes a conversation with his father after his first game for Stoke reserves at age 15 that suggests at a culture of respectability and self improvement under the guidance of patriarchal authority:

> Boy-like, I couldn't wait to get home quick enough to hear what my father thought. He was reading a paper when I got in the house and looked at me over the top of it. He said, 'Son, you'll play a lot better and you'll play a lot worse'. He paused, then went on 'Forget about the good things you did; remember the mistakes you made, study them, and correct them, then forget them completely. You'll never keep repeating them if you do that. Remember a man who never makes a mistake never gets anywhere. Have you got that, son?' I nodded and said, 'Yes Father'. 'Well, sit down and have your tea', he said, and together we discussed the rest of the game.[15]

Matthews was clearly brought up to believe in the respectable working-class virtue of thrift. When he first gets to play for the first team at age 17 he is excited about earning money, but his father insists that he puts half his earnings in a savings bank and gives the other half to his mother for his keep. As for pocket money for himself, his father says he will have to earn that by securing his win bonus. The point of these values of thrift, discipline and family respectability in Matthews' account is that they function to reproduce masculinity. Matthews comments, 'We won and my pocket money was safe. I didn't play for the first team again for the rest of the season, so I couldn't have had a good game. But I had gone on that field a youth and come off a man'.[16]

The world portrayed is one in which sexuality and the emotions are collapsed into domesticity and the work of domesticity includes the labour of emotion management. At age 19, Stanley is practising constantly to improve his game when his mother asks him what he feels about his girlfriend, Betty. She then says it is time he settled

down and that there are other things in life beside football. She reveals
that Betty was hanging around waiting to be taken to the pictures, but
Stanley was too busy practising and forgot all about it. Matthews
realizes then that he is in love, but Betty has gone to Scotland with her
father. Matthews makes a dash for the stairs and, as he recounts it:

> My mother called out, 'where are you going?'. I turned and said
> 'To pack a bag. You are right, I do love her. I'm going right up to
> Scotland to ask her to marry me, and shan't leave Scotland until
> she does so.' My mother said, 'Don't bother about packing a bag,
> son, I've already done it; it's behind the door.' I gave her a hug,
> picked up the bag, and I caught up with Betty in Scotland. We
> were married in the clubhouse of the Bonnyton Golf Club near
> Glasgow.[17]

In fact, Matthews or his ghost writer may have been putting a bit of a
romantic gloss on the story. In a later account, he writes:

> I was 19. Betty was the daughter of Jimmy Vallance, the Stoke
> City trainer. It was through Jimmy that we met. Jimmy was a
> good golfer and he invited me for a golfing holiday and we
> married within the year. Jimmy was such a keen golfer that the
> wedding ceremony was actually held in the club house at
> Bonnyton Golf Club near Glasgow – the place where Rudolph
> Hess landed after his fantastic flight from Nazi Germany in
> 1941.[18]

Notable in these narrativizations of Matthews' life is the contrast
between the masculine world of work and the feminine domain of
domesticity, the civilizing and rounding impact of women ('all work
and no play', Betty is recorded as grumbling to Stanley) and the
transition from carefree youth to family responsibility. The narrating
of Matthews' life takes on the character of a moral homily, illustrating
the rewards that hard work, discipline and thrift can bring. His
dedication and application to his career are rewarded with success on
the field and marriage and a family off it. Public and private lives are
both portrayed in terms of respectability and rectitude. In fact, the
mythologizing of Matthews, whilst re-inscribing these elements, has
served to erase any aspects of the Matthews story that do not neatly fit
the image, such as his divorce and his problems with football
management – a point I return to in the final section of this essay.

THE DEATH OF MATTHEWS:
RE-INSCRIPTION OF A MYTHOLOGY

Three themes were ubiquitous in constructions of the image of Matthews at the point of his death in early 2000. First, he was a gentleman – in some accounts 'the last gentleman of soccer'. He was a model sportsman – quiet, reflective, modest, reserved and courteous and of humble origins. Second, he was a genius, an artist. Third, he had rigorous self-discipline; he was never booked and totally dedicated. The picture that emerges is of Matthews as the working-class gentleman, who embodied the classic Corinthian virtues, is more idealist than archaic. Although in implying a contrast with the present, Matthews is inevitably cast in a nostalgic glow. Indeed the representation of Matthews at the time of his death serves as the point of condensation for a broader romantic and nostalgic image of English working class-ness, in which concepts of family, thrift, modesty and duty are central. Matthews is described as:

> the last gentleman of soccer; a player with artistry in his feet and integrity in his soul. He played in the days when love of the game was enough and the most he could earn was £20 a week ... But he was quiet with it, a reflective man who was never boastful and never gloated in victory. He was never temperamental. He did not argue with referees. He said it all with his feet. The son of a barber-cum-smalltime featherweight boxer, Matthews was brought up with an old-fashioned work ethic in the potteries. His first club was Stoke and he would run to the ground, weaving between people on the pavement, rather than take the bus.[19]

His talented artistry – 'the wizard of the dribble' – highlighted everywhere, was characteristically linked to his modesty. The *Daily Mail* reported: 'A genius and a gentleman: The magical mixture of Matthews'.[20] The *Daily Telegraph* proclaimed that 'He not only tormented and destroyed full-backs on a weekly basis but did it with a sportsmanship that emphasised the brilliance he tried to shrug off'.[21] His dedication was written in terms of hard menial work, tough journeys and privations, which are portrayed, not as manifestations of grinding poverty, but rather as character forming:

> He was taken on as an apprentice by Stoke, where every day he had to clean 46 pairs of the senior boots and sweep out the

dressing room after training. 'Then I had to walk home' he recalled. 'It was eight miles a day unless it snowed. Then my father would give me my bus fare. It was cold enough in those days without central heating and hot water but I used to pray for snow.'... And what did Matthews do when he got home? He went straight out into the street to practise his legendary dribbling skills with a pig's bladder under the light of a gas lamp.[22]

His preparation is constructed as one of monkish asceticism and self-denial – 'He maintained a strict diet which sometimes involved total fasting'.[23] The newspapers dwelt on this self discipline with a close attention to detail as if to reinforce the contrast with an undisciplined present:

> It required rigorous self discipline to sustain his speed for so many years, every day, during his professional career, his diet was the same: carrot juice at lunchtime, steak with salad for dinner, a fast on Mondays. And every morning there would be a training run.[24]

> He was totally and utterly dedicated to the game in a way that you just don't see nowadays. He was a self trained dietitian long before that science came into the game. He ate raw carrots and drank blackcurrant juice. Stan never drank alcohol, didn't smoke, and used to get up early every morning at Blackpool exercise on the beach before training.
> And despite his huge fame he was always modest, courteous and the epitome of the perfect gentleman.[25]

Characteristically, descriptions sought to combine the elements of 'gentleman', 'artist' and 'dedicated professional' in a composite picture of perfection:

> Sir Stanley Matthews was not just the most skilful footballer Britain has ever seen. He was a true hero, whose dedication, professionalism and lifestyle shame the overpaid, over-rated players of today. Thousands of fans flocked to matches just to watch the wizard of the dribble play for Stoke, Blackpool and England. He mesmerised defenders with the ball seemingly tied to his boot laces ... And though hard men tried to kick lumps out of him every week, he was never booked in a 33 year career.[26]

In his own case that mental superiority was never arrogant or vain. On or off the field he was a modest, reserved and courteous man. He was a scrupulously clean player who avoided physical contact; he never sought it, and his deceptive movements ensured that he rarely suffered it.[27]

But for many unconnected with the game, he was more than just a sport star, he was an icon revered as much for his quiet dignity and modesty as for his footballing skills.[28]

In most accounts there is a taken-for-granted naturalism that ignores the process of image construction that produces stardom. The myth of Matthews is as much a product of media construction as it is of the talent of the man. It is worth noting that for most of Matthews' career the majority of the public would have only been exposed to his exploits in written accounts, still images and very brief film clips:

You couldn't see your heroes on television in those days, but we knew what a great player he was from the clips we saw on Pathe news, at the cinema, reading *Charles Buchan's Football Monthly* and from information on the back of cigarette cards.[29]

Only the *Guardian* sought to situate Matthews in relation to the practices of representing fictional heroics:

Matthews was a hero of 1940s and 1950s children's cigarette cards and comic books as well as newsreels. He was the real life counterpart of Wilson the Wonder Man [*sic*], who – long before Roger Bannister – once ran a mile in a still unbeaten 3 min 43 seconds wearing a black, long-sleeved Victorian bathing costume. Matthews' wizard dribbles were viewed as almost as remarkable.[30]

Indeed the 'Matthews final' (when Matthews finally won an FA Cup Winners Medal) is, with the possible exceptions of Bannister's 'four-minute mile' and the 1966 World Cup Win, probably the most thoroughly mythologized moment in British sporting history. No wonder then that, as with Bobby Moore, the image of Matthews should become utilized so keenly as part of a rhetorical contrast between past and present.

COMPARISONS

The establishment of this image of the dedicated gentleman genius enabled the insertion of the narrating of Matthews into a discursive structure that compared sport's past with its present in order to produce a critical account of the present. The past was a time when footballers had a maximum wage of £20 a week and love of the game was enough. Played by men in baggy shorts, watched by men in cloth caps, football was a hard but fair physical contest, a working-class sport. England then was 'a country in which modesty was respected or worshipped almost as much as popular virtuosity'.[31] In the present day, players are portrayed as overpaid, over-rated, flamboyant, flashy and pampered, with their showbiz lifestyles and million-pound homes, Ferraris and celebrity wives. Football has become a 'money driven circus fuelled by dissent and deceit'[32] full of 'bad-tempered stars who regularly drag the game into the mire'.[33] According to these accounts, sportsmanship has gone from the modern game.

The *Daily Mail* recalls Matthews' FA Cup final victory, when: 'There was a spirit of manly sportsmanship in the mutual congratulations that is so wretchedly missing from the game today'.[34] In contrast, the modern game is characterized by cynicism and cheating: 'In his own 33 year career Matthews was never booked. He found intensely distasteful the way some players hurled themselves to the ground in the hope of getting a player sent off.'[35]

According to these assessments, money has corrupted football.

> Matthews never resented the wealth of the modern footballer. What he did resent was the way the game itself changed from a tough but honest sporting contest between men who took their knocks without complaint, to a money driven circus fuelled by dissent and deceit.[36]

The material rewards of the present day are opposed to Matthews' era when, supposedly, honour and glory were to the fore.

> Whether flying down the wing, hair immaculately in place, or smiling gently, presenting an award, he represented his profession with grace, charm, honour and integrity. In an age when many players are pampered millionaires criticised for being cut off from reality, Sir Stan – on £20 a week – represented another era when footballers were heroes.[37]

paid more in a week than he earned in a soccer lifetime. They may be more feted in an age of easy celebrity. But they are not fit to lace Sir Stanley's boots. He was an idol who truly deserved the fan worship that placed him on a pedestal. We shall never see his like again.[43]

The discursive structure that all this is fitted into is one that sutures gether themes associated with the decline of morality, the crisis of asculinity, the decline of Britain and the threat to family values. The clining power of authoritarian morality, associated with the pposed declining influence of the Church, the school and the family, ovides the structure of a traditional conservative cultural pessimism which television and conspicuous consumption are threatening ability. One way of understanding this is as a crisis of adaptation, arking the long historical decline of thrift and the work ethic. ccording to the *Guardian*, Matthews' death 'marked the passing of a fferent kind of England, one which was thought to have been almost rgotten long before he died, a country in which modesty was spected or worshipped almost as much as popular virtuosity'.[44]

Such qualities are not merely lost and mourned; there is a desire to surrect them, for they are seen as a necessary element in the battle ;ainst moral crisis. The Rector of Stoke, Canon Edgar Ruddock, escribed Matthews as a genius and added, 'We thank God for Sir tanley's skill, courage, energy, and example. We must reflect on how uch we need those characteristics in our personal community and ational lives today.'[45] Prime Minister Tony Blair, another figure whose iscursive style has religious roots, commented, 'Sir Stanley was and ill always remain one of the all time sporting greats. He was not only ne of the finest players this country has ever seen, he was also a model >ortsman'.[46]

The coverage, like that accorded the death of Bobby Moore, reveals ıe extent to which, in the context of the declining moral significance f Priest, Father and Teacher, sport stars are constantly looked to fill ıe void, constituting moral exemplars.[47] The regularity with which ıis pious hope is unfulfilled, with so many sport stars constituting >ad examples', has yet to make a dent in such unrealistic expectations.

Profligacy and extravagance, it is suggested, have brought :
conspicuous consumption and showbiz glamour that have (
sport.

> How different he was from the flamboyant, flashy, hi‹
> stars of today, with their Ferraris and celebrity wives. N
> ever miss a single day's training, which is why he was ‹
> on playing league football until he was 50, by which tin
> back again with Stoke.[38]

There were 'No Ferraris for Stanley, he trudged 16 mile‹
go training'.[39] Poverty here is transformed into a character
virtue:

> It was all a million miles from the perks of today's pamp‹
> with their Ferraris, showbiz lifestyles and million poun
> As a child, soccer-mad Stan would buy a pig's bladder
> butcher and use it as a makeshift ball. He said 'We could
> the real thing. I never saw a proper ball until I l
> schoolboy international'.[40]

Matthews is portrayed as an embedded figure, true to his ro‹
of the earth whose few perks came from sources with in
working-class credentials, 'And while modern idols lik
Beckham rake in fortunes from lucrative sponsorship the wii
was just grateful to get his football boots provided free by the ‹
A romantic nostalgia for the egalitarian comradeship of share‹
rarely to be detected elsewhere in the popular press trea
football fans, surfaces here:

> A gent on and off the pitch, he gave so much to soccer
> so little back – in stark contrast to today's overpaid bad-(
> stars who regularly drag the game into the mire. In l
> shorts and heavy boots, he was a true hero to legion‹
> capped fans – and earned little more than they did.[42]

Reasserted here is the concept of star as hero, deserving the ‹
and having a responsibility to be a good role model, alon
cultural pessimism that suggests that moral decline means 1
figures are situated only in the past:

> It is only right that his passing knocks the loutish anti
> likes of Collymore and Gazza out of the headlines. The)

ABSENCES

There is one other, curious, feature of the obituaries of Matthews and it lies in the lacunae, the significant absences. Three aspects of his life – his divorce, his managerial troubles and his curious relations with his father – are (as is, admittedly, conventional within the form of obituary) glossed over. His marriage to Betty ended in divorce in 1975 and he married a younger woman. Given that this divorce took place when he was 60 and that it potentially contradicts the image of honest, sincere integrity and therefore does not fit the dominant frame at all, it is not too surprising that most accounts ignored the event, or reduced it to a bland uninformative sentence.

In fact, at the age of 52, Matthews commenced an affair with a Czechoslovakian interpreter, apparently concealing the fact from his wife for over a year, before eventually divorcing her in 1975. Matthews and his new wife, Mila, eventually went public with their story in 1981, in the book *Back in Touch*. The tale of Stanley Matthews and Mila is pretty dramatic – it involves romance, adventure, danger, a life on the run, voluntary exile in Malta – and, in the context of Matthews' public image as a shy and reticent man, it is rather shocking. It has evident news value, which makes the erasure of the episode from the obituaries all the more striking.

The couple first met in August 1967, when Matthews took Port Vale to tour Czechoslovakia and also spent some time negotiating a football boot deal. Wandering the grounds of a grand house during a party, they became so engrossed in each other that they walked into the swimming pool. A supporters' history of Port Vale recounts that a pre-season tour of Czechoslovakia took place in August 1967 to help get 'the lads really match fit' and Vale were undefeated in their two games. They also visited the Cejakovice wine cellars and toured a giant footwear factory. The book quoted Matthews as saying 'It was the best tour I have been on'.[48] After reading *Back in Touch*, of course, the reasons for his enthusiasm for the tour are all too easy to understand.

Matthews returned to Czechoslovakia soon after this initial meeting and he and Mila spent more time together. When he returned to England they corresponded regularly and he sent her flowers every week. Before the end of the year, she had confessed to her husband that she was in love with Stanley and had paid a visit to England during which Matthews showed her around the Peak District, only a short distance from his home. On New Year's Eve, Matthews spent an hour on the phone to her and early in the New Year, in receipt of invitations to South Africa and Canada, he invited her to join him. By some moral standards, they behaved rather badly – Matthews was unable to face telling Betty about Mila for long after he and Mila had agreed that they wanted to divorce their partners and get married. Mila's husband George refused a divorce, so she tried to arrange for an actress to seduce him so that she could accuse him of adultery. It is not clear whether Matthews knew of this plan at the time.

Matthews was stranded in Prague for ten days in August 1968 when the Russians moved in. Soon after, Mila fled Prague for the west. Matthews abruptly left England later in 1968, leaving his wife, his home and his friends – in his words, 'everything I considered important' – to begin a life of hiding and concealment with his lover. During their time on Malta, an elaborate system of precautions and warnings provided by friends and neighbours helped them dodge the press. It was to be some years before Stanley and Betty divorced. The story does not fit comfortably with the Matthews mythology and the obituaries avoided any reference to the events, many of them avoiding any clear reference to the two women in Stanley's life.

Matthews' short career as a manager was effectively ended when his club were punished for breaking Football League rules, although he appears to have been an innocent party. Only one newspaper published any details of these problems:

> Spurning offers of international tours, Matthews became the manager of Port Vale, then a Fourth Division side. This proved a disastrous interlude. In 1968 due to a proposal to pay an illegal bonus to the players and to a failure to pay registration fees, the club was fined £2000 and expelled from the League.[49]

In fact, the Football League commenced an examination of Port Vale's financial records in November 1967 and the club were subsequently charged with several infringements of the rules:

• Several amateurs had received a weekly wage;
• Associate schoolboys had played for the club in contravention of the rules;
• Extra bonuses had been offered for a League cup win;

- Illegal bonuses were paid to two players; and
- Gifts were made to young players in contravention of the rules.[50]

The announcement of the investigation made headlines and Stanley Matthews, as the star name, became the focal point of the stories. Matthews recounts the impact the publicity had on him, 'the midday editions of the newspapers were out when I reached Euston. Placards and headlines screamed from all sides: "Football League to probe Stan Matthews ... Sir Stan on the mat ... Matthews in illegal payments scandal".'[51]

According to Matthews, the rule breaches were largely the result of administrative confusion and a degree of incompetence on someone's part. Paperwork relating to some players had not been filed as a result of negligence and this meant that some of their younger players had not been registered as professionals. Matthews recalls that the players requested a bonus if they won the League Cup Game against Chester; Matthews raised the issue at a board meeting; the Chairman asked the Secretary if anything in the rules prevented it and the Secretary said no so the Chairman agreed the lads could have a £10 win bonus – and this was recorded in the minutes. In the event the match was lost and so no bonus was actually paid. Matthews subsequently complained that the Chairman and Secretary refused to either make a public statement or give a press conference with him. Matthews struck a bitter note on the episode when he wrote:

> The headlines continued 'Matthews in Port Vale scandal' as much as saying I had been cheating or fiddling. The innuendo was I had been caught with my hand in the till. That was a joke! Quite apart from the fact that it rankled, it was downright ludicrous. The club was as good as broke. There was no money to fiddle and I hadn't even had a penny in salary since I joined.[52]

The Football Association had also called for an enquiry and eventually fined Port Vale £2,000. The Football League kept postponing their enquiry until in the spring of 1968 the club were fined £4,000 and expelled from the League for financial irregularities.[53] They were re-elected in June 1968 from the Fourth Division. Finally Matthews resigned, disillusioned at the lack of support from the Chairman and Secretary. Since he had still not been paid, he initiated difficult negotiations as to how Port Vale might pay the £9,000 they owed. Eventually the club agreed to pay £100 a month, but only during the season. This meant the debt (in effect an interest free loan from Matthews) would take around 10 years to pay off. The commentators' judgement on these events was that the rule breaches were associated more with incompetence than intent to deceit and that Matthews was not to blame. The relative absence of mention of these events in the obituaries stems partly from the conventions of obituary writing (glossing over the negative features of a career) and largely from the difficulty of fitting such events into an overall interpretative frame that portrays Stanley Matthews as the ultimate respectable sporting gentleman.

The power of interpretative frames is that material that does not fit into them is ignored, or marginalized. The incident in which Bobby Moore was accused of stealing a bracelet in Bogota, shortly before the 1970 World Cup Finals, was derided as a set-up by the British press. Moore was not charged with an offence and no persuasive evidence of guilt was reported. In representational terms it was almost inconceivable that it could have been otherwise; it would not have fitted the dominant frame of reference.

A similar incredulity initially greeted the accusations of ball-tampering in cricket involving England captain Mike Atherton, the first publicized positive drug tests by British athletes and the allegations of match fixing in football and cricket. Indeed cricket journalism, not noted for cynicism, is now struggling to come to terms with the escalating pace of match-fixing allegations and revelations. The British press, often quick to condemn the misdemeanours of those from other countries – Asian cricketers accused of ball-tampering, foreign athletes whose drug tests are positive – are more typically likely to assume the innocence of British stars. The relative lack of condemnation of British athletes with positive drug tests, such as Linford Christie, the double standards applied to foul play in football and the lamentable lack of enthusiasm for pursuing bribery allegations against English cricketers suggests a press whose national chauvinism and closeness to their key sources at times mitigates against the pursuit of journalistic imperatives.

A thoughtful assessment of the career and character of Matthews ought inevitably to consider his relationship with his father. Several accounts do mention the father–son relationship and some even mention Matthews' disappointment that his father never praised him:

> For years, Stanley believed his father had never once seen him play. 'When I came home from a match he never asked me how we got on, or if I did well' he recalled 'even when I was playing for England, he never praised me'. It was not until many years later that he learned how his father used to sneak away from his barber's shop on Saturday afternoons to watch him playing.[54]

> Sir Stanley did admit to one major disappointment in his life – the fact that his dad had never once told him 'well done'. He said 'For years he refused to come to any games, including England ones. When I came home from playing for Stoke City he would not even ask me how things had gone. When I played for England he never praised me once. It was only years later that my brother told me how my dad would sneak away from his barber's shop to watch me play. To me, he would sometimes be among the crowd – but never once did he say anything. After all these years I still don't understand why.'[55]

But none of the accounts seek to highlight this rather striking parental coolness. It represents a form of parenting that appears to fit well with the conventions of working-class masculinity that were dominant between the 1920s and 1950s. However, when observed from the perspective of the new millennium, even given the marginalization of the emotional in British working-class masculinity and the general lack of care given to the forms of emotional support that growing children and even young adults might need and thrive on, such emotional neglect, which might now be regarded by some as cruel, would seem to call for comment. Rather than simply modest and humble, we might speculate that despite his huge success, Matthews may have suffered from a bit of low self-esteem, given this withholding of the father's approval. However, such interpretation does not fit the over-arching frame of reference in which Stanley Matthews is idealized as a prime product of working-class respectability, thrift and commitment to the work ethic.

In the broader context, of course, there is a deeper irony in that a discourse that regrets the decline of paternal authority should in this instance have at its heart a figure whose own father, while probably a figure of authority, exhibited an apparent lack of parental warmth. Indeed, lack of emotional support from parents has, in recent years, been identified by many newspapers, various 'experts' and popular common sense as being at the core of the problems of that well known disfunctional family and most potent symbol of Britain, the Windsors.

The images and representations of sport stars are always complex assemblages, referring us, as they inevitably do, to discourses of national identity and gender and ethnic difference. In particular, in the context of perceived crises in morality and in masculinity, the images of sport stars are likely to be means by which concepts of morality and masculinity are worked through. The image of the sport star has become a significant point of condensation for social unease in which tensions about moral authority and manliness are addressed. In contrast to the images of 'pampered superstars' prominently featured in obituaries of Matthews, it could be argued that in fact today's top players work hard at their game – the training is more rigorous, the tactics more systematic and the knowledge of diet, sports medicine and even sport psychology is greater. Levels of fitness are considerably higher and the on-pitch work-rate is much higher than in the 1950s. The demands of the game are higher; the stakes have been raised. Self-discipline is now an expected prerequisite of the modern player. Far more games are played per season and for the top players more of these games are important ones against highly accomplished opponents. However, the discursive contrast between the ascetic Matthews training on cobbled streets with his pigs bladder and the overpaid players of today in their Ferraris has a stark tabloid simplicity that tends to mask the more complicated set of social changes through which modern football has been transformed.

NOTES

1. *Evening Standard* Sports Writers, *Sporting Spite*, 1991, back page.
2. Antonio Rattin, Captain of Argentina in 1966, quoted in C. Taylor, *The Beautiful Game: A Journey through Latin American Football* (London: Victor Gollancz, 1998).
3. Ibid.
4. See G. Whannel, 'Individual Stars and Collective Identities in Media Sport', in Maurice Roche (ed.), *Sport, Popular Culture and Identity* (Oxford: Meyer and Meyer, 1997), pp.23–36.
5. A. King, 'The Fining of Vinnie Jones', in *International Review for the Sociology of Sport* (Munich: R. Oldenbourg Verlag, 1996), pp.119–38.
6. Ibid., pp.122–3.

7. G. Whannel, 'Punishment, Redemption and Celebration in the Popular Press: The Case of David Beckham', in David Andrews and Steven Jackson (eds.), *Sport Stars: The Cultural Politics of Sporting Celebrity* (London: Routledge, 2001).

8. I explain the concept of vortextuality more fully in my book *Media Sport Stars: Masculinities and Moralities* (London: Routledge, 2002) and also in 'Punishment, Redemption and Celebration in the Popular Press' (ibid.). The growth in the range of media outlets and the vastly increased speed of circulation of information have combined to create the phenomenon of a 'vortex' effect, which I term 'vortextuality'. The various media constantly feed off each other and, in an era of electronic and digital information exchange, the speed at which this happens has become very rapid. Certain super-major events come to dominate the headlines to such an extent that it becomes temporarily difficult for columnists and commentators to discuss anything else. They are drawn in, as if by a vortex.

9. See Whannel, *Media Sport Stars*.

10. A. Davis, *Stanley Matthews CBE* (London: Cassell, 1962), p.79.

11. Stanley Matthews, *Sport Stars of Today: Stanley Matthews* (London: Football Monthly, 1963).

12. Ibid., p.3.

13. Davis, *Stanley Matthews CBE*, p.3.

14. Matthews, *Sport Stars of Today*, pp.3–6.

15. Stanley Matthews, *The Stanley Matthews Story* (London: Oldbourne, 1960), p.26.

16. Ibid., p.31.

17. Ibid., p.35.

18. Stanley and Mila Matthews, *Back in Touch* (London: Arthur Barker, 1981), p.87.

19. *Daily Mail*, 24 Feb. 2000.

20. Ibid.

21. *Daily Telegraph*, 24 Feb. 2000.

22. *Daily Mail*, 24 Feb. 2000.

23. Ibid.

24. *Daily Telegraph*, 24 Feb. 2000.

25. *Sunday Mirror*, 27 Feb. 2000.

26. *Sun*, 24 Feb. 2000.

27. *Times*, 24 Feb. 2000.

28. *Mirror*, 24 Feb. 2000.

29. Bobby Robson, former England manager, *Sunday Mirror*, 27 Feb. 2000.

30. *Guardian*, 4 March 2000.

31. Ibid.

32. *Daily Mail*, 24 Feb. 2000.

33. *Sun*, 24 Feb. 2000.

34. *Daily Mail*, 24 Feb. 2000.

35. Ibid.

36. *Daily Mail*, 24 Feb. 2000.

37. *Mirror*, 24 Feb. 2000.

38. *Daily Mail*, 24 Feb. 2000.

39. *Sun*, 24 Feb. 2000.

40. Ibid.

41. Ibid.

42. Ibid.

43. Ibid.

44. *Guardian*, 4 March 2000.

45. *Sun*, 4 March 2000.

46. *Express*, 24 Feb. 2000.

47. See J. Williams and R. Taylor, 'Boys Keep Swinging: Masculinity and Football Culture in England', in Tim Newburn and Elizabeth Stanko (eds.), *Just Boys Doing Business: Men, Masculinities and Crime* (London: Routledge, 1994), pp.214–33.

48. J. Kent, *The Valiant Years* (Stoke-on-Trent: Witan Books, 1990), p.220.

49. *Daily Telegraph*, 24 Feb. 2000.

50. Kent, *The Valiant Years*, p.222.
51. Matthews, *Back in Touch*, p.41.
52. Ibid., p.43.
53. D. Hayes, *Port Vale Football Club: An A-Z* (Cheshire: Sigma Leisure, 1998), p.84.
54. *Daily Mail*, 24 Feb. 2000.
55. *Sun*, 24 Feb. 2000.

5

New Media Sport

RAYMOND BOYLE and RICHARD HAYNES

> Forget television sets, set-top digital boxes and satellite dishes. Quite soon, sports fans who want to watch Arsenal, Tim Henman or Lennox Lewis in action will simply turn on their personal computers, access the Internet, select a channel – then break open the beers as usual.[1]

> Where there's passion, there's profit.[2]

The rhetoric that surrounds the new media environment is enticing. The prospect of being able to watch anything, anytime, anywhere makes the contemporary choice of terrestrial and pay-television channels seem relatively arcane. In this view of the new media order the use of information technologies is only restricted by our imaginations. Being online and being digital will be as natural as kicking off your shoes and flicking on the television with a remote control. The promise for sports fans is that they can indulge their passions to even greater degrees than at present. But how much of this futurology is reality and how much pipe dreams? What are sports organizations and media companies doing to accommodate such radical paradigm shifts in communications? What implications do global, networked multimedia-driven communications have for our experience and understanding of sport and media sport? This essay aims to focus on some of these issues and debates. In particular it will examine some of the changes in the UK football industry, one of the key sports in the new sports media economy. Initially however we want to identify what we mean by new media and indicate why it increasingly matters to sport.

THE NEW MEDIA LANDSCAPE

New media, particularly the internet, digital television and mobile telephony, are introducing new distribution platforms and services for the delivery of sports content. All these new services are characterized by the key processes of digitization, convergence and interactivity. Digitization has been characterized by Negroponte as the movement from 'atoms' to 'bits'.[3] Where traditional media are manufactured and shipped in a physical form or via analogue waves, digital media are broken down into intangible 'bits' of information that are easier to manipulate, distribute and reproduce via computer-mediated communication. Digitization is occurring at many different levels of the sports-media production process. Both the hardware and software used to capture audio-visual signals from sport have been digitized, from the capture of the moving image on camera to editing facilities.

The introduction of virtual advertising and sponsorship has added yet more layers to the information available on our screens, already laden with statistical data and channel branding. Moreover, the distribution of television can be digitized and compressed into a multitude of signals, increasing capacity for themed sports channels and bringing with it superior quality of sound and image. Similarly, traditional sports journalism is written, stored and manipulated for the internet at the same time as it is produced for print.

The global availability of sports information and analysis via digital networks is transforming the way in which breaking news about sport is gathered, selected and disseminated.[4] The speed at which journalists can send information to each other and to online media is radically altering our expectations of sports news and our capacity to consume it. Digitization also produces fundamental problems for the protection of copyright and other forms of intellectual property in sport. Regulatory and technical mechanisms (encryption) to control digital information are stretched as the ability to reproduce and distribute media content becomes easier and more accessible. The ability of the rights holders to leverage income from exclusive economic rents to 'digital property' is increasingly under threat. As more sports-related content is available on digital networks (the internet, mobile phones, digital television) and carriers (CDs, CD-ROMs and DVDs) the broader the possibilities for piracy and copyright infringement become.

Convergence and Sport

Convergence has long been the 'buzz word' of new media commentators. The process suggests the increasing integration of mass communication, telecommunication and data communication in the delivery of media content. Convergence would have a dramatic structural impact on all three industries at various levels. The *transportation* of sports media would no longer remain specified to television or the internet, but would become simultaneously available through both. Sports webcasting is already a reality, but the capacity of existing phone lines, even ISDN connections, make the 'streaming' of audio-visual content significantly inferior to viewing traditional televised sport (see below). Broadband transmission through fibre-optic cables or satellites with microwave transmission would deliver a truly converged capacity for what is referred to as the 'electronic superhighway'. However, the infrastructure for broadband networks is only just being built and is a considerable way off reaching the mass of the UK population. In the US, a more advanced market than Europe, one economy survey in the *Economist* suggested that only four per cent of US households had broadband access.[5]

Convergence is also happening at the economic level of media, telecommunications and computer companies. The merger of Time Warner and America Online (AOL) was an indication of the increasing conglomeration of communication industries around the world as they strategically align themselves in the new media environment. Convergence is also happening within the media sport industries as media organizations move to control or collaborate with sports organizations and companies in search of synergies and strategic partnerships (see below).

As the audio-visual spectrum has widened so the demand for quality content has risen exponentially. Sport is playing a pivotal roll in this converging economy, bringing a ready-made audience to new media platforms and delivery systems. Just as media companies can see the benefits of integration with sport so the sports industry itself has seen the potential benefits to be gained from exploiting their proprietary rights by developing their own media systems. Again, sport related pay-television channels, internet sites and telephone services using the Wireless Application Protocol (WAP) are viewed by many in the sports industry as a means of expanding business opportunities, in particular, the sale of sporting brands (see below).

Interactivity

The third process identified as key to the new media environment is interactivity. Where traditional mass media were about the one-way flow of information, new media incorporate the ability to interact with the medium in a two-way or multilateral communication without the control of intermediaries (producers, editors, schedulers and so on). By its very nature the internet incorporates elements of interactive media: hyperlinks between sites, electronic messaging (e-mail or bulletin boards) and other elements of e-commerce. Interactive television has also been launched within digital platforms, offering viewers a chance to react to the source content. For example, digital channels such as Sky Sports Extra launched in August 1999 allows its viewers to edit what they see; from the choice of camera angle (including a 'player-cam') to action-replays on demand and a rolling statistics service. As the branding of these services suggests, interactive television claims to offer extra choice and opportunities. The viewer is said to be in control, receiving added value for their additional subscription fee to the digital platform.

A further dimension to interactive digital television is the capacity to provide access to the internet. BSkyB's Open service provides prohibitive (or 'walled garden') access to online material, while Ondigital, the terrestrial digital platform, enables total internet access through its Onnet portal supplied through a set-top box. As the viewer of these new media services navigates through the interactive 'multiplex', pieces of embedded audio or video material pop up to view, save and paste into personal web space created by the television service. This technology broadens the scope for sports sponsorship and advertising to embed what is termed 'advertorial' content within a programme. During a televised sports event a sponsor's logo could appear on screen to act as a hyperlink to further information about the product or service. Moreover, the high-speed two-way links of interactive television could also provide exclusive access to video gaming that ties the sports event with other sports-related merchandise, introducing a complete sports entertainment package.

Interactivity is also a central component of the internet itself and the explosion of sports-related websites epitomizes the centrality of sport in the rolling out of new media services. One of the fastest growing areas in this respect is the emergence of online sports betting.

The betting industry is seeing a stream of new websites offering unlevied betting from tax havens located outside the UK. The combination of sports content and gambling is a potentially explosive mix. The internet's ability to provide informative data, sports webcasts and instant electronic betting has led to huge claims being made for the expansion of the sports betting industry and its online variant in particular. An example, in Scotland, is the launch of TSNsport.com by snooker agent and impresario Ian Doyle. The site brings together news and multimedia content on Doyle's stable of leading snooker professionals, including Stephen Hendry, and direct access to SportingOdds.com, an online betting service. The site will undoubtedly attract attention from Scotland, where snooker continues to maintain a healthy following, but its principle aim is to capture the massive audience for the sport in Asia. The website epitomizes the global reach of new media networks and the power that quality sport content brings to new media businesses.

The notion of interactivity is perhaps the most intriguing dimension of new media sport. It suggests a new way of consuming sport that is qualitatively different to anything that has preceded it. The transformation in the use of media forms and the impact of new media on our understanding of traditional media practices has reinvigorated debate on man's relationship with technology. As Negroponte argues:

> Broadcast television is an example of a medium in which all the intelligence is at the point of origin. The transmitter determines everything and the receiver just takes what it gets. Instead of thinking of the next evolutionary step of television as increased resolution, better colour, or more programmes, think of it as a change in the distribution of intelligence – or, more precisely, the movement of some intelligence, from the transmitter to the receiver.[6]

While Negroponte's analysis of television viewing is narrow and rather deterministic, his general point about the shifting of power to new media consumers would seem to have some grounding. The notion of the 'active viewer', which suggests audiences actively engage with television, is written into the new media services now on offer.[7] While it is not the focus of this essay, the study of interactive elements in sports websites, digital television, mobile telephony and the future advances in Personal Digital Assistants (PDAs) offering portable broadband technology, opens new ground for researching transformations in the consumption of media sport.

Understanding the economic and cultural context in which new media services are forming alliances with sport is an important starting point for this wider agenda. The remainder of our analysis attempts to build on this premise by focusing on recent developments in new media and its relationship with the football industry. Before moving on to a detailed case study of the UK football industry and the battle for control of broadcasting and online markets, it is instructive to look in more detail at some of the ways in which new media are being employed in the sports industry and traditional media.

Sport on the Web

The internet has undoubtedly had a dramatic impact on the environment in which the sports-media industry now operates. Throughout the late 1990s sports organizations and clubs developed websites to provide corporate information, breaking news and e-commerce (predominantly the sale of merchandise) to sports fans. It is no exaggeration to suggest that all major spectator sports now have a presence on the internet in some shape or form. The degree of engagement with new media clearly varies, but there is general consensus among sports organizations that the internet presents a range of new possibilities for communicating with various publics. This expansion in media capacity has brought with it a range of problems that sports and media organizations have had to resolve.

In relation to the production of content, sports clubs have had to invest in online sports networks including the development of new skills in the practice of public relations, journalism and design. Many sports federations and clubs have outsourced the development of websites to specialist companies – the number of which has mushroomed as the industry develops apace. Sports organizations are having to learn new business models and entrust the development of new corporate communications to new companies who do not have any pedigree in the sports industry.

There is a sense within this booming media sector that sports organizations are hedging their bets by investing in new media in the blind belief that any internet presence is better than none. Many clubs and federations are not strategically clear why they need a website or what function it has within the broader communication activities of their organization. The recruitment of public relations professionals and media managers with specialist knowledge of new media and e-commerce is becoming increasingly imperative for organizations to survive in a competitive environment.

There are several emerging models of new media sports enterprises that range from sports specific 'portals' acting as gateways to sports news (such as Teamtalk.com), to fan-related websites that have taken the concept of the fanzine into an electronic media environment (many of which are being brought under one umbrella by rivals.net). However, it is also interesting to briefly review the extension of traditional media – broadcasting and the press – into online activities that support mainstream coverage and journalism. An analysis of the transformations taking place in established media organizations provides a useful barometer of how new media are impacting on the traditional practices of sports broadcasting and journalism.

In the UK, the BBC have paved the way in the scale of their internet activity and the amount of resources they are prepared to allocate to new media. BBC Online has experimented with the 'streaming' of live commentaries from test cricket and football in order to fully exploit its increasingly limited portfolio of rights. The global reach of BBC Online is also a feature of the site. Global journalism has enabled the site to post almost instantaneous sports reports from anywhere in the world. For example, the landmark England test victory over Pakistan in Karachi in December 2000 was given extensive coverage in the hour following the close of play. The website included interviews with both captains, full colour photographs of the action, comment on the match by BBC correspondents and an opportunity for cricket fans to post their own messages regarding the future of English cricket. The website enables the BBC to interpose between the scheduled breaking of radio and television news and the traditional reportage of sports journalism. It can provide the depth of coverage missing from the brief sports bulletins of broadcast news and also the speed and global reach missing from the production of the sports pages of daily newspapers.

Of course, the press have also utilized the immediacy of online journalism with online versions of a newspaper providing wider scope for in-depth analysis. In this model of traditional-media-turned-new media-service, the internet acts as the 'hinterland' of sports reportage. However, as the scope and use of the internet grows, traditional media may see online coverage as the shop window for sports journalism. Where websites once provided a mirror image of the main newspaper, they are now evolving their own identities and brands (for example, *Guardian* Unlimited).

The broadening of sports coverage will clearly have ramifications for how sports journalists practise their trade – what deadlines they need to make and how they construct their copy. It also has implications for sports rights holders who are seeing a convergence in broadcasting and traditional sports journalism on the internet. Both media are using the internet in similar ways and may be forced to pay for access to certain events where previously they formed part of the press corps. The International Olympic Committee's decision to restrict internet coverage of the Olympic Games for the next decade is an indicator of the rights holders' growing fears that online sports coverage may dilute the exclusive rights they have licensed to traditional broadcasters.

It is against this backdrop that the second section of this essay is placed. We examine the trends emerging in the UK football industry as it adapts to this changing environment, looking particularly at the clubs of Manchester United in England and Celtic in Scotland.

THE UK FOOTBALL INDUSTRY: THE BATTLE FOR CONTROL

The 1990s saw an explosion in the business of sport in the UK. As broadcasting markets opened up, increased competition for viewers and subscribers has seen sport become the key element of 'media content/product' being used to build new audiences and income streams for media organizations.

The natural synergies of vertical integration between sports organizations and media conglomerates is easy to recognize when one understands the centrality of televised sport in the contemporary media environment. With the proliferation of television channels and heightened competition for an increasingly fragmenting audience, quality programme content is at a premium.[8]

Barclay Knapp, Chief Executive of NTL, the largest cable company in the UK, has been busy developing alliances with a range of possible content providers, including football clubs. NTL recognize that without content they may be the best store in town, but with 'nothing on the shelves'.[9] Thus sport, and in particular football, can provide a ready-made supply of attractive programming. One consequence of this shift in the economics of broadcasting markets is that a widening spectrum of delivery methods has placed more power in the hands of content providers.

The revenue from television has also fuelled a boom in related sports industries, such as merchandising. In the UK, the development of the sports economy has been uneven and the football industry has been the main beneficiary of this boom. For example, in 1999–2000 Manchester United PLC enjoyed a turnover of £116 million[10] – more than the total turnover of English cricket. Manchester United also became the first sporting club in the world to be valued at over £1 billion on the stock exchange.

One key area in this financial development has been the growth in the value of sports rights. It is the latent power of sport to withdraw altogether from the television arena, and the phenomenal hike in sports rights, that has urged media companies to look at sports organizations not as partners, but as integral units of their business strategies. One of the key areas to emerge has been the competition for sports rights, both national and global. Allied to this has been the selling and marketing of these rights by sports promoters operating in an increasingly global marketplace.

The market for sports rights has, therefore, become far more complex in the way rights are 'bundled' or 'unbundled' between live coverage, delayed transmission, recorded highlights and the increasingly important internet. The packaging of channels and sports rights across other distribution platforms means that both the sports rights sellers and television organizations get better value, effectively selling their product more than once, particularly where advertisers are concerned. Despite the collapse of ITV Digital in the UK in 2002, and the re-adjustment in football television rights across Europe, they remain a key element of the pay-television context.

Football as Media Content

Throughout the cultural industries the battle is on to forge alliances between content providers and new delivery platforms and distribution systems. Both new and old media recognize the importance of content, even to the extent that historic non-players such as telecom companies are increasingly expressing interest in securing television content and sports rights.[11] As Gerry Boon has pointed out with regard to football:

> Clubs have started to recognise their own power and have begun to use it. And power follows control of the commercial properties in the game: image rights, TV rights and so on. So it is all about a battle for control of those commercial properties.[12]

In material issued to season ticket holders, Celtic Football Club outlined its position by stating, 'Celtic's ambition is that, in the future, it will derive a much greater benefit for the club and its supporters from this intellectual property which, after all, ultimately belongs to the club'.[13]

This process has led to increasing the power of the top clubs at the expense of governing bodies. The continually evolving UEFA Champions league format demonstrates the extent to which UEFA are keen to appease these forces in the game and, in particular, to head off the threat of the top clubs, in association with a Milan-based sports marketing company Media Partners, breaking away to set up a separate European Super League.[14]

A major concern for clubs such as Celtic and Rangers in Scotland and the top clubs in Holland and Belgium is how they keep pace with the clubs in the larger and more lucrative (in television terms) leagues. While a club like Celtic may play in a small league (in terms of television audience) it has a large actual and potential fan base. Celtic earn just eight per cent of their total revenue from television rights, as opposed to 26 per cent in the English Premier League and 37 per cent in Seria A in Italy. This frustration was evident when a number of clubs from smaller European countries took part in discussions in Holland exploring other league formats that could boost television revenue (the so-called Atlantic League).[15]

The logical endgame for media companies is of course to own both the distribution network and the content providers. If BSkyB's attempted take-over of Manchester United in 1999 had been successful, not only would they have had control of the providers of content, but they would have had a key influence in the collective selling of media rights for the Premiership. The Competition Commission (formerly the Monopolies and Mergers Commission) blocked the move on the grounds that it would give both an unfair advantage to the company in the pay-television market and in the media rights negotiations with the FA Premier League. In addition it was felt that such a move would not be in the long-term interests of British football. Despite this setback and while it appeared that Rupert Murdoch had lost this battle, it soon became clear that the BSkyB endgame of securing exclusive live Premiership football rights was still very much on.

Media Stakes in Football Clubs

BSkyB has systematically built up its portfolio of investment in football clubs in the UK, a process Adam Brown has described as 'sneaking in the back door'.[16] By 2000, BSkyB controlled stakes in Sunderland PLC worth £6.5 million, 9.9 per cent of Manchester United, Manchester City and Leeds United. Granada media group had 4.9 per cent of Arsenal and 9.9 per cent of Liverpool, who appointed a brand manager to fully exploit the commercial potential of its brand. Since the downturn in the telecommunications market, NTL, as part of their debt re-structuring, has lowered its stake in Middlesbrough to 5.5 per cent. NTL's problems leave BSkyB as the dominant media player in the football market.

Also in early 2000, BSkyB purchased a 9.9 per cent stake (worth £40 million) in Chelsea Village, the holding company of Chelsea (the Premier League allows any one company to have up to a 9.9 per cent stake in a club). This gave the company exclusive media agents rights for five years and also allowed it to develop internet opportunities for the club. Vic Wakling, Managing Director of Sky Sports, commented: 'The club will be able to maximise its return from its media rights, sponsorship and advertising deals, and to develop broadband and new media opportunities, whilst remaining focused on its performance on the pitch.'[17] In the same month BSkyB also signed a five-year deal with Tottenham Hotspur (through the newly formed Sky Sports Ventures) to design and develop its website and announced that it would be investing £250 million in new media developments related to its Sky Sports websites.

Media companies were positioning themselves for the summer sale of English Premier League broadcasting rights, which fetched £1.65 billion in total. In short, these companies wanted to sit at both sides of the negotiation table; they became desperate to secure the media content rights to a sport they view as crucial if they are to develop or, in the case of BSkyB, simply sustain their market share.

A number of issues are worth noting about the summer rights sale of English football 2001–4. First, the Premier League sold their digital, pay-per-view (PPV), subscription, free-to-air and secondary recorded rights on behalf of the 20 clubs (these are known as the offline rights). However, a key second front was the online rights issue, consisting of broadband, internet and WAP. With clubs such as Manchester United developing their own media infrastructure, football clubs want to retain and exploit their online rights for themselves. BSkyB's monopoly on pay television initially appeared to be under threat from the increasingly complex 'unbundling' of the rights across differing platforms. However the collapse of the PPV NTL part of the deal in October 2000 suggested that companies involved in a largely untried market had actually paid too much for their PPV rights.

It is becoming clear that clubs require a multimedia capacity to be in a position to exploit the online rights that will only become more important as the decade progresses. Both Arsenal and Liverpool have developed broadband services in alliance with the Granada Media Group. In Europe, Inter Milan, AC Milan, Roma and Real Madrid have rolled out subscription television channels with various media partners. These developments mirror the most lauded club media enterprise, Manchester United's MUTV.

MUTV is a joint venture between the club, Granada and BSkyB and is viewed as a vehicle to drive the sale of the Manchester United brand around the world. However, financial results have shown a distinct lack of interest among the United faithful and the channel recorded losses of more than £2 million in its first two years of operation. The key to MUTV's success is the control of broadcast rights, currently shared among the entire Premier League rather than with individual clubs. The economic pressure for the collective group of Premier League clubs to release the rights to television broadcasts higher up the value chain to individual clubs is set to increase. Having a ready-made infrastructure and resources to exploit those rights, if or when they come, is foremost in the strategic vision of the major clubs.

Similarly, Manchester United's website, manunited.com, is a subsidiary of Manchester United PLC and operates as a separate company. The website reportedly receives more than 8 million hits per month, the vast majority of which are from overseas.[18] The global reach of this support was a significant reason for the club's strategic alliance with its sponsor Vodafone. Vodafone, one of the largest telecommunications companies in the world, bought the sponsorship rights to Manchester United for £30 million in February 2000. The deal takes Vodafone's relationship with the club beyond the traditional role of a shirt sponsor. Utilizing its wide-ranging expertise and resources in the telecommunications industry, the company intends to use the Manchester United brand to sell new products – including co-branded phones – and introduce new media services such as club-specific content across a range of platforms. This suggests that the deal can be viewed almost as a *franchise* arrangement, rather than a traditional sponsorship agreement.

Cross-platform deals of this nature are throwing up a range of new legal problems for football clubs to decipher. Licences for 'electronic rights' were previously another term for broadcast rights. However, in the new media environment 'electronic rights' have a broader significance and may now include WAP, internet, digital radio, or video gaming rights as well as the traditional broadcasting rights. To this end, rights holders and broadcasters are reviewing their existing licences to audit what rights have been pre-sold or pre-required under existing contracts. In the case of Manchester United, the publisher Kingfisher VCI have made claims that they are licensed to publish content related to the club including anything published on the internet and mobile phones. This is one of the many complexities football clubs find themselves in as they strategically build their communications infrastructure. As media markets fragment, football clubs are stretching their 'content' to migrate from one format to another. The contractual agreements that aim to exploit intellectual property in sport are demanding thorough policing of media assets.

Another related, and growing, issue for clubs also surrounds the online rights for individual players. In March 2000 it was reported that

David Beckham's agent was offering the rights to run the player's website to a number of ISPs.[19] This is another indication of the increasingly complex picture emerging with regard to copyright issues over online control of an individual player's image and how this should or should not relate to the collective rights of the club. This is something that is now being explicitly written into players' contracts. For example, in summer 2000 when Luis Figo moved to Real Madrid from Barcelona for £37 million, part of the contract involved Figo signing his online image rights over to the club.

Celtic PLC: A Multimedia Company

In 2000 the Chairman of the Celtic PLC Board could report that they were 'confident that a developed, global Celtic brand with its associated intellectual property will enable the company to take full advantage of the rapid changes taking place in the kindred worlds of sport, entertainment and communications'.[20] Celtic divide their commercial activities into five divisions:

- Ticket sales;
- Broadcasting fees and publishing;
- Merchandise;
- Catering; and
- Other commercial.

However, like other large clubs they are keen to develop their online and multimedia provision. Celtic was one of the first clubs in Britain to have a website (re-launched in December 1999). As noted above, an internet presence has become important both for merchandising opportunities and also for the webcasting of matches. Deals between sports web operators such as rivals.net and BSkyB, Yahoo and Cable and Wireless indicate that new alliances are being developed. The ability to control these rights and show live footage and/or edited highlights across the web will be the key to this development. Celtic have been at the forefront of carrying live audio commentary of matches through their website, initially in conjunction with Yahoo and more recently with Broadcast Europe, a subsidiary of Broadcast America. In addition the club has recruited a number of newspaper sports journalists to staff its newsroom, which is charged with generating content for the various media platforms that the club now controls (print, internet, radio and television).

The web also links Celtic directly with its supporters. Much is made of the revenue streams this potentially opens; for example, one can envisage that clubs such as Celtic will only sell their club shirts (sponsored by Umbro) via the internet, mail order and their own superstores. Celtic make in the region of £3.8 million per annum from this sector of their activity and, although Manchester United make over £20 million, this figure compares well with other Premiership teams.

However it would be a missed opportunity if clubs simply used the new media to sell goods and services to fans. As noted above, one of the key features of the new media landscape is the extent to which it can be interactive and can bypass more traditional media outlets. We would like to see clubs use their websites to engage in a dialogue with supporters. Celtic recently used the web to elicit feedback on their system for allocating tickets for a Cup final and then acted on the feedback from supporters on this issue. To confine debates on new media solely to income streams would miss the opportunity to build trust and new communications networks between football and its fan base.

Celtic TV (Speakeasy Productions)

Celtic TV broke new ground in October 1999 when, using its own in-house multimedia production company, it beamed the League Cup match from Ayr United back to a paying audience at Celtic Park. Beam-back matches have become increasingly common among the two big Scottish clubs Celtic and Rangers, given their large fan base (almost 100,000 season ticket holders between them) and the difficulty these fans have in getting tickets for away matches. In the first five months of the 1999–2000 season, Celtic beamed six matches back to the stadium to a total paying audience of 45,469 supporters.[21] While in the past pictures have been bought from traditional broadcasters, Celtic, with their own communications and broadcasting staff (Speakeasy Productions) have begun, where appropriate, to beam back using their own broadcasting facilities. They also use in-house facilities for their internet audio webcasts.

In December of 1999, Celtic became the first British club to screen live video coverage of their home UEFA Cup match against Jeunesse Esch through their website. The game attracted 35,000 requests, of which it was estimated that 70 per cent came from outside Scotland.[22]

While there are clearly advantages for clubs in these developments, in particular when they control their rights and start to charge for access, it is vital for the long-term health of the game that a variety of media platforms are used to promote the clubs and the game. Without some free-to-air access, what happens to the more general football/sports viewer or the viewer/listener with only a passing interest in a major media event (as is often the case in international sports)? By reaching these groups the game and the club is continually promoted and the next generation of fans is nurtured. New media offers ample opportunities to individualize and customize the sporting experience by giving additional information to the die-hard fan, but football cannot afford to become a ghetto sport. While much has been made of the potential to deliver content via mobile phones (the appeal of images via WAP technology has been massively overstated), clubs must maintain a profile and presence outside of these groups. They underestimate the appeal of the collective televisual viewing experience of football at their peril.

There appear to be two models of media/sports club development emerging. In one, clubs are increasingly viewed as part of wider media organizations; for example, in the US where baseball clubs such as the Atlanta Braves are owned by Time Warner. In the other, clubs are developing multimedia strategies either by themselves or in conjunction with new (and not so new) media companies, as they aim to exploit their online rights. As they control the content the newly emerging distribution systems and technologies are desperate to harness, why (they ask) should they not simply deliver it themselves? It is clear that every major club is keen to develop its media capacity for fear of being left behind when the projected revenues (and, like a lot of dot.com financial analysis, 'projected' is all they are at present) begin to materialize.

CONCLUSION: EVERYTHING TO PLAY FOR?

As we have argued, the extent to which the media landscape has altered over the last decade or so is such that standing still is not an option for football or its clubs. However, there is a real danger that something intrinsic to the game will be lost in the scramble to cash in on the opportunities offered to football by the economic shifts in the media and related industries. 'Tradition' can be a double-edged sword, both mobilized as a force to retain important aspects about the meaning of the game and also as an excuse to stifle progress.[23]

Not so long ago, football fans in the UK were told by those who ran the game that they preferred to stand and watch football in decrepit stadia because it was traditional. Few fans would want to return to the days when clubs patently abused their loyal support. New opportunities offer new patterns of exploitation. Disconnect the club from the community within which it is located, and the supporters who have sustained it during the lean years, and the gains enjoyed during the boom may be short lived.

Competition remains vital for football to flourish. Unlike most markets, the sports market will collapse if the strong dominate and take-over the weaker market participants, something that is realized even in the highly commercial world of American sport. As money drifts to the elite clubs, there remains a concern that the grass roots of the game are in need of attention if the long-term future of the sport is to be sustained. There is also the danger of over-exposing football, both in terms of excessive matches and television coverage, a concern both in the UK and elsewhere in Europe.[24]

Sport, New Media and Collective Identities

The origins of sports clubs in previous centuries were bound up with notions of community. The football club often became a public projection of the community's wider collective sense of itself. It might be argued that we now live in an increasingly networked society in which new media technologies construct new patterns of community. Yet in many ways it is the appeal of that actual sense of community, which being a football supporter offers, that makes it such a potent cultural force in an increasingly fragmented and turbulent social and economic world. People like to feel they belong and sport offers a highly charged emotional public area within which to express this sense of belonging, even if at times this carries with it negative aspects.

Football still occupies a central position in many communities in Britain. Even in the global economy, this remains linked with a sense of place and identity. The stadium fans remain the backdrop onto which the game is projected; football as a televisual spectacle becomes redundant if it is played in front of half-empty stadia. Football has a responsibility to look beyond the next season and the next television deal (something it has not previously been very good at). If the game is unwilling to do so then it should be required to act through governmental intervention. The rights of supporters who invest both emotionally and financially in the clubs are vital for the long-term health of the game.

Many of the potential developments outlined in the opening section of this essay are also dependent on the creation of a robust and open broadband network, something to which the UK government has committed itself in terms of rhetoric, but not as yet actual investment. We are at the start of a process and it may take at least five years before clear winners and losers emerge.

We are not arguing for some nostalgic return to the past. By and large, the experience of going to a football match has become safer and more enjoyable, if more expensive, over the last decade. However we now stand on the verge of the next stage of the development of the sport, driven by changes and opportunities that the evolving media landscape offers. Football needs to ask itself who the game is for and who are its stakeholders in the twenty-first century. We would argue that broadly speaking the relationship between football and the media (television, radio and the press) has been good for both institutions; it has opened up new audiences and brought the game to a large global audience.

However, contemporary media culture increasingly views sport as commercially important, but not necessarily socially or culturally so. The market value of football is high precisely because people view it as culturally and socially important. If that affiliation is not nurtured, developed and respected, then the result may be disappointing for many.

Football is too important to be left solely at the mercy of financial analysts, global media companies and internet start-up firms. It offers a rich arena of myth, image, narrative – a compulsive world of story-telling. At a cultural level the images that a community projects on to the sporting field, and the manner in which these images are refracted through various media, tell us much about our individual and collective identities. They also expose our values, priorities, hopes, dreams and aspirations in a very public manner. It is these very factors that make sport such a compelling media 'product'; strip that away and very little of interest is left.

New media developments offer very real opportunities for the clubs of the twenty-first century to reconnect with their supporters and communities, both local and global. To restrict that debate solely to one of revenue generation is to misunderstand the business of being a football supporter. For those of us who care about the game, the ultimate challenge in the new century is to develop strategies that embrace these new opportunities, while retaining those elements of the game that make so many of us committed to these clubs in the first place.

NOTES

1. Denis Campbell, *Observer*, 8 Aug. 1999.
2. A. Fynn and L. Guest, *For Love or Money* (London: Andre Deutsch, 1999), p.11.
3. See N. Negroponte, *Being Digital* (London: Coronet Books, 1996).
4. J. Herbert, *Practising Global Journalism: Exploring Reporting Issues Worldwide* (Oxford: Focus Press, 2001).
5. E. Duncan, 'Media Madness', *Prospect*, 56 (Oct. 2000), p.13; 'A Survey of the New Economy', *Economist*, 23 Sept. 2000, 1–52.
6. Negroponte, *Being Digital*, p.19.
7. S. Livingstone, 'New Media, New Audiences?', *New Media and Society*, 1, 1 (1999), 59–66.
8. R. Boyle and R. Haynes, *Power Play: Sport, The Media and Popular Culture* (London: Longman, 2000), pp.206–24.
9. *Broadcast*, 17 March 2000.
10. B. Warner, 'Net Strategy With Balls', *Industry Standard Europe* (2 Nov. 2000), 54–61.
11. *Financial Times*, 15 March 2000.
12. G. Boon, 'Football Finances: Too Much Money?', in S. Hamil, J. Michie, C. Oughton and S. Warby (eds.), *Football in the Digital Age: Whose Game is it Anyway?* (Edinburgh and London: Mainstream, 2000), p.33.
13. Material issued to season ticket holders in Oct. 2000, entitled *Team Celtic: Pointing the Way Ahead* (Celtic Football Club).
14. Fynn and Guest, *For Love or Money*, p.300.
15. This remains an ongoing debate as the clubs and UEFA battle with each other to re-structure European competitions.
16. A. Brown, 'Sneaking in Through the Back Door? Media Company Interests and the Dual Ownership of Clubs', in Hamil *et al.*, *Football in the Digital Age*, p.83.
17. Reuters, 6 March 2000.
18. B. Warner, 'Net Strategy with Balls', 54–61.
19. P. Kelso, 'A further £8m in the pipeline for Beckham on the net', *Guardian*, 25 March 2000.
20. CFC, *Team Celtic*.
21. Ibid.
22. Ibid.

23. See R. Boyle and R. Haynes, 'Modernising Tradition: The Changing Face of British Football', in G. Lines, I. McDonald and U. Merkel, *The Production and Consumption of Sport Cultures* (Brighton: LSA, 1998), pp.21–36; D. Conn, *The Football Business: Fair Game in the 90s?* (Edinburgh and London: Mainstream, 1998); P. Dempsey and K. Reilly, *Big Money Beautiful Game: Winners and Losers in Financial Football* (London: Nicholas Brealey, 1998); J. Williams and S. Perkins, *Ticket Pricing, Football Business and 'Excluded' Football Fans: Research on the 'New Economics' of Football Match Attendance in England* (Leicester: Sir Norman Chester Centre for Football Research, 1998); J. Williams, *Is it All Over? Can Football Survive the Premier League?* (London: South Street Press, 1999).
24. See I. Bell, 'Just how much more football can we take?', *Scotsman*, 5 April 2000. The proposed re-structuring of the UEFA Champions League in 2003 is in part driven by a concern about over-exposure of the tournament on television.

6

Meeting the Industry:
An Interview with Alex Gilady

ALINA BERNSTEIN

The growing body of literature addressing a variety of issues related to the media–sport relationship in modern society devotes a relatively modest place to the perspective of the people who actually work in the media industry. Arguably it is important for academics interested in media and sport to interact with the people who, in many respects, shape the reality we analyze, in order to gain a better understanding of the professional motivations behind mediated sport. Actually meeting with such people and asking them what they think is an important step towards understanding the past, present and future of this relationship.

The interview that forms the basis of this piece is an attempt to narrow the gap by seeking the view of a high-ranking television executive, who although certainly – as this contribution demonstrates – possessed of his own views and unique style of expressing them, represents an important view within the industry. In this context, Alex Gilady seems an especially well positioned interviewee since he is able to provide a broad view of the production of televised sport in the US, Europe and Israel (a useful example of a small country). Specifically, Gilady is best positioned to discuss the relationship between television and the Olympic Games, while his views of more general aspects of the relationship between commercial television and sport provide a much needed insider's insight into televised sport.

RESEARCH METHOD

This interview took place in Alex Gilady's office in Herzliya, Israel on 27 November 2000. The hour-long interview was conducted in Hebrew[1] and was based on a list of open questions that I had prepared in advance. These questions were grouped into themes, which are reflected in the structure of this essay, and included general questions about media and sport, NBC sport and globalization, media and sport. More specific questions dealt with the Olympic Games and the Sydney Games in particular, the internet and its role in the future of mediated sport (mostly in relation to the Olympic Games) and sport in the Israeli media.

In many instances, answers to a given question lead to a discussion that did not necessarily follow the pre-prepared line of questioning. Indeed, in some cases I asked one broad question – for example, 'how do you see the internet, you personally, and/or what is NBC's view' – and the long, detailed answer given actually covered most of the further questions I intended to ask. Overall, I would say I was able to lead the interview in the directions I was interested in, but the interviewee controlled the specific paths followed within each theme.

After transcribing the entire interview I edited some of the answers in order to provide a coherent discussion of the main themes I had initially structured it around. This resulted in relatively few omissions – the essay reports on nearly the entire interview – but necessitated some moving around of answers, or parts of answers, to fit more coherently into a written argument. As well as the interview itself, this essay includes my own critical discussion of some of the answers given. It also refers to various further sources, which, in some cases, contradict the interviewee's answers, or simply shed more light on them.

It is important to emphasize that one of the main aims of the interview was to reveal the type of motivations dominating television executives' decision-making processes regarding the coverage of sport and the questions were formed accordingly. My own prior view, which emerges from the essay, is that the media, including commercial television, should assume (at the very least some) social responsibility. My questions were therefore aimed at assessing whether economic logic was the main, or even only, factor guiding the industry's decision-making, or whether further factors were also at play. There is therefore a structured tension in the interview between, broadly speaking, a public service expectation of television on the part of the interviewer and its rejection by the interviewee.

BIOGRAPHY

Alex Gilady was born in 1942 in Tehran, Iran to parents of Polish origin. Since immigrating to Israel as a small child he has always kept a home there. He has been a journalist, a television sports commentator and was the Israeli television Channel 1 Head of Sports in the 1970s. He is currently Senior Vice-President of NBC Sport (for global operations; he has been Vice-President at this American network since 1981), Chairman of the IAAF Radio and TV Commission (since 1985), member of the International Olympic Committee (IOC) Radio and TV Commission (since 1985) and member of the IOC (since 1994).[2] He owns a six per cent share in Keshet Broadcasting Ltd., a franchisee of the second television authority in Israel (the commercial Channel 2). He has been awarded three Emmy Awards for the production of NBC's Olympic broadcasts of Barcelona 1992, Atlanta 1996 and Sydney 2000.

TELEVISION AND SPORT: THE VIEW FROM NBC SPORT

I began the interview by asking Gilady about the structure of NBC Sport. He explained that:

> NBC Sport is divided to two separate divisions, one is NBC Olympics since for the first time in history the Games were sold for 13 years. The deal was made in 1995 till 2008 inclusive, a deal which includes three summer Games and two winter Games [see below]. The Olympics division works separately, NBC Sport takes care of everything else and sells advertising time for all the sports it holds the rights for, including the NBA, [American] football (I am not sure they have the football now), golf (very strongly) and abroad tennis, especially the French Open and Wimbledon and the golf's Riders Cup, and the Athletics World Cup, which NBC had very often – this is an international event, but has never had a lot of success in the US because athletics is declining there. The American television is mainly concerned with sports that will generate an income bigger than what they cost. That is NBC Sport.

Clearly then, within the American context, NBC is investing in the big and successful sports. When asked whether there have been any attempts to introduce new sports to their audience Gilady stated:

> No. Television is not an experimental channel; commercial television is not experimental.

In fact, whichever way I tried to assess whether NBC Sport might undertake an educational role within the world of mediated sport Gilady shrugged it off (see below). For example, I suggested television could show more women's sports; he responded:

> OK. The WNBA is an excellent example; David Stern decided that he would make this business grow. So he forced NBC because of the deal with the men's [basketball]. So what? If he stopped it today we would stop it immediately, immediately! It has no value and no money.

So the only way to get a not-already-popular sport on television is if someone 'crazy' decides it is important to him and has the power to force networks?

> Yes, absolutely, and people crazy for a cause can make many things happen.

Even when I suggested that some sports might be worth at least a try, not in order to experiment but, for example, simply because someone else has acquired the rights for the more lucrative sports, Gilady said:

> No. For the time being NBC is sitting well, with the Olympics till 2008, Wimbledon and the French Open, NBA (which is very strong), the college basketball, the college football (which is also strong in the US) – these are American things I am not very well informed about because that is a whole independent market, a huge market bigger than the entire world put together and they deal with that, I deal with what they do outside the USA.

Indeed, Gilady's 'ministerial responsibility', as he put it, is 'all the NBC productions outside the US, apart from the Olympic Games in which in fact I am also involved like in the coming Salt Lake City Games'. Thus, much of the interview focused on the Olympic Games and/or on the Games as an example for wider issues. However, as mentioned, NBC sport does cover further events that take place outside the US:

> Wimbledon, for example. We transmit the women's and men's finals live although it is 9am in America and the figures are very low, but we take that into consideration. We dub it 'Breakfast at Wimbledon' … the number of people who are devoted tennis fans in the US is relatively small.

In this context it is worth mentioning that American television does currently show some international sports, such as the top European and

South American soccer leagues, Formula One and (occasionally) cricket and rugby.

A couple of further issues regarding NBC's sports coverage in general were also discussed later in the interview. For instance, when I asked whether this network's broadcasts were transmitted outside of the US, Gilady explained:

> No, only the designed international channels like CNBC, MSNBC, for example, which is an international news channel, not NBC.

And do these international channels cover sport?

> Yes, a lot. Golf and other suitable sports.

What exactly are 'suitable' sports? Suitable for the European market?

> No, to the American market. Things like golf ... All these channels speak to very few people, economics and stuff like that and golf goes well with economics, it's the same audience.

So, I asked, there are no attempts to make the programming more localized?

> To make it more localized you need money and the resources to cover that are not there. The first, second, third and tenth options of Mrs Tenardier in Marseille is not English, so it would be silly [to invest in that].

Furthermore, one of the reasons NBC itself cannot broadcast sport outside the US is because:

> NBC has broadcasting rights only for the USA, that is exactly why we don't allow moving pictures on the internet, because the internet is international and then you step on somebody else's rights [see below]. ...
> [Moreover,] if you are an international channel, who will give you the rights for the entire world? And how much are you willing to pay for them? Rights are sold *territorially* if you have merchandise that is worthwhile. If it is much less valuable merchandise it doesn't really matter, so it will be shown on CNBC on a Sunday afternoon.

Speaking of the relationship between local audiences and global sports more generally I mentioned football (soccer), to which Gilady immediately reacted by saying that:

> Football, first of all, is king. When the European Cup is being played or the World Cup a huge audience watches together the same match and then to the next match since usually they play one match after the other. It is not like the Olympic Games, which divides the audience. The audience is united for the opening ceremony, but then the audience is fragmented; there are 297 gold medals to give away between 200 countries so each country is covering the things it is interested in. In the football World Cup it is, at the end, one match of one sport and one medal. That is true to some extent for tennis too: it is one sport and one prize, one cup. That is why it is much easier to bring a large unified audience to this type of event than to an event like the Olympic Games in which the audience is divided by the nature of the event – each country wants its flag, its athlete and its anthem.

And what about American sports?

> OK, let's look at what happened with the NBA, that is a very interesting phenomenon. Until six/seven years ago, the NBA was very successful in Europe and in Israel too. Why? Because the important games were broadcast in Israel around 10.30pm because NBC – or CBS, whoever had them – showed them in the afternoon. Now NBC has paid the NBA a lot of money for the 40 most important games and scheduled them in prime time in order to make the money back. They took them from Saturday and Sunday afternoons to the prime [time], that means 3.00 or 4.00 in the afternoon in Europe and Israel. The NBA lost interest in these countries because these are not attractive hours. It is true that there will always be the devoted fans that will wake up at any hour [to watch], but these are very small numbers.

So, I inquired, sport is different to movies where Hollywood no longer looks at the rest of the world for 'gravy', but actually aims at international audiences? (In recent years Hollywood has recognized 'the rest of the world' as a major source of revenue for its movies, much more than simply an additional source of income to the US market, as in the past.) The NBA doesn't care much about its international audience?

They do care, but $500 million are $500 million and nothing the world can pay will get even near to that [amount of money paid within the US].

And are there any other American sports that are popular outside the US?

So what? The NBA is the top of the international, American football is not.

Why not, I asked. In England, for example, Channel 4 invested in it and tried to generate an interest in this sport.

So what? Leave it. That is a negligible sort of rating, all of Channel 4 is negligible; it returned the money because the rights were cheap not because it is an important sport. They actually formed an entire league and still play the sport, but it is all very marginal. Like soccer is in the US, the stadiums are full, but in fact all the fans are there and there is no one left at home to watch it on television …

In this case it is important to note that Britain's Channel 4 is a unique and significant television channel in many respects, including the place it has given to sport in accordance with its commitment to innovation and experiment. It is worth mentioning that it, for example, was the television channel that introduced Japanese sumo, within its cultural context, to audiences in Britain, which in turn sparked a world-wide interest in the sport.

When asked whether he had an idea as to why certain sports are popular in certain cultures and not in others Gilady replied:

Not really, every place is different. You can see that in countries where the Brits were, cricket is still important and baseball cannot get off the ground.

So, if your view is that 'foreign' sports will always remain marginal for a broadcasting channel, which are the most important sports for a given channel?

Television needs to make a list, 'what are the things I must have on my shopping list'. Local football – that is what interests the audience in a certain country, after that international football and maybe after that one other sport, like Maccabi Tel Aviv basketball is here [in Israel, see below], which for 30 years now has been of such interest that it is a major television asset not related to anything else.

NBC AND THE OLYMPIC GAMES

The Olympic Games are surely also top of the 'shopping list' of any broadcaster interested in sporting events. As previously mentioned NBC's major sport asset is the Olympic Games, it currently owns the exclusive US television rights to the Olympics through to 2008. In fact:

> NBC paid $705 million to the International Olympic Committee for the Sydney TV rights, a total of $3.55 billion for Sydney and the four games after, and estimates it will face $100 million in production and administrative costs next year. The network depends on advertising to cover those costs and, it hopes, to turn a profit. The 1996 Atlanta Games finished $70 million in the black.[3]

It worth mentioning that some controversy surrounds Alex Gilady's role in this context since he is both a high ranking official of NBC Sport and a member of the IOC. As Frank Deford of *Sports Illustrated* put it:

> Years ago, in Olympic circles, Alex was facetiously known as 'the delegate from NBC'. He is, most prominently, an official of that network, and he was a ubiquitous Olympic presence. Then, one day, the delegates arrived at a meeting to learn that His Excellency [Juan Antonio Samaranch] had determined that Alex should become a genuine member. So overnight, the honorary delegate from NBC became the real IOC delegate from Israel.

> Naturally, in the fuzzy Olympic world, where everybody seems to have a second or third agenda – some concealed, some brazen – Mr. Gilady continued to work for NBC, even as NBC purchased Olympic rights for 10 years at $3.5 billion in secret negotiations that denied all other networks any opportunity even to bid.

> But then, that's the way that business is carried on in the Samaranch regime.[4]

Put simply, Alex Gilady was 'wearing both his NBC and IOC hats at the same time Samaranch was cutting a secret deal with NBC giving them ten years worth of Olympic rights without the other networks even having a chance to bid'.[5] In fact, according to reports, Gilady sits in on

IOC-NBC contract negotiations.[6] Indeed, in an Israeli television interview he told the story of an otherwise uneventful dinner he had with Samaranch, which actually lead to this deal.[7] During that meal, Gilady recalled, Samaranch told him how tired the IOC was of having to re-negotiate broadcasting rights for each and every Games, which made Gilady think that the IOC might be open to the idea of a long-term contract.

Gilady himself does not see this as a conflict; when asked about it in the Israeli television interview he said:

> I started at NBC, 14 years. The trust the IOC had in me lead to me being elected as a member, it is not that I was first a member of the IOC, and NBC thought 'ah, you are a member of the IOC so we can surely benefit from your contacts', it happened the other way round.[8]

One could, of course, raise an eyebrow at this explanation and ask in what way it actually dissolves the conflict. Be that as it may, Gilady is indeed well positioned to discuss the relationship between television and the Olympic Games.

THE 2000 SYDNEY GAMES

Reports in the American media clearly indicated that ratings for the Sydney Games were low (see below). I asked Gilady whether, especially in the context of the long-term contract between NBC and the IOC, a smaller success, like Sydney, changed matters for NBC?

> No. That is utter stupidity, Sydney was a big success, the 14 hours [time difference] didn't make a difference. What did make a difference? The fact that it was September and in September people go to work in the morning and the children to school, so at 11 at night the ratings dropped no matter what you did. Since we managed to 'make good', namely sell advertising time to advertisers in time, NBC's revenue was as it had been the day before the Games opened. Now the effect may be on future Games, for instance, we won't be happy for the Games to take place in September or October again, but nobody is happy with that because the world is round – that never changes. No matter where the Games go, somewhere around the world it will be very late at

night and somewhere else it will be very early in the morning. The President of the IOC has been trying for the past three years ... he lectures about this passionately, that the Games must be in July–August since then they disturb all other sports around the world the least and they don't clash with anything else and that too affects viewing figures.

I thought Sydney was an exception because of the weather, not that there was an intention to move the Games to September?

But Seoul was also in September, Melbourne was in November, the same in Mexico ... These are indeed the exceptions, but in Melbourne and Mexico the amount of money wasn't so big that you immediately went and checked what happened. Here when you paid $705 million only for the US, every move is meaningful and you need to correct it.

In relation to these responses it is worth mentioning that even prior to the Sydney Games one article suggested that:

The network is expecting a dip from the 21.6 average rating for the Atlanta Games because network television viewership is generally declining and because fewer Americans are interested when the games leave the United States. Ratings for the Barcelona and Seoul Olympics were between 17 and 18.

NBC's specific prediction of the ratings for Sydney, which it won't reveal, is important because if the numbers fall short, the network will owe its advertisers concessions, such as free commercials on future programming.[9]

Indeed, the televised Olympics *were* a ratings disappointment in the United States – they were in fact the lowest US television ratings for any Olympics, summer or winter, since the 1960s. However, in some countries – like Japan and Britain – they were very successful in ratings terms and have actually risen in many cases, for example (in spite of the instance provided by Gilady, see below), in Canada.[10]

One further reason provided by journalists for the fact that the Sydney ratings were low in the US, which appears valid, was that the broadcasts were recorded. When I asked Gilady about that he retorted bluntly:

Why do they need to be live?

They don't need to be live? It doesn't matter? I asked, surprised:

Not at all. You know that in Atlanta they were not live?

But, I said, in Atlanta they were 'seemingly live'.

Kerri Strug jumped her famous vault with the broken leg at 6.20 in the afternoon, Dick Ebersol [President of NBC Sports since 1989] put her on screen at 10 minutes to midnight with 38 ratings. The Americans want their stories 'chewed and digested' from 7 or 7.30 till midnight. If they are at 11pm that makes the average fall. The Canadians, for example, went live and they had 300,000 viewers in a country of 30 million. Journalists write – but what they write is not always important, they don't really understand. If we had broadcast live we would have lost our pants and shirts.

Indeed, the result of this view was a very heavily edited and packaged coverage, Gilady claimed:

It is always packaged; it was like that in Atlanta too.

He articulated again the ideology behind the NBC's coverage of sport, 'chewed and digested'. Clearly NBC cannot afford to abandon this philosophy as the next summer Olympics, in Athens in 2004, will again require use of taped events because of the time difference. So, I asked, there are cases then where NBC takes smaller and less popular sports and covers them as small drama?

That is during the Olympic Games, these are the only two weeks they do this for these sports, you cannot do it even a day later.

As someone who isn't very interested in fencing, I told Gilady, when it was presented to me in a dramatic package I was fascinated.

For how long? The human being chooses his areas of interest, you can help him understand more, but you cannot force things on him. It is voluntary, watching television is voluntary. It is a Bolshevik attitude to enforce rules and laws like they are doing here now with the new channel [referring to Israel's third channel which started broadcasting in 2002 – see below], they cannot tell people what to watch so they tell the people who want to broadcast what to transmit. Like the viewer, at the end of the day, will not have a say. 'We will show you things and you will watch them.' The point that this is irrelevant doesn't guide them and that is why we [Israel] are not exactly a place people learn about when they want to learn how to make television. It is a good example of how not to do television.

When I tried again to suggest that television might have an educational role to play in society, Gilady said angrily:

You are exactly one of those people who want to rape the medium in an unnatural way and to make it do things that it doesn't know how to do. There are sports that … are not interesting. Most sports are not interesting. You know there are 93 international sport federations? How many of them are people interested in? At the summer Olympics there are 28 sports and at the winter Games there are eight – altogether there are 36 out of 93, so most of them are not even in the Olympics.

… The number of sports that are attractive to both the advertisers and the viewers is very small, very small. See, there is a problem with the gymnastics World Championship, it doesn't interest anyone. As part of the Olympics gymnastics is of interest, but the gymnastics World Championship is not covered in the US.

By this stage Gilady was truly angry with my 'nagging' about minority sports, women's sport, the possible educational role of televised sport and so on. It is not possible to report the entire dialogue that followed, but I would like to quote one comment, which seems relevant to any academic attempting to study the industry:

The question is who are you? I have two Emmys [by the time of writing he already had three], I have been through 13 Olympic Games, I lead television to the organized and excellent sports coverage you see today and you say we have different views. Why aren't you thinking that you don't have the right to differ?

This comment should not give the wrong impression – most of the interview was amicable and Gilady was very co-operative – but I believe academics should be aware of the way they are perceived by the people who see themselves as 'doers'.

THE INTERNET

While discussing the Sydney Games the issue of the internet's role in the media/sport world came up frequently. When asked of his views on the internet, both personally and as an NBC executive, Gilady replied:

> Much is unknown. Next week there is a major IOC conference in Lausanne about the internet with all the major internet players. But the internet was a great disappointment in Sydney ... newspaper journalists wrote that Sydney was going to be the spring board, from then on things would be different. IBM.com had all the results directly from the Games, the same was true for NBCOlympic.Com. Everybody and every-nobody had a website that gave the Olympic results, but the IOC forbade moving pictures because of the reasons I explained [see above] and there were 1,800 court cases around the world that stopped these website from showing pictures. Now, how many visitors were there, in all the sites accumulated, over 17 days? 15 million. That is nothing, when you consider the fact that these Olympic Games had, altogether, 68 billion television viewers [different figures were supplied by the Chairman of the IOC and confirmed by other sources – see below]. That means that the internet does certain things, but not others. It is certainly not yet a form of entertainment and the pictures it shows cannot compete with the wonderful television pictures – not yet. What will happen with it in the future? It [the internet] will get onto the screen too and then if you wish to get the data parallel to the good quality television pictures that could be a different thing. But really you cannot know, no one can truly tell you what will happen. What is already clear, though, is that it is not what people thought it would be.
>
> [Moreover,] most people want to be couch potatoes. The couch potato wants to be a couch potato. Really, when you think about it 15 million visits to the Olympic websites mean in some cases the same person several times. All in all that is a very small figure.

And yet, I inquired, NBC keeps a very impressive website.

> NBCOlympic.com cost $40 million! The thing is that precisely because nothing is clear or certain we cannot afford *not* to be there. These are two different things.

Indeed, during the Sydney Games, the IOC allowed online video coverage of events only on NBC and then only after a 24-hour delay to a highly restricted audience (see below).[11]

The two-day internet-related IOC conference of sports officials, broadcasters and promoters of the new media that Gilady mentioned has now taken place in Lausanne and has resulted in the reaffirming of the IOC's 'determination to keep streaming video and audio of the Olympics off the Internet until at least 2010'.[12] As is also clear from Gilady's position, this 'decision was made to protect the enormous investment television networks and consortiums have made to purchase the rights to the sights and sounds of the game. As such, it seems to make business sense'.[13] Clearly, 'Olympics officials are loath to jeopardize their income from TV rights, which accounted for 51 percent of all its revenues from the Sydney Games, $1.33 billion of the overall $2.6 billion'.[14]

For the time being, the main IOC reason for not allowing pictures on the internet, as also expressed by Gilady, is that the television audience is much greater than the internet audience. Dick Pound, Chairman of the IOC internet group, said that for the Sydney Games: 'Some 3.7 billion people watch television as opposed to 25 million Internet users.' Furthermore, in the US '185 million people watched NBC's television broadcasts of the Olympics, while 5.6 million clicked on to the network's Internet site' – MSNBC is a joint venture partly owned by NBC.[15]

And yet, in further contradiction of Gilady's assertions, it can be argued that:

> Television viewership in the United States declined drastically for the Sydney Games. Internet use expanded. By 2008, the last Games to which the current ban applies, Internet use will have multiplied exponentially. And if NBC and the IOC learned anything this year, it is that dedicated fans do not want to wait to see the tape-delay of events that occurred a dozen or more hours earlier on the other side of the globe.[16]

Although Gilady insists there is no way of knowing what the future holds, others strongly believe that there is no way of stopping the internet.[17] As Phil Dwyer, Managing Director of Jupiter Research Europe, which specializes in the new media analysis, put it: 'You cannot put a lid on it.'[18]

Clearly, the IOC is not simply waiting to see what the future holds. At the internet conference the IOC announced that it was considering allowing internet companies to broadcast small sports on the web.[19] Furthermore, the IOC is already looking into filtering software that limits access to Olympic websites to geographic regions, which will enable territorially restricted access to moving images.[20] This is related to the fact that, as is clear from the entire discussion, the main point of argument is the moving pictures that the IOC is currently unable to limit to geographic regions, as is possible with television. Thus, as long as the technology does not allow video to be restricted, live video put on the internet by a provider in one country could pre-empt the taped and delayed coverage – like that NBC used in Sydney. Therefore it seems obvious why NBC will continue to support the IOC's blackout of video on the internet.

As far as text is concerned, every newspaper that received credentials to cover the Sydney Olympics was able to put coverage on its website immediately. However, it is worth mentioning that:

> Internet news companies, including MSNBC, were not allowed even a credential to view a live event. MSNBC was able to provide stories and commentary by reporting from NBC's newsroom, where live feeds from every venue were available. Other providers with no connection to a rights holder had to settle for wire service stories.[21]

This meant that for the Sydney Games newspapers still had the upper hand.

To conclude this theme, the official IOC reasoning for not allowing pictures on the internet, as also expressed by Gilady, is that the television audience is much greater than the internet audience. However, the actual reason for the ban, as many have noticed and Gilady also referred to, is that the international and broadcasting rights to the internet are sold *territorially*. Overall, it seems that American television and the IOC – as reflected by Gilady's views – tend to downplay the role of the internet, but at the same time are threatened by it mainly, I would assume, because of the ways it might interfere with the hegemonic position they have established.

THE ISRAELI CASE

By way of context for this section, but without getting into an in-depth description of Israeli television, it should be mentioned that several channels transmit sport in this country:[22]

- IBA – Israel Broadcasting Authority, a public service broadcaster, better known to its audience as Channel 1 – was the first television channel in Israel and started broadcasting (after a long public debate) in 1968. This channel still owns the rights for major sporting events such as the Olympic Games, but during the 1990s it lost the rights for many of the sports and events it had previously broadcast, such as the Israeli Football League. In an overall fading viewership, some of the channel's most watched evenings are those in which they broadcast Maccabi Tel-Aviv's basketball games in the European League (in some cases this channel owns broadcasting rights jointly with Israel's Channel 5, see below).

- Channel 2 – Israel's commercial channel started broadcasting in 1993. The channel is operated by three franchisees who share the days of the week, changing the days periodically. A separate body produces the news for all the franchisees. This popular channel (slightly less popular since mid-2001) never invested heavily in sport, the one asset it did and does fight for are the rights for the Israeli Football Premiership League and the national football team's international matches. Indeed, since its inception it has broadcast, in most years, the central football league match on Saturday afternoons or evenings, as well as many of the Israeli internationals (in some cases this channel owns the rights jointly with Channel 5, see below).

- Channel 5 – a thematic sports channel transmitted by cable and, more recently, satellite. From a relatively modest start in the early 1990s, this channel has become an important player and currently owns the rights (in some cases jointly with other bodies, including Channel 1 and Channel 2) for the Israeli Football Premiership League, various European Football leagues, the Israeli Basketball League (both women and men), the NBA and WNBA, the Athletics Golden League and more. Productions also include a daily sports news bulletin, studio-based programmes, which accompany the transmission of football and basketball matches, and occasional documentary films.

- Channel 10 – in 2002 a second commercial channel started broadcasting and received a very cool welcome from both critics and audiences. At the time of writing the future of this channel is unknown, though it continues broadcasting. In an attempt to win over audiences, this channel bought the rights for the crucial football matches of Hapoel Tel Aviv in the 2002 UEFA Cup and indeed, as the team proceeded to the highest achievement of an Israeli team ever, the channel reached its highest ratings to date.

Several international sports channels are transmitted in Israel by cable and/or satellite, these include Eurosport, EuroSportNews, ESPN, Extreme and Fox Sport. Certain Israeli channels transmitted via satellite occasionally include sports programming, for instance, 'Briza' (an entertainment channel with a 'Mediterranean' agenda) has shown the Turkish Football League since 2001. The Turkish league has become of interest to Israeli fans since Haim Revivo (one of Israel's leading footballers) joined the high profile Fenerbahçe club in 2000.

As mentioned, Alex Gilady has been very much involved in Israel's television, first in Channel 1 and later in Channel 2. Whenever he is interviewed in the Israeli media, and this is relatively often, he voices a very critical view of the country's television industry. For example, at one stage of this interview he said:

> Everything here [referring to the television in Israel] was born out of the law and out of the womb. Everything.

Later he added:

> Everything here is crocket, bent.

However, for the purposes of this essay I asked him mainly about sport. Although the Israeli case is specific, I believe that at least to some extent it reflects more generally on the television–sport relationship in small countries.

According to Gilady, the 'must-have list' of the IBA (Channel 1) should not:

> include the NBA, for example, and not the lower football leagues or the basketball league. [However,] for Channel 5 the basketball league is on the 'must-have list' since their options to get more major sports are small, although now they have the rights for the football league. This channel actually caused a major shift here [in Israel], but that is due to the nothingness of the people who are in charge of football in this country. The Israeli football should have

been on YES [the satellite operators]. YES made a big mistake [by
not fighting for it] ... because football is a major distinctive feature.
They won't have the Olympic Games; the football World Cup
cannot play a similar role to the Olympics – it is only 120 hours
once every four years, that is all that is in it and the most important
games (according to FIFA rules) must be transmitted to everybody
over the air. That is in contrast to the Olympic Games, which
produce 3,500 television hours in half the time! That is the
dilemma, what is your strategy. The strategy of the cable channel
was right and left everybody at the sideways, especially Channel 1,
whose stupidity made them lose, for a difference of half a million
dollars, the central football match. This makes it an outcast except
for Thursdays [when they transmit Maccbi Tel Aviv's European
basketball matches].

So what will happen to Channel 1 in the future? I asked.

It doesn't matter, it doesn't matter, this channel isn't relevant, it
doesn't matter.

But doesn't this have to do with a more world-wide question, namely the
place of public service broadcasters in today's television?

The public service ... that is exactly the point, the entire world
waits to see what will happen with the BBC ... Someone will say:
'close this story, what is this story? Close.' This is a tax that you pay
for them to transmit television. There is nothing like that in the
US. There is nothing like that in most of the South American
countries, including Brazil, but it does exist in the rest of the world
because governments always think they can use this tool, but this
tool declines to rating levels that are frightening. I will show you,
turn off the tape.

I stopped the tape and Gilady showed me confidential documents to
prove the very low rating figures for the Israeli Channel 1. His view is
very clearly that PSB is a thing of the past and should be abolished. I did
not get into a further discussion with him here on this matter despite my
intense disagreement. Instead I asked, as far as sport is concerned, where
do things currently stand with Channel 1?

They have the rights for the Olympic Games till 2008, inclusive.
But they have these rights because of the EBU [European

Broadcasting Union], not in their own right. But see, recently they had to negotiate on their own for the Football World Cup and they said 'we cannot pay'. Any time this channel stands on its own …

So who will show the World Cup on Israeli television?

I don't know, it will be interesting. In my opinion Channel 3 [by the time of writing the World Cup had already begun transmission on Channel 10 – see above], for example, cannot show it because Channel 3 will be transmitted only via cable. According to FIFA's rules, the opening match, the two semi-finals, the final and all the matches of the local team must be transmitted free over the air and Channel 3 will not be free at all.

Talking more generally about sport on television, in the Israeli context as well as world-wide, he added:

Football is very difficult to justify financially, that is why Channel 2 finds it difficult to pay the money for football on Saturdays, since they cannot make the money back by selling commercials. That is why, not only in Israel, football works well on cable or satellite, which are paid [for] – people will pay for that even if they don't have enough money for food. It works well in certain places, but the sports that really work well [on television] are golf, for example. There is no problem to include commercials in it and the sponsorship is strong since the CEO of this or that company will bring all the directors to see Tiger Woods play. Make money? Very few [sports] actually make money. The people in the sport itself? Very few make money. [Martin] Edwards, [former Chief Executive] of Manchester United, makes a lot of money, but Manchester United is an unusual phenomenon in the world. The owners of the Chicago Bulls have to pay millions to the players. For them it is part of enjoying life, like Simon Mizrachi in Maccabi Tel Aviv, he makes money? It costs him money. It is part of life, of ego, of all sorts of things, but the number of sports that are attractive to both the advertisers and the viewers is very small, very small.

So that is why Channel 2 isn't involved in much else other than a little football?

It also has to do with the stupid idea that sport productions are not considered local [original] Israeli productions, even when made in

Israel, even the football league. Two hundred Israeli workers went out to cover the league and we filmed 60 hours of football a day – it wasn't considered a local production. Who is the idiot who made this decision? ... So what sort of incentive does Channel 2 have? Moreover, there is no Channel 2, that is your mistake, it is fragmented between seven different elements, I [Keshet] have two days a week, five hours of prime, that is all, so I have to make as much money as I possibly can during this time. [This furious comment refers to the fact that sport productions are not 'counted' as part of the quota of original productions Channel 2 is obliged to produce by law.]

In the future, will much sport be shown on cable and satellite channels?

In the US, ESPN, for example, has ESPN 1 and 2, in fact there are nine of them and they make more money than ABC, their parent network, and that is because they operate on subscription fees. Here we are not yet at the stage where you pay for what you want to watch; you pay for the entire package.

But we have it on a small scale – we even had one attempt of showing boxing on 'pay-per-view'.

Yes, with a 25-year delay. We will get there eventually because there isn't any other choice. They will close the channels and you will decide what you are willing to pay for and what not. It is your privilege, you are the customer, you are the one who pays. Why are you allowed to choose at the supermarket and on television you are not?

PAST, PRESENT AND FUTURE

Finally, I asked Gilady whether he thought television influenced sport in any way over the years.

First of all, yes, but not in a very meaningful way, that was the most beautiful and most catholic wedding in the world. Yes, we need them and they need us. But the concept 'sport' – be careful with it, there are several things that work well [on television] but others that do not. See boxing, all the professional boxing is not [working], any fight is the marketing of the next fight, that is all it is. That is why it is on pay-per-view and some people are willing to pay for that, but there are also people willing to pay for the WWF which, as everybody knows, is not a sport. The boundaries blurred, but there are places where they didn't blur. The sports that really generate interest are very few.

So if we stick to the popular sports, do you think television pushed them more towards entertainment?

No, it didn't touch on any area of entertainment. It made it faster, basketball, [the time provided for a given play in Europe is now] 24 seconds; it wasn't able to change football, to this day, there are no time-outs for commercials. [Furthermore,] even the role of refereeing was not yet given to television, in order to leave the whole thing human, with human mistakes.

In fact, Gilady has expressed his views of the future of sport on television on several occasions. For example, in a speech delivered to the General Association of International Sports Federations he said, among other things:

We in television must produce better pictures all the time. Our production must be more and more detailed, and we must surprise and please the viewers more and more ... TV production ... will have much more electronic means that will attract viewers and which will replay mistakes, the replaying of performances will have to be quicker and will have to be much more clear.[23]

When I asked about the future of televised sport he emphasized one point:

We will all pay more for the sports we want to watch in the future, much more, because it will all go to cable.

Everything? But there are still rules of nations and of federations, lists of events that are supposed to be broadcast free over the air...

They make lists of events they have no control over, they have control of the football World Cup? It's silly.

Interestingly, in his own speech to the General Association of International Sports Federations he summed up thus:

I say that broadcasting, free over the air, will remain the carrier of big sporting events and will pay for them, well into the next century. I say that narrowcasting, cable, satellite, will continue to grow and will continue to want more programmes and more sports programmes. I say that pointcasting, the infostrada, will present new challenges in both the statistics, the archives that can be retrieved through the screen, and maybe also for live.[24]

This shows that Gilady does not stick to expressing the one given opinion. He might have changed his views on this matter to some extent or, it could also be speculated, he might be presenting slightly different opinions on different occasions.

To conclude, I believe that above all the interview with Alex Gilady reaffirms the notion that from (commercial) television's perspective televised sport is a business, driven almost entirely by economic logic. This will in fact continue to shape it, so much so that in the (near?) future our experience of televised sport will indeed resemble a supermarket – to use Gilady's metaphor – and we will have to pay for each and every item we wish to enjoy.

Final Thoughts

I would like to re-emphasize that we – academics researching mediated sport – need to have these types of interactions. Of course interviews like the one I described in this essay need then to be reported critically and any answers given should also be confronted by information gathered from further sources. In fact, it is worth noting that in some cases Gilady provided data that is not supported by other sources (for example, about the 'success' of the Sydney Games on American television and/or their failure on Canadian television). In this context it is also worth mentioning that in this interview, as well as on various public appearances and newspaper interviews, Gilady seems wilfully to voice extreme and controversial opinions that may very well be his views, but that are amplified by the persona he 'wears', so to speak, on such occasions. Thus I feel that some of the comments he made in this interview should be taken with a pinch of salt (as I have attempted to do in reporting it).

Having said that, this interview voices a coherent set of views of a television executive in a position of power within the television/sport industry and provides a challenge to the ways in which the academic community views the role of broadcasting. Clearly, this essay opens up many more questions than can be asked or answered in any one interview. Thus I would suggest that a broader empirical process is required – including further interviews with television executives from a range of television organizations in addition to participant observation – in order to produce further evidence of the (varied and possibly dissonant) views of the industry.

As willing as we might be to listen to them, it might take more convincing on our part to make television executives actually listen to us, but we should at least try. I don't think we will be able to change their world, but we might have a little more impact on it if we share our research-based views with the people in charge of the industry.

NOTES

I would like to thank Alex Gilady for taking the time to grant me the interview that formed the basis of this piece and also my co-editor for his help.

1. I take complete responsibility for the translation of this interview (and some of the newspaper and television material used) into English. I believe that although not always straightforward, the translation maintains the spirit of the original.
2. This biographical information is based mainly on Alex Gilady's IOC webpage, www.olympic.org/uk/organisation/ioc/members/bio_uk.asp?id=67 (1 Aug. 2002).
3. 'NBC Betting Viewers, Sponsors Forgive and Forget Oly Scandals', The Associated Press, Saturday 6 March 1999, www.sltrib.com/1999/mar/03061999/business/88374.htm (15 Sept. 2000).
4. Frank Deford, 'A Matter of Honor', *Sports Illustrated*, Wednesday 10 Feb. 1999, http://sportsillustrated.cnn.com/inside_game/deford/990203/ (1 Aug. 2002).
5. United Electrical, Radio and Machine Workers of America, 'Integrity, Anyone?', *Short Takes*, http://www.ranknfile-ue.org/contract2000_shorttakes.html (1 Aug. 2002).
6. See www.breadnotcircuses.org/jennings2.html (15 Sept. 2000).
7. Television interview with Yair Lapid on Israel's Channel 3 (cable), 14 Jan. 1998.
8. Ibid.
9. 'NBC Betting Viewers, Sponsors Forgive and Forget Oly Scandals'.
10. John Rice, 'Olympic Ratings Said Great Worldwide', *Associated Press Information Services*, 30 Sept. 2000, http://special.northernlight.com/olympics/ratings.htm (1 Aug. 2002).
11. Associated Press and Reuters, 'Net video for small sports pondered: IOC's Pound relents a bit from proposed 10-year web ban', www.msnbc.com/news/498345.asp (5 Dec. 2000).
12. Mike Celizic, 'IOC's Internet policy leaves fans in cold: Olympic committee ignoring viewers by concentrating only on TV', www.msnba.com/msn/498822.asp?cp1=1 (4 Dec. 2000).
13. Ibid.
14. Associated Press and Reuters, 'Net video for small sports pondered'.
15. Celizic, 'IOC's Internet policy leaves fans in cold'.
16. Ibid.
17. Alex Gilady, 'Sport and Television', Speech delivered to the General Association of International Sports Federations, http://archive.www.worldsport.com/worldsport/gaisf/publications/sport_television/sport_television1bis.html (24 Dec. 2000).
18. Celizic, 'IOC's Internet policy leaves fans in cold'.
19. Associated Press and Reuters, 'Net video for small sports pondered'.
20. Ibid.

21. Celizic, 'IOC's Internet policy leaves fans in cold'.
22. For a much more in-depth description and analysis of this, see Yair Galily 'Watching Sport in Israel: The Transformation from Single to Multi-Channel Society', in M. Lammer (ed.), *Proceeding of The History of Sport in the Jewish Nation Congress, Wingate Institute, 13–15 July 2001* (forthcoming).
23. Gilady, 'Sport and Television'.
24. Ibid.

7

Attribution of Failure:
A German Soccer Story

HANS-JOERG STIEHLER and MIRKO MARR

Sport is not only a matter of competition and results, it also produces many ways of talking about sport.[1] On the one hand sport is a social system of its own: for those who are active in it as well as for those who are only watching it, sport includes many varieties of social behaviour. On the other hand sport is a specific area of sense-making. There is a need for a broad public to receive explanations that make rules and results understandable.

Today's mass media can be seen both as a form of public observer and as a producer of sport events.[2] The media have already put these two ideas together – they satisfy the need for discussion, as much as the demand for practical interpretations of the results. The 'sport communications' branch splits into two parts: the first is orientated toward media structures and formats, but also creates new types of texts other than the report, such as the framing coverage around live-reporting, sport comment, sport talk shows and so on. In a second development, sports communication leads to a differentiation of journalistic roles – today there is not only the reporter who comments on the game, but also the moderator who talks to experts and the experts, or co-commentators, themselves. The demand for these new forms is based on the entertainment dimension of sport in the media. The discussion and analysis of sport is embedded somewhere between everyday communication and professional analysis. This provides a context for the following analysis, which concerns the live television coverage of three consecutive games of the German national soccer team at the World and European soccer championships in 1994, 1996 and 1998 and is realized in two parts.[3] In some areas we have included data from the European Championship of 2000, when Germany was eliminated in the first round.

The first section of the essay analyzes the institutionalization of communication about sport in television: as a special point of focus we chose the pre- and post-event coverage of the three games. The explosion of costs for transmission rights in the last few years have forced the television stations to create informative and entertaining evening schedule-filling programmes often just around one national or international sport event; this means that the sport event is embedded in presentation frames with pre- and post-event coverage. Even though the competition itself is the main point of interest, it takes up barely more than half the time of the programme. The question we pursue is what happens in this coverage on a formal level and how can it be described in an adequate analytical way.

The second section of the essay focuses on the process of analyzing the game. We examine the logic of media interpretation of sport results, an investigation that contains the analysis of patterns of story-telling and attributions. In 1996 the German team won the European championship, but in 1994 and 1998 they lost in the quarter-finals of the world championships. The German public was extremely disappointed by those two defeats, which is understandable once one is aware of the important role of soccer within Germany. There were many ups and downs for the German national team in the 1990s – begun at the European championship in 1992 when the Germans were surprisingly defeated by the Danish in the final – and the events were a source of great public interest and massive media coverage. The media coverage can be reduced to a set of 'stories' that were told during the decade:

- The meaning of the typical German 'Tugenden', that is, virtues like strength, discipline, team spirit and so on;
- The German national team as a team that plays excellently in tournaments, getting better from game to game; and
- The coach Berti Vogts who began his career in 1990 after the team had won the world championship under the direction of the legendary Franz Beckenbauer (*Der Kaiser*).

FRAMING THE EVENT

First we describe the framing of the event as the programme context, where the attribution process, to be analyzed in the second section of this essay, takes place. This description is based on a content analysis of written recordings including the pre-match, half-time and post-match coverage of the three games. To protect the comparative dimension we consider only German television stations (ARD/Channel One and ZDF/Channel Two). We begin with the presentation of some basic data. The complete reporting of the three games took 683 minutes, an average of nearly four hours per game. Only 51 per cent of the reporting time was filled by the game itself, that is, by the live reporting of the competition. The remaining 49 per cent was used for framing: 27 per cent for the post-match coverage, 18 per cent for the pre-match programme and four per cent for half-time.[4] While the time relations between live reporting and framing remained constant over the three games, the length of the framing parts differed (Table 1).

TABLE 1

DURATION OF VARIOUS SEGMENTS OF COVERAGE

	Germany vs. Bulgaria (1994)		Germany vs. Czech Republic (1996)		Germany vs. Croatia (1998)	
	Minutes	%	Minutes	%	Minutes	%
Live match	107	49	134	52	110	52
Pre-match	27	12	61	24	37	18
Half-time	3	1	10	4	15	7
Post-match	82	37	51	20	48	23
Total	219	100	256	100	210	100

With regard to different presentation forms, the 334 minutes of the framing can be classified in four main categories (Table 2). With a duration of 196 minutes the live talk is the most important of these categories, 69 minutes were reserved for prepared videotapes and 38 minutes for several entertainment segments including the rare (in comparison to private stations) commercials. The remaining time of 31 minutes was for routine presentation (announcements, introducing guests, filling time and so on). The distribution of the presentation forms varies considerably between pre- and post-match coverage. Prepared videotapes occupy 40 per cent of the reporting time before the game, but only nine per cent after the game. In contrast the proportion of live talks grows from 45 per cent to 68 per cent.

TABLE 2

PRESENTATION FORM IN THE FRAMING COVERAGE

Form of presentation	Minutes	%
Live talk	196	59
Videotapes	69	21
Entertainment, commercials	38	11
Presentation/moderation	31	9
Total	334	100

The whole process of framing the event is characterized by the investment of great effort by the television stations. This effort is first of all attested by a large number of live switches between the several studios: a home studio in Germany, a main studio in the respective host country of the tournament and a studio in or adjacent to the stadium where the game is played. In addition there are several live reporters in the tunnels or on the touch-line, in the town or city hosting the game and also in German towns catching live statements and atmosphere.

The large number of live switches is dependent on a remarkable contingent of journalists, reporters, presenters and technicians involved in the framing process. This crew is completed by the so-called experts – usually former players or coaches – who interact with journalists in the live discussions.

For every game the television stations pre-produce about ten videotapes, which are spliced into or between the live talk, mostly in the pre-match coverage. These tapes provide pictures from the team's hotel and the latest activities of the opponents. They summarize the previous performance of the teams in the tournament and they ask players, coaches or VIP's to guess the outcome of the game. There is no pre-match coverage without a tape about the town hosting the game, preferably including details of its cultural traditions, its sights and its typical food. Normal parts of framing coverage are reports about the fans' mood before, during and after the game. In some cases we perceived prepared comedy interludes, live appearances of entertainment stars, quizzes for the audience and telephone polls. The co-ordination of these different programme segments is lead by the presenter.

The most obvious effect of this effort is a strong segmentation of the whole programme. Apart from the live discussions, segments rarely last longer than two minutes. The consequence of this segmentation is a dynamic rhythm of transmission and a great variety of presentation forms. At the same time, the television stations use traditional presentation forms of media sport, as well as elements of media entertainment, and so join the general trend of convergence of originally different programme formats, which can be observed, for instance, under the label of 'infotainment' in news coverage.

The course of the analyzed television frames follows a programme logic, which can be described as 'zooming in' and 'zooming out'. This logic is mainly realized by the live switches, which lead the audience from the studio in Germany to the venue. The prepared videotapes support this logic by accompanying the two teams in the last training session, on their last evening in the hotel and on the journey from the hotel to the stadium. After the game the logic runs in reverse, bringing the public back 'home'.

AFTER THE GAME: BACK TO THE GAME

Problem and Approach

There are two main topics to be dealt with after a sport event. The numerical result is defined by the media as a social fact. Most of the time the result is clear – there are winners and losers – but its meaning can be unclear and, metaphorically speaking, can have different flavours. The different actors – the players, the coach, the journalists and the public – compare the game and the result against their expectations, which can be very different. A narrow defeat can be quite a success to an outsider and a victory can be something astonishingly normal to a fan. Every actor has his/her own perspective on the tournament and therefore might label the same result differently – 'the earned victory' or the 'lucky punch'.

The competition and its result are also being analyzed. This is the hour of the professional and amateur experts (of whom there are thousands in the sport business) and of course they always know exactly why the game arrived at the result. So far as science is concerned, these attributions are nothing but speculations and hypotheses; they must be stated in simple terms because the event itself requires a quick explanation in terms of its result. These quick interpretations can be called a 'battle of interpretations' – a common expression in the analysis of election campaigns.[5] It is a battle in so far as the national prestige of the country, the expenditure of quite a lot of money and the approach of the coach and the players are being defended by the interpretations. The differing interests and points of view the actors may have concerning the tournament and the result can result in fairly controversial interpretations. The 'neutral observer' is too seldom an element in this performance to be mentioned.

There are social-psychological theories of attribution that look for 'causal explanations' to interpret everyday life on the basis of cognitive theory. 'It is their goal to describe the principles of interpretation of causes for individual behaviour.'[6] In this context the expression 'causal explanation' is very complex and there are many definitions.[7] One thing those definitions have in common is the question 'why' and the relationship between the *explanandum* (the topic one wants to explain) and the *explanas* (the explanation itself). Wienold states that 'the explanation needs to put the topic into context with principles and rules of a general character'.[8] This gives the explanation a theoretical basis. One needs to differentiate between causal explanations and descriptive explanations.

Descriptive explanations help to characterize events, persons and situations. The classification they follow is 'what is happening here?'.[9] Examples of descriptive explanations that are common in sport communications might include: 'this is off-side', 'the pitch is rough' or, more generally, 'the winner takes all'. Descriptive explanations help to actualize the frame of the event, for example, the rules.

At this point we would like to summarize some basic ideas about theoretical concepts for attributions. Theories about attribution are models of a specific type of information processing, concerning the inference between the present information and the attribution that is mentioned.

> The person who wants to explain some behaviour or an event in his/her surrounding does this on the one hand by the pieces of information that are present at the moment and on the other hand by the background of already existing convictions and motivations.[10]

An important question of attribution research is how far the explanations are given rationally by the observer. This question was raised by Fritz Heider, a founder of the approach.[11] His idea was to define human beings as 'naive scientists' who draw their conclusions from intuition, but also in a logical and enclosing manner. This picture has changed over time: Boehm later names the former naive scientist a 'cognitive miser' who is unable to use all the pieces of information he has and tends toward biases because of motivational factors.[12]

Many of the models in attribution research are orientated toward the causal understanding of John Stuart Mill (1806–73) who developed a so-called differential method.

> This method says that the cause for an effect is always the one that comes along with the effect. This means whenever the effect can be observed there is also the cause and when there is no effect there is no specific cause to be observed.[13]

The most important difference between those models that focus on ascription of causes is the presence of pieces of information about effects and their causes. From the range of given information one can differentiate the principles of covariance and configuration.[14] In the first-mentioned case, covariance, the idea follows the model of Mill whereby one looks for linkages within several observations and draws conclusions. A typical example for theories of covariance is Kelley's ANOVA model.[15] This states that the observer of social behaviour of one person knows more or less exactly whether the person would behave in the same manner this with other stimuli (distinctiveness), whether other persons show the same behaviour (consensus) and whether the same behaviour will occur in other situations with different circumstances (consistence).

All this information is added together to form a naive analysis of variance, which allows the cause to be identified as the person, the stimulus, the circumstances, or the combination of some circumstances. Those theories of covariance implicate complex knowledge structures, that is, knowledge about relations of causes, patterns of covariance and so on, but overall they stress a data-based attribution process.[16] The differentiated systems of hypotheses provide an indication (depending on the information available) about the direction of attribution.

There is an obvious reason for using these kinds of models for the explanation of sport events: sport statistics give information that is critical for covariance models, anyway. The comparison between the current result and an earlier one, the comparison between the players and the teams, as much as the creation of relationships between the present-day result and short- or long-term trends – all are part of the event and its presentation in the media.

The second type of model – based on configuration theories – compares observations against internal variables in order to ascribe causes. Common sense, which is understood as a causal scheme, has a significant influence on the attribution.

> Schemes are developed from experience, preconceptions, assumptions and maybe even theories about causal interactions. They try to achieve a certain effect. An observer is able to integrate pieces of information by comparing them to a scheme and by their integration into the scheme.[17]

These kind of causal explanations are seen as conceptual or theoretical explanations.

No matter how much he is involved in the event himself, an observer dispenses with information from covariance. He explains the event with causal explanations, as there are theories from everyday life or from scientific sources at his disposal. Sport especially is a field of historically grown 'causal scenarios' and 'prototypes of explanations'.[18] Those common explanations are often used in sport communications, that is, 'the referee was unfair to us', 'the team did not play to their usual standard', 'playing this team is difficult for anyone'.

To conclude this section, one has to state that these models pose difficulties when it comes to empirical validation in sport communications, as distinct from some fields of interpretation of communications. They do not really give us the chance to predict attributions.

However, there is one model, created by Weiner,[19] which is very popular in research on sport achievement.[20] Weiner integrates attributions into his model of achievement and combines the possibilities of attribution by locus of control (external vs. internal), by the stability of causes (stable vs. variable) and by their means of control.[21] From a methodological point of view, the bi-dimensional classification of attributions in sport communications makes this model superior to the others. Biases are a matter of special interest, a deviation of the attributions of rational explanations. They are often designated as mistakes of attribution, even though they follow a specific causal scheme.[22]

There are only two biases that it is normal to find embedded in sport communications. The so-called fundamental bias of attribution concerns itself with the general overestimation of internal dimensions (within the person).[23] In sports this would be the internal attribution of the achievement to the actors as a norm and the avoidance of external attributions (circumstances).

Self-serving biases are those attributions that increase self-esteem by attributing success internally and that protect self-esteem by attributing defeat externally.[24] The latter have been especially observed after defeats in sports in various studies, although there are also other areas where this scheme has been proved to function successfully.[25] Nevertheless it is difficult for actors to use self-serving biases in public because they can be interpreted as exaggerated self-praise as much as a refusal of responsibility.

There is a close relationship between attribution and sport research in at least two subjects. The mental processing of victories and defeats, as much as sporting motivation in general, are important fields of research in sport psychology.[26] Sportsmen and -women need an optimum self-confidence that can be influenced by the attribution of success and failure. Sports have also been identified as a field for 'spontaneous attributions'. They can be studied without any reactive research conditions but,[27] in this context, mediated attributions seem to be an enlargement of the database for social psychologists in their own discipline – their specific media dimensions are only side issues for most researchers. Empirical research on attribution theories in media communications has developed only slowly.[28]

Until recently the role of the media in the definition and explanation of sport competition was only of indirect significance to social psychologists. The media themselves implicitly frame sports competitions, and their expert interpretation, as an aspect of sport communications (in other words making the mediation process less, rather than more, visible). The following section of the essay seeks more specifically to clarify the role of the media in the attribution process.

The media have three functions in the attribution process. They provide a basis for the attribution process by transmitting sport events. The core element of nearly every attribution theory is information, which may be compared against other pieces of information or other former events. The presentation of sport competitions in the media, and the complete set of sport statistics available, form the basis for any information about consistence and consensus. (This also happens indirectly by influencing expectations about sport events or a specific team.)

Television mediates the ascription of causes by actors and therefore becomes an 'arena' for the conflict-interpretation of sport events and their results.[29] These arenas are represented by the post-event coverage and analytic programmes on the following days. Both types provide a chance to involve representatives and experts who can fulfil their function and interpret and analyze 'live'.[30] The daily and weekly press are also 'arenas'. Nevertheless, the editorial selection determines the choice of non-editorial interpreters.

The media have their own patterns of interpretation and their own actors (journalists, commentators, experts and so on). The comment or the interview are the preferred journalistic forms for stating explanations or for giving patterns of reaction in coverage by the media. In fact there are also different genres and types for every kind of attribution. This short analysis makes clear that there are at least three different media functions impacting on attributions in sport. The different perspectives and interests of the actors can lead to many attributions and therefore there tends not to be one all-explaining attribution.

However, there are other specifics that distinguish the ascription of causes by the media from other interpretations and arenas, such as discussions among friends in pubs, or private reflection about sport results. It should be remembered that there are types and genres of reporting that are rituals, that is, there are a lot of journalistic routines, which are used automatically and independently of the actual object of reporting. A typical example of such a ritual is the 'why' question as one of the five classical questions of journalism, which is a stereotype and an inherent part of all post-match coverage. The root of this ritual can be seen in the history of the media and its genres. The genres and formats frame the vocal input and they limit length, style and forms of interpretations and explanations.

Participants must recognize the seriousness of the report situation. The actors have to accept the rules of the genre being used and behave within the rhetorical demands of the culture. The actors need to have special knowledge as well as an objective and balanced way of interpreting sport results. The need for seriousness limits by common sense the attributions that serve only the self-esteem of the interpreter. Other essentials for explanation patterns are 'the limited understanding of the audience'[31] and the preference for 'deterministic causal models'.[32]

There are many patterns of explanations that fit more or less well with those multiple criteria and this gives their selection different probabilities. The explanations are limited by different news considerations and the media select sport events with such factors in mind. News values like importance, cultural distance, conflict, prominence, negativism and the factor of surprise can easily be been seen operating in sport communications.[33]

The above three criteria lead to specific dimensions of the ascription of causes in the media. This makes media sport different from the attributions of everyday life. The following hypotheses can be derived from the above criteria:

Hypothesis 1 (common sense): the ascription of causes in the media follows the rules of attribution of everyday life according to the covariance model.

This hypothesis is derived from the demand of seriousness. On the one hand this necessity meets the expectations of everyday life of the spectators and on the other hand it respects the values of sports, such as fairness, respect for achievement and so on. Following the covariance model for uncompleted information (see above) there are some hypothetical solutions. In the game between Germany and Bulgaria, for instance, the consensus information, which refers to the performance of teams comparable to Germany, was contradictory because some other favourites lost too, but some won. The distinctiveness (how Germany was playing in comparable situations) was very high in correspondence with the image of the German team as a tournament team, famous for the ability to raise their game on the big occasions. Finally, the consistence of a German defeat was low because the team had won most of the games against Bulgaria in the past. In this constellation the covariance model predicts an explanation with specific circumstances. Table 3 lists dimensions of information and hypothetical attribution for every game. The corresponding hypotheses derived from the model of Weiner are mentioned in brackets.

TABLE 3

HYPOTHESES OF ATTRIBUTION FOR SELECTED GAMES

Game	Year	Consensus	Distinctiveness	Consistence	Attribution
Germany vs. Bulgaria	1994	+/-	h	l	C (external)
Germany vs. Czech Republic	1996	l	l	+/-	P (internal)
Germany vs. Croatia	1998	+/-	h	+/-	SC (external)
Germany vs. Portugal	2000	h	l	h	P (internal)

Notes: +/- = no/ambivalent information
       h = high
       l = low

Hypothesis 2 (self-serving bias): in case of defeats the actors (players, coach) attribute external circumstances more often. In the case of victories they attribute internal factors more. Presenters, reporters and (neutral) experts attribute by the norm of internality and less by self-esteem.

The first part of this analysis showed that there are different actors with different attributions (and evaluations) in television. The subsequent classification indicates that the actors have different roles: journalists in general, then commentators of the game, the presenter and his/her editorial team and the actors, especially the players and the coach. Then there is a 'third party' group of experts (such as former players and coaches), sport functionaries, politicians and so on. These roles are of a different order of closeness to the game and follow different demands. Journalists and experts are observers just as much as politicians; they have a perspective of their own, for example a national perspective, but they have less of an interest in attributing specific forms of causality than the participants do. Normally they are professionals within the media. The players or the coach talk about an event they were a part of a short while ago. We can assume that the expenditure of great physical and mental effort makes them less neutral.

Hypothesis 3 (perspective): the attributions given by the media differ by country.

Huge sport events can be seen world-wide and are judged by different audiences. Another point of contact in sport communications is the international market for players and coaches, which produces commentaries traversing national boundaries. Germany, Austria and Switzerland have a lot in common, both politically, historically, and in sports. At the same time, each country has its own national perspective of the German team. Austria and Switzerland are famous for malice in the case of a defeat of the 'big neighbour'. This gives motivation for references and for a specific point of view, which ought to influence the attribution process. (That is why we have extended our analysis to include the coverage of Germany versus Croatia in 1998, on Swiss and Austrian television.[34] The comparison between this and the German broadcasting coverage allows a test of Hypothesis 3.)

Hypothesis 4 (story-telling): attributions are embedded in a pattern of story telling that was developed before the game.

One has to differentiate between attributions from narratives that are based within sports and those that are offered by the media.[35] The media give a specific framing to sport events, for example, by emphasizing particular parts of the event in the pre-event coverage. Post-match attributions refer to these and so may form a specific meaning. Table 4 provides an overview of which hypothesis is tested on which game and coverage.

Method

The attributions for all matches were recorded, from immediately after the end onwards, including the final summary of the commentator. A unit of analysis was an expression that contained a cause or verbalization

TABLE 4

DESIGN OF TESTING

Game	Year	Result	Channel	H1	H2	H3	H4
Germany vs. Bulgaria	1994	1–2	ZDF/Germany	x	x		x
Germany vs. Czech Republic	1996	2–1	ZDF/Germany	x			x
Germany vs. Croatia	1998	0–3	ARD/Germany	x	x	x	x
Germany vs. Croatia	1998	0–3	SF/Switzerland	x		x	x
Germany vs. Croatia	1998	0–3	ORF/Austria	x		x	x
Germany vs. Portugal	2000	0–3	ZDF/Germany	x			x

of the result or some other sportive aspect of the game, or when there was a connection between result and cause. If the expression could be transformed in a causal sentence without loss or change of meaning it was coded as an attribution.36 If there were many causes in one expression or causes were interacting within one expression, the expression became part of several categories. The identified attributions were classified by the models of Kelley (team 1 [P = person], team 2 [S = stimulus], circumstances [C] and Weiner (external/internal, stable/variable).

Given the constraints of space it is impossible to list the statements we gathered as evidence, however two worked examples should make our method more understandable. In 1994 one expert stated: 'Our team didn't play the game it is able to play and so we have to go home.' 'Going home' is just another expression for losing in the quarter-final. This negative effect is explained by the fact that his team was unable to show its true ability. So in the model of Kelley the attribution is team 1 and in the model of Weiner the cause is 'internal' and (as the general ability to win the game is not denied) 'variable'. After the same game another expert concluded that: 'We have to accept [after this game] that other countries are playing football very well too.' The cause named here is the Bulgarian team, so in the model of Kelley the 'stimulus' is the opposition. In the scheme of Weiner, Bulgaria stands for the difficulty of the task and was coded as 'external' and 'stable'.

To concentrate on attributions televised immediately after the match brings both advantages and disadvantages. One advantage is the concentration on those moments that form the picture of the game, within the television audience and other media. Many people watched these three games.37 The soccer-orientated audience had a chance to gain a live impression of the game and of the post-match coverage. The other media relate to the television transmission and its analysis afterward (that is, interviews and press conferences). One disadvantage is that at this stage there are not too many expressions with attributions that can be categorized.

It is difficult to fit the attributions of sports events into the classification systems mentioned above. First, the results do not arise from individual actions ('Jeremies is angry at the referee'), but rather from interactions ('Every player is as good as the competitor gives him/her the chance to be'). Experience indicates that attributions by the media are simplified and interactions of causes often are split (that is, the action of the referee, individual and collective mistakes and so on). However, there will still be multiple classifications.

Second, it is a characteristic of the media discourse that attributions are also neglected ('Let's not blame the referee', 'the team is not the problem' and so on). These indirect attributions are not to be classified by the existing categories. They have several meanings because they state what is not the cause and they must be taken into account because they are part of the media discourse.

Third, attributions depend on their speakers' perspective, therefore one effect can be the base for several attributions.[38] As in the case of all content analysis, analysis of attributions encloses hermeneutic text interpretations, that is to say, there are cultural interpretations embedded in the attributions.

Finally, the categorization of attributions within the widespread models of Kelley and Weiner does not take their 'narrative character' into consideration. External variable attributions are often used in verification: a mistake by the referee, bad conditions, the fateful turnarounds of sport ('someone has to lose') or systematic discriminations. Any of these causes can have different functions in different patterns of narration.[39] One has to add the quantitative recording of attributions in order to define the stories that form the media framing of sport events.

Results

Hypothesis 1 supposed that actors explain events in the media by using the 'common sense' mode. The statements put forth by attribution theory support this mode, here shown in the data-regulated variant of the covariance model (Table 5). First of all, we notice that in German television each of the three matches has a comparable number of attributions, this corresponds with the comparable frame of reporting in all three games. In both Swiss and Austrian programmes there are fewer attributions, this is mainly a result of the fact that post-match reporting is shorter.

If one compares the direction of attributions with the hypothesis, one notices that in all four matches internal attribution was primarily carried out in regards to the German team (or 'person'). A higher value for external attributions (of the circumstances) was only detectable in the third game (and even this attribution was partially denied). This dominance of internal attributions only corresponds with the hypothesis

TABLE 5

ATTRIBUTIONS AFTER FOUR GERMAN GAMES

Versus	Year	Channel	Actors of attribution	Hypotheses	Attributions (%) (Kelley's Model)				Dominance*** (Weiner's Model)
					Team 1 (Person)	Team 2 (Stimulus)	Circum-stances	Other*	
Bulgaria	1994	ZDF	all	Circumstances	75	16	3	7	Internal/variable
Czech Republic	1996	ZDF	all	Team 1	80	5	15	0	Internal/stable
Croatia	1998	ARD, SF, ORF	all	Team 2/ Circumstances	54	11	27	8	Internal/stable
Portugal	2000	ARD	all**	Team 1	65	17	12	6	Internal/stable

Notes: * other = neglected or controversial attributions.
** attributions only on elimination.
*** dominance = majority of attributions.

in Germany vs. Czech Republic, the final game of the European Championship, which Germany won. The other two matches do not support the hypothesis. Neither in 1994 when Germany lost against Bulgaria did circumstances as attributions play a great role, nor in the 1998 game that Croatia won, in regards to the Croatian team, which was to be expected according to the covariance model.

The comparison between four German defeats is notable, especially if one takes into consideration Weiner's distinction between variable and stable causes. In 1994 there is a clear dominance of variable internal causes – above all, indicators of some mistakes, or lack of usual form. 'We didn't play as well as we can', was German team captain Lothar Mathäus' main statement, which denies any problem in the German team. This serves to comfort spectators, promising better results next time. In 1998 and, even more so, 2000 one can see a shift to stable internal causes. In this 1998 match, the team's age and (old-fashioned) style of play are given responsibility for the defeat: Germany's soccer team is in a crisis for which there is no immediate solution. The crisis was continued at Euro 2000.

On the whole, the data can be interpreted as proof of a causal theoretical scheme, namely the internality norm. In the attribution of sporting events, on the one hand the performance of one's own team is considered first – a fact that also dominates in neighbouring countries.[40] On the other hand, sport results are viewed primarily as the performance of the actors, external circumstances being considered second. The explanation of the result is traced back to external variables (circumstances) if other explanations are less plausible. We can thus conclude that 'common sense' would have another type of logic in sports.

Hypothesis 2 refers to the concept of self-serving attributions that can usually appear after (unexpected) defeats. Precisely because we are dealing with public attributions in the medium of television, there can be modifications. We have only investigated the German defeats of 1994 and 1998 and summarized all attributes that point toward this conclusion (Table 6).

Circumstances (Kelley) or external variable causes (Weiner) can be viewed as attributes that supply their own self-esteem. Taking this into consideration after the 1994 defeat, the difference between both large actors' groups is slight. Attributions applied to the German team's insufficient performance dominate. The cause is viewed by the sport

TABLE 6

ATTRIBUTIONS AFTER DEFEAT BY DIFFERENT ACTORS

Versus	Year	Actors of Attribution	Attributions (%) (Kelley's Model)				Dominance** (Weiner's Model)
			Team 1 (Person)	Team 2 (Stimulus)	Circum-stances	Other*	
Bulgaria	1994	German Players/Coach	67	25	8	0	internal/variable
		Experts/Journalists	78	13	0	9	internal/variable
Croatia	1998	German Players/Coach	23	9	59	9	external/variable
		Experts/Journalists	58	10	24	8	internal/stable

Notes: * other = neglected or controversial attributions.
** dominance = majority of attributions.

actors, more frequently than by experts and journalists, as alterable. One has been eliminated from competition and blames oneself. We can only speak of the existence of self-serving attributions in a subtle form, as far as avoidable individual mistakes led to defeat, or as far as general optimism regarding the future flourished.

The 1998 defeat paints a completely different picture. The difference between players/coach and experts/presenters is extreme. Fifty-nine per cent of attributions of German sport actors are attested to circumstances or external variable causes (observing actors: 24 per cent). After the game in which the Germans were judged by both locals and foreigners to have played best, considerable dissonance between the positive judgement of the play and the clear defeat arose, which must be rationalized. Whereas the players blamed the referee for the defeat, the coach looked to conspiracy theories for the answer. By contrast, experts/presenters used these attributions only 23 per cent of the time, looking 58 per cent of the time for causes arising from within the German team. This latter group often argues against placing the blame on circumstances. Hypothesis 2 may thus be confirmed: in 'case of emergency' (that is, failure), sports actors use more or less subtle, more or less convincing methods of self-justification and means to cope with defeat. These differ from the explanation patterns of the observing actors and experts.

It is rather more difficult to test Hypothesis 3, which (using the example of the 1998 game) claims that there are differences between the television stations in various German-speaking countries. All three programmes have comparable dramaturgy (a studio with experts), but each allows a different amount of time for post-match reporting. Second, each gives the involved sport actors a different amount of on-screen time. Third, experts, reporters and presenters demonstrate a different amount of 'closeness' to Germany. Therefore, we have decided only to considers the hosts'/experts' reports and to sum up the reports on Swiss and Austrian television (Table 7).

Table 7 highlights a few differences, based upon each separate perspective, although the German team's defeat is the event to be described in all three channels (see note 5). From the outside perspective the Croatian team's performance is clearly more frequently mentioned, while this cause is only mentioned in passing in German television (24 per cent compared with six per cent). Experts and presenters on both foreign programmes also tend to negate the idea, placing the blame on

TABLE 7
ATTRIBUTIONS FROM DIFFERENT PERSPECTIVES FOR GERMANY VS. CROATIA (1998)

Channel	Perspective	Attributions (%) (Kelley's Model)				Dominance ** (Weiner's Model)
		Team 1 (Person)	Team 2 (Stimulus)	Circumstances	Other*	
German television	Inside	50	6	33	11	internal/stable
Austrian/Swiss television	Outside	62	24	3	11	internal/stable

Notes: * other = neglected or controversial attributions.
** dominance = majority of attributions.

circumstances or external variable causes, which is more often practised on German television. This hypothesis can thus be supported by these facts: in this case it is not only crucial that there was a partially different 'ensemble' of explanation givers, but also that there was supposedly the more distant neutral view, existing in Germany's neighbouring states.

Hypothesis 4 postulates the embedding of the attributions, after the game, in narrative patterns that were developed in the pre-reporting segment. In a strict sense, this hypothesis can only be illustrated using the following cases.

From the German perspective there are two stories that have been told over of a number of years and have become embedded in the explanations for victories and defeats. One of these is the myth of the 'tournament team' that grew out of many championship games. A 'tournament team' demonstrates improving results from game to game and can compensate for the loss of players. In difficult situations, a tournament team possesses the 'luck of the hard-working'. This story is simultaneously the 'German virtues' – fighting strength, discipline, the ability to perform well as a team – with which the team asserts itself against football 'artists'. A second theme, rather further below the narrative surface, is the question of whether or not Berti Vogts would succeed in winning important tournaments and step out from behind Franz Beckenbauer's shadow.[41] The stories are bound together with the trainer figure as he, in his active playing days, represented these 'virtues' with especial emphasis.

In 1994, both of these stories took a negative turn. The comforting explanation, that the performance potential was not exhausted to the utmost, helps to get past the first disappointment: 'Once again, we didn't play as well as we can' (Matthäus). In the following week the 'coach question' was discussed. The year 1996 represented a triumphant interlude. German virtues were the deciding factor in the championship victory in England: 'My star is the team' (Vogts). Television broadcasts show Vogts cheering in front of the fans in Wembley stadium; he is forgiven the defeat in 1994. The German chancellor Helmut Kohl was reported as praising him personally after the televised game, 'That is a man with persistence and character – this is his hour, his day' and all media commentators and other experts were with him.

1998 saw the stories turn into catastrophe. The 'German virtues' were sufficient only up until the quarter-final and the 'tournament team' was defeated. The German television expert Günther Netzer and Otto

Baric from Austrian ORF (a native Croatian coach), judged the defeat nearly identically: 'And finally their luck ran out'. During the press conference after the game, the coach said: 'We have to go home, for whatever reason, other people will have to take the responsibility.' In terms of narratives, Vogts tried to establish a new attribution pattern, which constructs an international conspiracy. At this point he obviously ignored the demands of 'seriousness' and 'plausibility'. The tabloid *Bild* ended this discussion on the Monday following the game with the front page headline: 'Stop moaning!'

Instead of complaining about conspiracies, two other discourses were set in motion after the World Championship of 1998: one concerned the future of German soccer and the other dealt with the role that the federal coach, who was still at his post, was going to play. It was the end of an era. The Euro 2000 tournament in Belgium and the Netherlands is also history now. Germany lost in the first round – their worst performance at an international tournament in over a decade. Gary Lineker's statement that football consisted of 22 people running after a ball and Germany winning at the end had lost its validity. Thus, the attribution of failure had to be continued in the usual way and by the same media staff. 'You're an embarrassment!', the tabloid *Bild* cried after the miserable defeat against Portugal.

If one looses in the early rounds of three out of four tournaments, common sense (represented by failure attribution theories) will say that it was one's own fault. In 1998 Günter Netzer, the German television chief analyst, could still talk of an 'end to luck', but now the 'end of excuses' had come, that is the end of external attributions. The experts rated German soccer at its 'absolute worst' (Jupp Heynckes). An out-of-date approach to the game, lack of creativity, poor promotion of young talent, the media's over-rating of the national league, too many foreigners in important team positions, bad management of the German Football Association (DFB) – little was left out of the crisis discussion. Several hours after exiting Euro 2000, Dieter Kürten, a long-time ZDF commentator, stepped in front of a board. On it, he had noted the experts' optimistic hypotheses regarding the final result of the game against Portugal; on a sudden sarcastic impulse, he crossed them out and wrote instead 'Forget it'.

After Euro 2000 the management changed again. After the double victory of a team almost identical to the one that lost in Euro 2000 the new coach, former striker Rudi Völler, became the darling of the media and the masses. His new status of national hero appeared imminent. The crisis seemed to be over and now appears only as a footnote to the actual media coverage. Oblivion overtakes the sports discussion of the media and public – until the next disaster.

The results of our four case studies show (with a small but complete database) some inconsistencies. While the data support Hypotheses 2 and 3, derived from attribution theory, they do not support Hypothesis 1. In this hypothesis we assumed data-orientated (vs. schema-directed) attributions, following the covariance model. In two of four cases (German failures) the hypothesized attribution to unfavourable circumstances did not happen. We can offer two separate explanations for this. First, in cases of mediated sport events, the attributing actors – players as well as spectators – may base their judgement not only on the results, but also on the perception of the whole event. Therefore the actors have more information than the covariance model supposes: a hypothesized attribution could be justified by the result of a game and by information about the course of a game. However, in cases of media sports – a sphere with highly ritualistic communication – we should now also be working on the assumption of dominance of causal schemes. This means above all that it is the norm to make internal rather than external attributions, to start explanations from the performance of the actors and to admit external causes only under specific conditions and in a few cases of the 'incredible'. In this way actors in the media meet with the demands and norms of media coverage.

CONCLUDING REMARKS

If the question beyond that of the formal structural features is to be followed, namely what is actually going on besides the additional coverage, there are many descriptive perspectives to be brought in. For our purpose of characterizing the media explanation processes, it turned out to be fruitful to apply the general procedure of attribution research – which consists of comparing ordinary people's explanation processes with those of professional researchers – to the programme formats of the additional sport coverage. Although the attribution models may be not very successful in predicting concrete attributions in media sport, they allow a precise and adequate classification of explanations after sport events. These models appear to be useful in detecting ritualistic patterns and schemes in mediated interpretations of events.

From this perspective, the phases of coverage can be related to the conventionalized course of scientific research processes. Thus, the pre-match coverage that is based on forecasts about the outcome of the game is equivalent to the process of hypothesis formation. The running commentary (or live reporting) depicts the field research, during which the course of the game is established, advance information is updated, expectancy is modified and the interim score is passed on. The subsequent reflection serves finally as result interpretation – the fundamental meaning-variety of the numeric end result and the following evaluation of possible influential variables is reduced by the process of cause attribution. The outcome of the game gains some social reality and can find its way into the forecasts of future game outcomes. The same people forecasting the outcome of the game are usually included in the interpretation process once the score is set and therefore their own forecast and the score explanation are both evaluated.

The proposed analogy of sport reporting and scientific research might seem rather speculative at first sight. As a whole, the differences are probably considerably bigger than the common ground, but we wish to retain our claim that the framing coverage on live events is borne principally by an analytical basic 'gestus' of all participants. Following attribution research again, we call the result of this basic gestus 'pseudoscientific' or 'pararational' sport coverage. Its function can be described in various dimensions:

1. The analytical basic gestus of pararational coverage ensures a coherence among the different stages of the programme as a whole, especially the initial treatment and the post-match coverage. In that way the constraint on plausibility is still dominant, whether there are defeats to be digested or triumphs to be celebrated.

2. Sport coverage, especially of international competitions, has the tendency to focus on one's own national team and is therefore under the suspicion of violating the basic professional norms of objectivity, independence and balance. However at the same time, the national position has to be accommodated as an important prerequisite for audience feedback. The pararational coverage can be interpreted as a strategy to dodge role conflicts on the surface, without giving up the support for one's own team.

3. The pararational coverage distinguishes itself by its high rate of adaptability to everyday communication about sport. The speculations on, and the search for, the cause of the outcome, especially the way they are articulated within the circle of experts, represent the continuation of 'alehouse talk', but under mass-media conditions.

4. The pararational coverage alongside this analytical discourse creates an independent event within the event, a competition over forecasting and interpreting, besides the actual sport event. The players and coaches in particular, but also the experts, expose their assessment to another assessment, which can lead to notable distinction or disgrace. The audience, which is attributed an unusually high expertise in the sport sector, gains additional gratification when able to relate its own interpretations to that of the mass-media participants. The discourse of explanation offers the media itself an event that can be the object of future reporting, like the competition itself.[42]

5. Finally in the case of defeat of the national team, the form of the pararational coverage is well adapted as a ritual discourse framework and the irritation about German defeats can be bridged with its help. Explanations serve to make the incomprehensible comprehensible. Experts and journalists express their analytical posture in the role of the therapist who can not undo the defeat, but can make it understandable. The audience may also gain some gratification from this.

To sum up, additional sport coverage equals the actual event reporting in terms of programme length. It is marked by a strong effort involving the programme's resources and personnel, a strong segmentation and dynamics during the course of the programme, a variety of presentation forms that contain elements of media entertainment, a display logic concerning the zooming-in and the zooming-out and, finally, by the dominance of the pararational gestus. These aspects generate various forms of audience gratification. This includes rich diversions and entertainment as well as extensive information about the game. The creation of an additional event through the process of pseudoscientific reporting must always be an appealing proposition; even if the home team fails there is still a chance of an entertaining discourse.

NOTES

1. K.-H. Bette, 'Sport als Thema geselliger Kommunikation: Zur Choreographie mikrosozialer Prozesse', in W. Kleine and W. Fritsch (eds.), *Sport und Geselligkeit: Beiträge zu einer Theorie der Geselligkeit im Sport* (Aachen: Meyer und Meyer, 1990), pp.61–80.
2. See L.A. Wenner (ed.), *MediaSport* (London and New York: Routledge, 1998).
3. 1994: Germany vs. Bulgaria (quarter-final, 1–2).
   1996: Germany vs. Czech Republic (final, 2–1).
   1998: Germany vs. Croatia (quarter-final, 0–3).
4. Only sport-related programmes were taken into account, that is, newscasts in the half-time break were left out.
5. J.-L. Missika and D. Bregmann, 'On Framing the Campaign: Mass Media Roles in Negotiating the Meaning of the Vote', *European Journal of Communication*, 3, 2 (1987), 289–309.
6. G. Boehm, *Die kognitive Struktur kausaler Alltagserklärungen* (Frankfurt am Main: Peter Lang, 1994), p.31.
7. G. Reinhold (ed.), *Soziologie-Lexikon* (München: Oldenbourg, 1992).
8. H. Wienold, 'Erklärung', in W. Fuchs-Heinrich, R. Lautmann, O. Rammstedt and H. Wienhold (eds.), *Lexikon zur Soziologie* (Opladen: Westdeutscher Verlag, 1994), p.179.
9. Boehm, *Die kognitive Struktur kausaler Alltagserklärungen*, p.31.
10. Ibid., p.32.
11. F. Heider, *The Psychology of Interpersonal Relations* (New York: Wiley, 1958).
12. Boehm, *Die kognitive Struktur kausaler Alltagserklärungen*, p.33.
13. E. Witte, *Sozialpsychologie: Ein Lehrbuch* (München: Psychologie-Verlags-Union, 1989), p.301.
14. M. Hewstone and F. Fincham, 'Attributionstheorie und-forschung: Grundlegende Fragen und Anwendungen', in W. Stroebe, M. Hewstone and G.M. Stephenson (eds.), *Sozialpsychologie: Eine Einführung* (Berlin: Springer, 1996), pp.177–218.
15. H.E. Kelley, 'The Process of Causal Attribution', *American Psychologist*, 28, 1 (1973), 108–28.
16. Boehm, *Die kognitive Struktur kausaler Alltagserklärungen*, p.61; Hewstone and Fincham, 'Attributionstheorie und-forschung', p.185.
17. Hewstone and Fincham, 'Attributionstheorie und-forschung', p.184.
18. Boehm, *Die kognitive Struktur kausaler Alltagserklärungen*, p.54.
19. B. Weiner, *Motivationspsychologie* (Weinheim: Psychologie Verlags Union, 1994).
20. D.L. Wann, *Sport Psychology* (Upper Saddle River, NJ: Prentice Hall, 1997).
21. In various combinations of the first two dimensions the causes are ability (internal stable), effort (internal variable), difficulty of task (external stable) and luck (external variable).
22. Terms like 'mistake' or 'bias' are disputed subjects within theories of attribution because of their normative tendency. Since they are used within social psychology, we want to keep them in this text.
23. L. Ross, 'The Intuitive Psychologist and his Shortcomings: Distortions in the Attribution Process', in L. Berkowitz (ed.), *Advances in Experimental Social Psychology*, Vol.10 (New York: Academic Press, 1977), pp.173–220; Hewstone and Fincham, 'Attributionstheorie und-forschung', p.190.
24. G.W. Bradley, 'Self-serving Bias in the Attribution Research: A Re-examination of the Fact or Fiction Question', *Journal of Personality and Social Psychology*, 36, 1 (1978), 56–71.
25. Hewstone and Fincham, 'Attributionstheorie und-forschung', p.194.
26. S. Biddle, 'Attribution Research and Sport Psychology', in R.N. Singer, M. Murphey and L.K. Tennant (eds.), *Handbook of Research on Sport Psychology* (New York: Macmillan, 1993), pp.437–64; J. Möller, 'Attributionsforschung im Sport: Ein Überblick', *Psychologie und Sport*, 8, 1 (1994), 82–93; Wann, *Sport Psychology*.
27. B. Weiner, '"Spontaneous" Causal Thinking', *Psychological Bulletin*, 97, 1 (1985), 74–84.
28. R.R. Lau and D. Russell, 'Attributions in the Sport Pages', *Journal of Personality and Social Psychology*, 39, 1 (1980), 29–38; J. Möller und H. Brandt, 'Personale und situationale Leistungsbegründungen in Fernseh- und Zeitungsberichten', *Medienpsychologie*, 6, 4 (1994), 266–77; M. Marr and H.-J. Stiehler, 'Zwei Fehler sind gemacht worden, und deshalb sind wir

nicht mehr im Wettbewerb: Erklärungsmuster der Medien und des Publikums in der Kommentierung des Scheitern der deutschen Nationalmannschaft bei der Fußball-Weltmeisterschaft 1994', *Rundfunk und Fernsehen*, 43, 3 (1995), 330–49.

29. F. Neidhardt, 'Öffentlichkeit, öffentliche Meinung, soziale Bewegungen', in idem (ed.), *Öffentlichkeit, öffentliche Meinung, soziale Bewegungen: Sonderheft 34 der Kölner Zeitschrift für Soziologie und Sozialpsychologie* (Opladen: Westdeutscher Verlag, 1994), pp.7–41.

30. Ibid., p.14.

31. Ibid., p.13.

32. Ibid., p.19.

33. J.F. Staab, *Nachrichtenwert-Theorie: Formale Struktur und empirischer Gehalt* (Freiburg: Alber, 1990).

34. Public stations were responsible for the portrayal of the championship games in both countries. In Switzerland, SF DRS and in Austria, ORF.

35. See A.A. Berger, *Narratives in Popular Culture: Media and Everyday Life* (Thousand Oaks, CA: Sage, 1997).

36. Marr and Stiehler, 'Zwei Fehler sind gemacht worden', 330–49.

37. In Germany, 1994:
     * Germany vs. Bulgaria was seen by 20.01 million people (77.9 per cent of the market);
     * Germany vs. Czech Republic was seen by 28.44 million people (76.3 per cent of the market); and
     * Germany vs. Croatia was seen by 23.26 million people (72.4 per cent of the market).

     These are average numbers for the coverage, for example, 32.86 million people watched the 'Golden Goal' in 1996. In 2000 the ratings for Germany vs. Portugal (12.89 million people, 38.4 per cent of the market) were disappointing and indicate that a great part of the public did not expect the 'wonder', that is, Germany beating Portugal and Romania beating England.

38. A good example is the treatment of the foul in the Germany vs. Croatia match in 1998 that led to the dismissal of the German player Christian Wörns. Nearly all commentators flagged this event as very important for the result of the game. German speakers tended to believe that the dismissal was unfair (external attribution: referee), while others more often felt it was justified (internal attribution: mistake of the player).

39. Friedrich, 'Self serving bias in medialen Attributionen bei Erfolg und Mißerfolg im Mannschaftssport: Untersuchung von Attributionsprozessen in deutschen und italienischen Printmedien zur Fußballeuropameisterschaft in England' (Unpublished manuscript, University of Leipzig, 1996). Friedrich showed in his analysis of the Italian press after Italy's exit from the 1996 tournament that the coach Arrigo Sacchi was first treated as part of the team (internal attribution) and later as scapegoat (external attribution).

40. Eighty-six per cent of attributions concerned the German team: 86 per cent on German, 73 per cent on Austrian and 92 per cent on Swiss television (Game 3, Germany vs. Croatia).

41. Franz Beckenbauer, who won the world champion's trophy as player (1974) and as coach (1990), figures as a national symbol for success in both soccer and management of the media.

42. The aforementioned newspaper headline, 'Stop moaning!', refers explicitly to the attribution process, rather than the game itself and illustrates this point.

8

'Witches of Our Age': Women *Ultras*, Italian Football and the Media

RINELLA CERE

Women have not been on the streets for very long ... it is probable that women could also elaborate a model of violence of their own in the future.[1]

International football support has been interpreted has having three modes of development: the British (English) model, the Italian model and the South American model.[2] The British model is more individualistic in style and still very few women are part of it. The Italian model will be discussed at length in this study, but we can say initially that the term and culture of the *ultras* has travelled beyond Italian national boundaries and to other Mediterranean countries (France, Spain, Portugal and some countries of eastern Europe), in the same way as the English model has been adopted by Scandinavian countries, Holland and, anomalously, Greece. The only exception is Denmark with the *Roligans*, a peaceful type of football supporter and a play on the word 'hooligan'.[3] The third, the South American model, also called '*bailado*', is the most lively and cheerful support in the world and includes many women in their ranks; many of their spectacular 'choreographies' have also been introduced into the culture of the Italian *ultras*.[4]

Ultras/Ultrà is a term adopted to describe dedicated football supporters who, in addition to supporting their team, go to great lengths to enrich the experience of the match for themselves and others. In recent years, the media has represented only negative offshoots of the *ultrà* culture. The terms *ultrà* and *ultras* are used interchangeably and without regard to the singular or plural. In Italy there are in fact two kinds of football supporters: *ultrà* and official. *Ultrà* fans are normally very contemptuous of the 'official' supporters' experience. In a study conducted by Roversi one respondent (interviewee No.20) stated:

These people [the official supporters] are not needed by Bologna [football club] … The only really serious supporters are us [the *ultras*], and I am not talking about the violence here but about people whose support on the ground [on the '*curva*'[5]] for the team goes beyond everything and everybody. They [the official supporters], in my opinion, are parasites.[6]

The main distinction immediately perceivable is the *ultras*' dedication to their team, a support that goes beyond winning or losing. In concrete terms this means spending a good part of the week, if not all, preparing the 'choreography', organizing the trip to the away game or collecting money from the members. It is an elaborate operation, which requires an enormous amount of dedication from the members of the group and especially the '*direttivo*' (a kind of organizing committee).

Another aspect of the *ultrà* world is the extensive literature published. Practically all groups, even the smallest ones, produce a fanzine. In fact at European level there is an elaborate map of publications exchanged through which *ultrà* football supporters get to know each other's culture. This has now extended to websites and is a fast-growing activity (however, I have not yet seen a website linked to women-only *ultrà* groups).[7] In Italy there is also a biweekly *Supertifo*,[8] entirely dedicated to the activities and culture of the *ultrà*. Much of the magazine is often dedicated to the images of the various '*curve*' and their 'choreographies'. The 'spectacle' aspect is undoubtedly the most important to the supporters and also in terms of the message it sends out to the opposing teams. In some groups women are often in charge of the 'choreography' (see below). This is how one official Bologna supporter described the joys of a successful 'choreography': 'I feel a million miles away from them, but without them the stadium [spectacle] would be nil'.[9]

This brings us to the final important feature of the *ultrà* culture discussed: the '*gemellaggi*' (twining) between teams and their *ultrà* supporters. At least at the beginning of the *ultrà* support in the 1970s, the *gemellaggi* certainly had its roots in political allegiances (see below), although more recently this has given way to a more 'intricate map' of twinning, which is not always based on political sympathies.[10] The twinning phenomenon is not exclusive to the football world, but it has taken on characteristics that have determined new enmities as well as friendships. It is not unusual therefore that the help to the 'twinned team' goes well beyond even the call of duty of an *ultrà*. Normally this means supporting the twinned team in a fight against what may not previously have been a common enemy, or even going in *curve* together. There is presently no information available on *gemellaggi* between women-only groups and whether these are different from the men, but there is increasing new twinning at international level, which often takes place in an *ad hoc* fashion.

WOMEN AND *ULTRÀ* CULTURE

The single most important thing to note about female football support is its 'invisibility' in Italian society at large, and that of *ultrà* supporters in particular, in all areas of social communication, the mass media included, and of course, as a consequence, in cultural and sociological studies of sport practices. Like the story of witches, uncovered in the last few decades by many feminist researchers as women who did not submit to the will of man and Church,[11] the women *ultrà* are on the whole seen as 'different' because the association of 'women' and *ultrà* is viewed as an unlikely one.

That very little has been written and researched on women football supporters is hardly surprising, given the sport under discussion and the larger question of gender division within sport and society. Women football supporters are still a minority in the make-up of football support; a fact that should be considered in the context of past lack of leisure in women's lives.[12] In fact among the many changes that the world of football has sustained in the last 20 years, one is the increase in women following football. Some studies have tended to read this development as part of the 'embourgeoisement' of football,[13] rather than as a genuine process of change involving women from different social backgrounds. This may be true of Britain, but it seems less true of Italy.

The *ultrà* phenomenon has a peculiarly Italian character, tied to the specificity of football support in Italy and the political and cultural climate in which the phenomenon was born. It is also the case that football support in Italy has commanded rather more female support than in other equivalent European societies, although it remains a small percentage in comparison to male support, with some regional variation. There are 35 women-only groups in the whole of Italy and they are networked in the *Associazione nazionale italiana femminile sostenitrici di calcio* (National Italian Association of Female Football Supporters).[14]

The study of women *ultrà* groups presents a number of problems to the feminist researcher, the first is of a theoretical nature and it concerns the nature of the *ultrà* culture. For example, is women's membership of *ultrà* groups, which are predominantly male, a reinforcement and a reproduction of structured gender power relations? Alternatively, how may this membership be seen as a form of resistance to such power relations? Some of the research and experiences described later will seek to answer these questions.

The second problem is tied to the fact that this discussion is an exploratory study of female *ultrà* football support in Italy, as hardly any systematic empirical research has been done on the subject. As a result it is very difficult to discuss the specific type of football support that goes under the name of *ultrà* not only because it has been primarily the domain of 'boys', but also because there is a general lack of relevant research and literature. Having said that, it is known that alongside the *ultrà* groups mainly composed of male support there is a sizeable female support and, furthermore, for some years, women-only *ultrà* groups have been established, either operating in conjunction with male *ultrà* support, or separately – but nonetheless inhabiting the *curve* of the Italian stadium.[15] This research is a start in the direction of comprehending the women *ultrà* phenomenon; all the literature available on the subject has been scanned and in addition some information has filtered through various pieces of research that have not been gender-specific.

Some of the questions addressed will raise issues about gender differentiation: for example, are the women-only *ultrà* groups different from the men's, given the characterization of *ultrà* football support as male and violent, what Marchi has termed SMV (*Stile Maschio Violento*)?[16] Not that problems are absent in the studies of *ultras* in general; many of the studies produced have concentrated on violence within the world of *ultras*, thus giving a skewed version of the movement as a whole. This essay considers this skewed version particularly in relation to the mass media and the perceived bias in reporting about the *ultrà* support, normally perceived as men's support, or certainly support by males. Nonetheless, this essay does not overlook the fact that violence has become more of an integral part of *ultrà* culture, especially in the last decade.[17]

Through the short history of the movement, the essay traces some of the important changes within society that have affected the *ultrà* culture as a whole, moving it in a racist and politically right-wing direction; while at the same time women-only groups with a predominant, albeit not entirely, generally peaceful culture have entered the *curve*. The next section will also consider the relationship between *ultrà* culture, violence and the media. Many of the changes will be evaluated through the eyes of women *ultrà* supporters in the existing literature.

HISTORY OF THE *ULTRÀ* MOVEMENT

Most historical studies locate the rise of the *ultrà* groups as beginning in the early 1970s.[18] Some earlier forms, which did not go under the name of *ultrà*, are identifiable in the late 1960s. In 1968 the '*Fossa dei leoni*' (lions' den) was formed by AC Milan, followed by the supporters of the other Milanese team, Inter FC, a group called the 'Inter Boys'. The 'Red and Blue Commandos' of Bologna were also formed around the same time, but the actual term *ultrà* was first used by Sampdoria supporters in 1971. The term itself (often perceived to have the same meaning as 'hooligan' and – wrongly – used interchangeably in many studies) is associated with left-wing politics of the 1960s and 1970s. As was briefly mentioned above, groups were commonly referred to as 'ultra-left' both in Italy and France.

The link between the term *ultrà* as football supporter and *ultra* as political activist is, however, not purely semantic. In the early days of the *ultrà* phenomenon, there were clear links between one's politics and the support on the *curve*. In a similar way the names of the various groups reflected the political language and struggles of the time, so on the left there were groups of supporters using titles such as '*Fedayn*' and '*Tupamaros*' and on the right there were the '*Folgore*' and '*Vigilantes*'.[19] The militancy associated with ultra-left groups was extended to the football environment: 'If a member of an official football club can be said to be a citizen of the football world, an *ultra* has to be considered as a militant.'[20]

Podaliri and Balestri[21] describe the *ultrà* phenomenon as unfolding in four phases. The first of these phases is clearly embedded in the period of protests that in Italy involved both workers and students alike, what Paul Ginsborg[22] has called the epoch of collective action (1968–73). This ranged from the student protests of 1967–68 and the '*autunno caldo*' of 1969, a period of workers' protests and strike actions, to the period of consolidation and reforms, albeit often limited (and in some cases a complete failure).[23]

This mixture of political action and counter-cultural movements spilled onto the football culture and the stadium:

> It is clear that besides the not infrequent contiguity between curve supporters and people taking part in the demonstrations, the *ultrà* groups tended to conform to the style of these groups, adopting their organisational and structural characteristics together with some counter-cultural features.[24]

However, it is important to distinguish between *ultras* that were allied to extreme left-wing groups and *ultras* that were allied to extreme right-wing groups. This is for two reasons, first because left-wing groups 'never carried out systematic recruitment campaigns in the stadia' and normally exercised a kind of 'passive' influence, unlike the extreme right. Second, many *ultrà* groups were actually formed by far-right leaders (the most important in terms of size and violent propensity were Inter Milan, Lazio and Verona), hence the systematic recruitment practices ascribed to right-wing *ultrà* groups.[25]

The second phase occupied the period between 1977 and 1983. Although still very much influenced by counter-cultural movements of the left, these movements have changed dramatically from the late 1960s and early 1970s. They are characterized by a rejection of all the values that were intrinsic to the new left of the previous decade:

> The '77' [as it is called now] is the first large mass movement of republican Italy that does not have any other country as a model. In fact it is the first movement which is fully conscious of the 'irreversible and utter failure of the communist revolution in the world'.[26]

The other political failure is the 'parliamentary' road to socialism. The possibility of a left-wing government is dashed by the electoral failure of the New Left and the Italian Communist Party's strategy of the 'historic compromise'.

An important trait of these movements, which is of relevance to our discussion and related to the role that feminism has played within general transformations and thematics in culture, is the idea that the 'personal is political'. It has also been argued that because of 'their counter-cultural tendency, the *ultrà* groups accepted a fairly remarkable number of women absent in most other European groups and carried out direct membership activities, as with political organization'.[27] Of course this was only true of groups associated with left-wing politics, we do not yet know whether it was true also of the groups with right-wing allegiances, given their less than open embrace of feminism.

In the world of the *ultras* the names and symbols seen in the stadia were very much those adopted by sections of the left-wing – names such as Brigades and a five-pointed star symbol, which belonged to a left-wing armed terrorist group called the Red Brigades. Che Guevara figured prominently as an image on the 'red *curve*'. That is not to say that right-wing terrorism did not have its equivalent. Right-wing *ultrà* groups often adopted the two-edged axe emblem, which belonged to Ordine Nuovo (an extreme right-wing group operating in the 1970s). However, as Podaliri and Balestri have argued:

> It is true that the *ultrà* groups traditionally controlled by the right strengthened their position, however, the leisure time and 'the world of imagination' were still completely controlled by the left, and groups which were strongly leftist were not threatened by any kind of penetration by the right.[28]

The organization of *ultrà* groups also based itself on similar structures present within extreme left-wing parties and used the same terms to describe them; the word '*direttivo*' is one such and is still in use today.

The third phase, the 1980s, marked a fundamental change in the composition of *ultrà* membership. The movement extended beyond its established field of recruitment, new groups set up around lower division clubs and newcomers were also younger and much more differentiated in their social background. Gone was the *ultrà* traditionally associated with the political protests of either the 1960s or 1970s and the struggle against a society based on unequal material access, aware of the contradictions inherent in football, where players earned vast sums (although not as much as now). 'The logic of the "*curva*" as a liberated space is replaced by that of the "*curva*" as a "small mother country", which produced a clannishness, a cult of toughness and paramilitary organisation.'[29]

Varied factors contributed to the above changes. The rise of new political movements with a regional character (such as the Lega Nord, with their open prejudices and xenophobic attitudes) have played a part in changing the culture of some *curve*, especially northern ones (Atalanta-Bergamo and Brescia are two prominent examples of this phenomenon). Back in 1993, Ilvo Diamanti defined the Lega Nord as a movement whose real strength lies in having undermined the political identities previously in circulation. Referring to the *leghe*'s, that is all the different regional *leghe* that make up the larger body of the Lega Nord, he stated that:

> Their principal innovation has consisted in the ability to break with the traditional basis of political identity ... religious, secular and class inspired; in their place, they [the *leghe*] have introduced other reference points, recouped from ancient contradictions within Italian society: the contrasts between centre and periphery, North and South, private and public, civic society and traditional political parties.[30]

In recent years the Lega Nord has often accused the public service broadcaster RAI of not allowing their party spokespersons any of the allocated airtime for political news,[31] however alternative channels were certainly provided by Berlusconi's commercial television stations after their electoral coalition with his party Forza Italia, respectively in 1994 and 2001. The Lega Nord has also built up a considerable media base of its own. It owns a television and radio station, respectively called Telepadania and Radio Padania Libera, publishes a daily newspaper, originally titled *La Padania*, as well as a political-cultural weekly, *Sole Delle Alpi*, and a quarterly journal, *Quaderni Padani*, which is the 'intellectual' backbone of the party. They use the above media to full effect by, on the one hand, compounding the stereotypical dichotomies, admittedly in circulation long before the Northern League voiced them, between the north and south of Italy and, on the other hand, openly attacking the 'new communities' of immigrants, which in Italy are termed '*extracomunitari*'.[32] Their ongoing media tirades about 'the inefficient centralized state' and what has been called, in rather racist terms, the 'Africanization' of the cities, has been an arbitrary association that foments intolerance and phobias and associates the sub-proletariat *extracomunitario* with the proletariat and petite bourgeoisie of the south.

In addition, this relatively new local xenophobic culture of the Lega, alongside the more established nationalist and racist culture of 'Alleanza Nazionale'[33] (paradoxically in political contradiction with the Lega's separatist objectives yet political allies with them in the centre-right coalition 'La casa delle Libertà' led by Berlusconi's party Forza Italia[34]) have together intensified racism on the terraces. The culture of the above political parties, like some of the *ultrà* groups to which they are associated, is overtly masculine. There are women who are part of that culture, but not as a critical force of some of the male-orientated practices. There is a general consensus that women could play a positive role within the culture of the *ultrà* in general, especially in relation to violence and racism. This is certainly suggested by more than one writer in the *ultrà* world; among the immediate solutions to stamp racism out of the stadia Roversi suggests creating 'incentives to raise the numbers of women going to the stadia',[35] but this seems to refer more to the 'traditional' woman fan than the *ultras*.

The remarkable changes in Italy in the 1980s have been interpreted as part of a wider 'discontent' with politics, yet I would argue that the recent phenomena in Italy, which voice the revival of regional identities, are indeed political. They are, in fact, part of an attempt to dismantle what are considered 'myths' surrounding the Italian national unification process and the perceived wrongs perpetrated in achieving and maintaining it.

The fourth phase of the *ultrà* culture, the 1990s, was even more marked by a clear bifurcation of the movement into, on the one hand, the *ultrà* groups that have 'a social conscience' and, on the other, those that are only interested in actions of a 'military' or paramilitary kind. According to Podaliri and Balestri, the beginning of this new phase was marked by a serious incident: the murder of a Genoa *ultrà* member before the match with AC Milan on 29 January 1995. The Milanese *ultrà* group, which carried out the attack, had modelled itself on the British 'casuals':[36] they travelled incognito to Genoa by train without any visible sign of their being football supporters. Interestingly, Podaliri and Balestri refer to them as 'superhooligans', a term also widely used by the media.[37] What distinguished them, however, was the fact that they carried knives; for most traditional *ultrà* supporters this was considered an act of infamy, as harmful weapons such as knives or guns were not perceived as part of the confrontational culture of the *ultras*. Vincenzo Spagnolo (Claudio), a young man of 24, died of a stab wound. This was not the first serious incident, deaths had also occurred in the late 1980s and early 1990s,[38] but it coincided with a sudden awareness that the *ultrà* movement was no longer evolving along the original criteria: 'Under the knock-on effect of the increase in right-wing symbols and culture, even "*tifoserie*" – traditionally left-wing – vacillated.'[39]

Balestri, as privileged observer and co-ordinator of the Ultrà Project,[40] cites recent examples of this transformation, found even within *ultrà* groups traditionally considered entirely left-wing, such as Bologna. Following a racist attack by extreme right-wing offspring calling themselves 'the Mods', he notes that:

> In the wake of the incident the Bolognese *ultrà* world split ... on the one hand there are groups who offer a strong identity to their members on the basis of a series of initiatives and activities [including even the social field, carrying out collections of second-hand clothes for war victims and fundraising for children's charities] and, on the other, there are groups which are mainly orientated towards a military confrontation.[41]

Interestingly, a historical explanation can be found for this development: as the extreme left was repressed during the 1970s and early 1980s, the right continued to flourish within the *curve* and inevitably is now the single largest problem as it also feeds on racist culture. Admittedly, as Bruni has pointed out in his history of the *ultrà* movement, Italy is not witnessing an infiltration of extreme right-wing organizations of the type seen in Britain. Nonetheless fascist symbols on the *curve* accompanied by racist banners are far more common, even if this does not necessarily correspond to 'a real political militancy on the far right'.[42] On a more positive note, it is also true that in spite of the perceived 'depoliticization' of society and of young people in particular, which has often meant a flirtation with extreme right-wing culture, political left-wing alignments of some of the largest *ultrà* groups have survived to this day.

The above bifurcation has clearly not interested women as much as men, but it is impossible to say whether they could also act as the counter-influence mentioned earlier as they are rarely part of any media representation. There are clearly three opposing centrifugal forces operating in the stadia. The first of these entails 'a greater degree of active participation, and even some democratization among fans. This process is evident in the increase in the number of women in soccer.'[43] The second is tied to the commercialization of football (as never before), principally associated with the televising of football and sport in general:[44] the increasing presentation and marketing of football for a passive, 'respectable' audience sitting either in executive boxes, all-seater stadia, on sofas at home, or at the bar watching on 'deregulated' television'.[45] The third force is constituted by the fomentation of hatred and violence against adversaries and players based on xenophobic and racist ideologies, often the only aspect of football support reported in the media.

For example, it is common knowledge that Verona *ultrà* supporters have often opposed the management in the purchase of black and Jewish players. A recent racist event reported in the media, involving Verona, implicated President Giambattista Pastorello himself. When asked if he was going to buy a black player Patrick Mboma, who was at that time playing for Parma, he responded that he could not buy black players because the Verona supporters did not want them: 'How can I buy a black player with the type of supporters we have' (*con una tifoseria così* ...).[46] In a recent European-wide survey on racism and football conducted by the *International Herald Tribune*, covering 16 countries, Italy not only had the longest list of racist incidents at matches, but was also described as the 'epicenter of racist abuse in soccer'.[47] At the same time in the same issue, another article by the same journalist mentions Italy as one of the countries at the forefront of combating racism in soccer with a number of anti-racist activities, such as the one organized by the Progetto Ultrà.[48]

THE 'PARTIAL' EXPERIENCE: WOMEN, *ULTRÀ* CULTURE AND THE MEDIA

Mainstream media have completely ignored women's football support and women *ultras* in particular. Given the stereotypes adopted in the media about *ultras*, predominantly about violence and machismo, it is hardly surprising that the invisibility and silence persists along gender divisions. It is also clearly part of a wider, tacit collusion with news values, which ignore the positive experiences of both men and women as *ultra* supporters. The only material available on women *ultras* and their experiences is to be found in alternative media and some glimpses can be had in some mixed sociological studies (see below).

THE ALTERNATIVE MEDIA ON *ULTRÀ* WOMEN

One document that comes closer to describing the experience of women *ultras* was published in *Noi Donne* in April 1995.[49] It is a discussion of the experiences of six different women's groups: supporters of Lazio,

Genoa, Cosenza, Avellino, Parma and Reggio. What is perhaps not surprising is the way in which their experiences are very different, yet still recognizably linked to the political allegiances of the team. For example, the Lazio supporters – with a traditional right-wing support – have established a women-only group, the '*Irriducibili* Girls' (although this is deferential to their male counterpart, the *Irriducibili*). In the interview one supporter talks of 'respect' for what she perceives as 'essentially a male world' where you are not really 'allowed' to behave independently:

> One is a woman and a Lazio supporter, but one has to keep one's place because you are in the way. If we go all together to an away match and something happens, it's obvious that the men have to protect us.[50]

In contrast, a Genoa supporter sees the women's role in the fights as one of help and support to defend the colours, but always within 'the unwritten rules' of *ultrà* fights (knives are not allowed).

The '*Donne Rossoblu*' (Cosenza), a sizeable and well-organized female *ultrà* group, was established in 1989. They are described as a peaceful group, which organizes accommodation and food for opposing teams (in conjunction with the well-known figure of Cosenza support, the Capuchin friar Padre Felice Bisceglie, also mentioned in Tassistro's study). However, one supporter is keen to point out that this should not be interpreted as 'maternal', but simply the rule of 'hospitality'. Like the women mentioned in the first study looked at above, these supporters stress that it has been difficult to establish themselves within the larger male *ultrà* world, but that commonality has prevailed: 'The love for the team and the rejection of the official supporters' club.'[51]

There also appears to be more disillusion among the women *ultras*, for example, one Avellinese supporter has abandoned the *ultrà* support because of what she sees as a general corruption of the ideals, 'The free tickets for some, the financial support from the team management for away games, dirty play in the name of victory, etc.' and what she calls the 'triumph of business over football'. One Reggio supporter expressed similar sentiments, she feels that the *ultrà* experience does not carry the same values; she sees them as being no longer those of the 1970s. This particular interviewee is one of the 'historic' leaders of the *ultras* of Reggio and although she is still part of a women-only club (the group Carmen Borghi, one of two women-only official clubs in Reggio) she feels the *ultrà* experience is over, at least for her. This can also be interpreted in the light of the generation change mentioned above.

The experiences seem more positive in all the female *ultràs* within the Parma 'All Girls' supporters group, but then female support in Parma is amongst the highest in the country – women account for 40 per cent of the stadium and even organize activities with their male counterparts (mainly the match 'choreography'). There is no friction between any of the groups in Parma, *ultrà* and *non*, although the women-only groups have hinted that on away matches the women within the male *ultrà* groups are very much subordinate (*fanno solo da seguito*).[52]

Another media document (incidentally, one of the first pieces of research on *ultras* in Italy) was produced by Daniele Segre between May 1977 and May 1979. Segre collected interviews and photographic material, which formed the basis of two documentaries: *Il potere deve essere bianconero* (1978) and *Ragazzi di stadio* (1979). A book detailing all the research was subsequently published in 1979 and it is in this work that we first detect a real presence of women supporters, not just as subordinates – for example, as *donna del capo* (the leader's woman) – but as supporters and organizers in their own right.[53]

Amongst the *ultras* of the Turin team, the leaders and organizers are equally men and women although the tasks appear to be divided along gendered lines: the women look after the 'choreography' of the *curva* (the flags and the drums, the aesthetics, as it were) and the financial aspects, while the men see to public relations and particularly to relations with the club. However, this is not perceived by the women as a gender-constructed division, but rather as a result of not having held a prominent role for as long as the men. Nonetheless, one female interviewee states that this has come about as a result of a certain amount of assertiveness on their part and through real necessity. They have always been part of the organization, but they had never been recognized as such.[54]

Another woman interviewed by Segre acknowledged the difficulties of being a woman *ultrà* when she first started frequenting the *curva*, but also claimed that where women were growing in numbers the climate, and as a consequence, their role was changing, with perhaps one exception, their relationship to violence. As mentioned above, the 'scuffles with the enemy supporters' are not quite part of the culture of the women *ultras*, although it appears from the interviews that the women are present in the background, as a helping hand either to bail someone out or to act as a 'base' and hold onto the banners and drums. In the culture of the *ultras* a stolen banner is like a war lost. Segre's study broke new ground with its informal and in-depth interviewing method and lack of set questions. He allowed the fans to speak at length about their experiences as *ultrà* supporters and their way of life, without the interference of the usual prejudices that were circulating in society and especially the mainstream media.

SUB-CULTURAL AND SOCIOLOGICAL STUDIES AND WOMEN *ULTRAS*

Colombo and De Luca's *Fanatics* is another important document as many of the testimonies are from female Genoa supporters, a traditionally left-wing *curva*.[55] One interviewee talks about the position of women within the *ultrà* organization, which she calls the *tifo organizzato*, and asserts that while women remain a minority there has been a 'feminization' of the *curve*.[56] Another testimony from a female Genoa supporter also touches on the link between politics and *ultrà* culture:

> Political allegiance was far more important in the past, the '*gemellaggi*' were based primarily on that ... there was an ideological motivation behind the skirmishes. Then the twinnings were broken [for example, with Milan and Rome] and ideology became less relevant, many 'curve' lost their political identity. This has taken place because of a general crisis of ideologies and an upsurge in right wing positions, of right groups, the 'skins' phenomenon, and so on.[57]

A third interviewee articulates some of the concerns about the new legislation introduced in 1995 during Berlusconi's Government and the related policing activities:[58]

> Police only increase the tension. It [policing] is not capable of solving difficult situations arising and often it is not there where it is needed. Fortifying the stadia is no solution ... rather than criminalize, more opportunities should be offered to young people to socialize, right now the stadium is one of the few places where young people can meet.[59]

All these young women *ultras* seem very articulate and clear about the changes taking place within society and how these are affecting the *ultrà* culture in terms of gender. They are also clear about the obstacles posed by some of society's institutions (the essay will explore how the media is believed to be part of these obstacles below). They are also aware that these changes may spell the end of the *ultras*' particular kind of football support, including that of women and its intrinsic difference.

There is also an unpublished academic study of Genoa fans, which is based on individual and collective interviews as well as a questionnaire.[60] As in the other sociological studies, there is a 'female component' to the sample, albeit only 15 per cent.[61] Unfortunately very little is said about their experience as women within the Genoa *ultrà* groups. All the individual interviews were conducted with male supporters; not a single interview was conducted with a female supporter, although they are clearly present numerically in the collective interviews. It is of course striking that in this study nothing transpires about women's experience, especially since the work discussed above is particularly rich in the experiences of Genoa supporters who are women.

Dal Lago and Moscati include some data about women's interest in football, but the section of the study entitled '*Tifo* and Social Stratification' is mainly concerned with male football support.[62] Its methodological bases are dictated by the interest in the stratification processes that have changed the traditional binomial of the working class and football. Only one of the tables considers the interest in football in terms of sex differentiation, although the data presented show some increase in women's interest in football. Certainly in the 'fairly interested' category the difference in percentages is very small, 29 per cent of men against 20 per cent of women. In the 'very interested' category there is a much larger gap between women and men, 37 per cent of men against seven per cent of women (data based on attending at least one football match in 1984).[63] However, the study considers football support in general, rather than *ultrà* support.

On the other hand, the research undertaken from an *ultrà* and gendered perspective by the 'Istituto Cattaneo' of Bologna in 1990 with the *ultras* of Bologna, reported in Roversi's study, is of particular interest to this essay.[64] This is a particularly useful study with which to evaluate the female component of *ultras* culture; the sample is based on 264 *ultra* supporters, 45 of whom are women. Roversi estimates the number of women involved as relatively high: 17.1 per cent, a sizeable percentage in women *ultras*' terms. According to Roversi there are a number of specific factors that contribute to this number: more than half of the 45 women stated that they did not belong to any previously constituted group and therefore had not encountered the opposition of a strongly masculine culture.

Of these 17.1 per cent, 65.9 per cent declare themselves to have been part of the *ultras* for less than three years. Roversi calls this section of the sample the 'weak segment' (*segmento debole*), in contrast to the 'strong segment' (*segmento forte*), which is composed of women who have been part of the *ultrà* culture for many years and who have never held roles subordinate to men. Bologna is also one of the teams that has an exclusively female *ultrà* group, the 'URB Girls'. (Other cities have similar women-only *ultrà* groups, such as the '*Monelle*' of Inter Milan and the '*Oche*' of Vicenza.[65])

The above figures and interpretation are also ascribed as part of a 'rooted culture of female support' in Bologna (*radicata tradizione di tifo al femminile*).[66] However, many of the women of the sample are young and are not part of the 'traditional' groups. It is later stated that some of the women involved in two historical *ultrà* groups in leadership roles have provided role models to younger women, but in this sample it is important to note that the younger generations hold a different attitude towards violence. In Roversi's study, most of the people involved in violent episodes are very young, 21 and under (64.7 per cent), and again it is significant for us to note the very small, but nonetheless important, percentage of young women involved (8.4 per cent).[67] Among the sample of interviews there are some testimonies from women *ultra* about their experiences of violence going to an away match.[68] The other study mentioned in Roversi is on Pisa's fans and here, as with Bologna, there is a significant female component, 13 per cent, but again no specific questions addressing their experiences as women *ultras*.[69]

THE MEDIA, WOMEN, VIOLENCE AND *ULTRÀ* CULTURE

Women's *ultrà* support is practically invisible in the mass media, rarely are they discussed in the sports pages of the national newspapers or even in the three sport-dedicated dailies available in Italy.[70] The same is true of radio and television, even though now women have started fronting sport programmes in Italy.[71] It is certainly the view of one of the women interviewed in *Noi Donne* that 'support is only ever represented in terms of men' (*tifo al maschile*),[72] although she admits that this is not a 'privilege' as it is often in relation to violent events. The mass media does not usually occupy its time covering the world and culture of the *ultrà*, the beautiful spectacle they put on, unless violence is involved. Yet the *ultrà* support has also functioned as a 'containment and control' over violence, although this is less true today.[73]

The equation is simple: women *ultrà* are rarely involved in clashes with opposing teams and therefore rarely discussed in the public sphere. (Nonetheless, as we have seen in Roversi's study above, women are sometimes involved in violent clashes). On the whole, girls are not the standard bearers of those codes and masculine values central to football support, believed to be 'a form of entertainment based on clashes learnt on the streets'. Women 'have not been on the streets for very long ... it is probable that women could also elaborate a model of violence of their own in the future'.[74] They are also less likely to be involved in racist attacks, a phenomenon that has become more prominent in the last decade, as we have also mentioned above. However, in the survey conducted by the *International Herald Tribune*,[75] the co-ordinator of Football Against Racism in Europe, Michael Fanizadeh, cited an example of racist abuse involving women (and children) experienced while watching the match between Inter Milan and Lazio: 'Jungle noises aimed at Inter's Dutch player Clarence Seedorf were not just coming from right-wing, male skinheads ... the problem is worse than that. A lot of women and children were joining in the abuse.'[76] Lazio has well-known right-wing support, including many women who share the racist ideology of their fellow *ultras* while at the same time, as seen in the *Noi Donne* interview above, accepting their role as subordinate – also part of extreme right-wing ideology. Lazio's *curva* is often in the media for its racist chants and '*striscioni*' (banners) against black and Jewish players such as at the derby between Rome and Lazio in 1998[77] and on the terraces of the Lazio *curva* in April 2001, which got them banned from playing in Rome.[78]

Studies have been undertaken in terms of the newspapers' coverage of incidents where *ultrà* groups have been involved. One worth mentioning, as a sizeable sample of newspapers were selected over a long period of time (seasons between 1970/71 and 1989/90), is that conducted by the Istituto Cattaneo in Bologna. This study (quoted and analyzed in Roversi), shows a marked increase in incidents over the years, which would perhaps justify the 'intensification' of coverage of violent episodes relating to *ultrà* football support generally. However, not all the figures are rising, for example, there is a decrease in incidents in the Turin support and a stable pattern in Sampdoria (a Genovese team).[79]

As it happens, Marchi's work also includes a discussion of how violence is at the centre of most descriptions and discussions about British studies of fan hooliganism, not just in the media but also in most sociological studies.[80] The critical study conducted by Ingham *et al.* in the 1970s stands against these tendencies and is still of relevance today, particularly Stuart Hall's study of the press, which lays open the usual prejudices of the mass media and state institutions.[81]

In Tassistro's study the diffidence of the mass media is explicitly articulated by many Genovese fans and the theme is returned to in many of the interviews.[82] In one particular interview the opportunism of the media and the ways in which the political forces 'criminalize and emphasize' the '*guerricciole inutili*' of *ultrà* supporters are mentioned: 'it is more comfortable, for them [the politicians] to have youngsters, preferably unemployed, who beat each other up in the name of football, a closed space easily controllable for the police.'[83] In another interview, other fans denounce the media stereotype of the *ultras* as 'intolerant and aggressive fighters'. The same media refuse to acknowledge the positive things that *ultras* engage in as organized groups of people, for example, when fans collected money for the Gaslini Hospital in Genoa they invited the local Genovese paper *Il secolo XIX* to report on it, but were told that 'unless there were fights the paper had no interest'.[84]

A similar view is expressed by a Turin supporter in Segre's study, but in this case it is more specifically addressed to how powerful teams, such as Juventus, get preferential treatment in reports on the negative aspects of the *ultras* world. This question is addressed by a Turin supporter, also a journalist for the local paper, in a comment to a colleague from a national paper:

> I don't understand why when there is a scuffle in the Turin camp it gets two or three pages' coverage [the underlying point of course is that it is negative coverage]. But when Juventus *ultras* have a fight, two or three lines discharge the whole incident.

The response from the national journalist is particularly illuminating: 'I don't want to be transferred to Sardegna.'[85]

CONCLUSION

Most of the works looked at in this essay widely acknowledge that the female component is much more visible than in other European '*tifoserie*', with the exception of the Danish '*Roligans*'. More importantly, I hope it has become apparent that women *ultras* are not only present in an ancillary function for the men. It is certainly astonishing that in Bruni's excellent study of the Italian *ultrà* movement the only reference made to women is that they are there 'to sew the flags and banners, to sell the promotional material [stickers, T-shirts and banners] which the *ultrà* produce to finance themselves'.[86]

It is equally worrying that in Roversi's study, the section quoted from Segre's interviews omits the details about the '*direttivo*' being composed of men and women in equal numbers and highlights only the perceived 'secondary roles' that the women have within the organization. This is in spite of the fact that many of the contradictions about the gendered roles – undoubtedly in existence – are opened up and discussed in the collective interviews. Yet Roversi himself acknowledges that there is an important female component (in the Bologna support), which has been fully part of the '*ultrà* universe' without being relegated to secondary roles.[87]

Certainly in future research it will be important to explore the ways in which women *ultrà* negotiate the symbolic world of 'hard masculine' identities. It seems clear that women-only *ultrà* groups, as well as women within the male groups, are already part of the process, which may bring positive changes to the *curve*, especially in the light of the increase in racist and violent culture among some groups. We have noted that there are exceptions, especially within groups that have a racist and right-wing orientation, where women are clearly still considered either in terms of utility or adornment. However, the heterogeneous nature of the *ultrà* movement should not be seen as an excuse to view football and its *ultrà* support as 'forever masculine'. In the same way, the mainstream media have been equally guilty of silencing women *ultras* to fulfil the so-called 'media logic' of monopolistic media[88] and the patriarchal requirements that expect women still to keep out of sight, or to be present only as a 'female spectacle'.[89]

NOTES

1. V. Marchi, cited by D. Cannizzaro, A. Di Pietro, C. De Michele and P. Gabrielli, 'Tutte in curva, girls', *Noi Donne* (April 1995), 45, my translation. *Noi Donne* was a monthly publication by the Communist Women section of the former PCI (Partito Comunista Italiano), now called DS (Democratici di sinistra). It has now closed down.
2. D. Colombo and D. De Luca (eds.), *Fanatics: Voci, documenti e materiali dal movimento ultrà* (Roma: Castelvecchi, 1996), pp.150–57.
3. A. Dal Lago and R. De Biasi, 'Italian Football Fans: Culture and Organization', in R. Giulianotti, N. Bonney and M. Hepworth (eds.), *Football, Violence and Social Identity* (London: Routledge, 1994), p.79.
4. 'Choreography' is a term used to describe the elaborate and spectacular preparations for a match, which consist of banners, choruses, musical instruments (normally drums) and coloured smoke bombs. One particular model adopted in the Italian *'curva'* is the *'barras bravas'* from Argentina, which consists of strips of colourful material covering from one end to the other of the *curva*. Another is the Mexican *'ola'*, which is cascaded down the steps rather than displayed horizontally.
5. The end of a football ground is termed *'curva'* in Italian. It is the place in the stadium that normally 'belongs' to the *ultras*. Hence many of the denominations for *ultrà* groups use the word *curva*. However, *curva* has also come to mean the space of the 'choreography'.
6. A. Roversi, *Calcio, tifo e violenza: Il teppismo calcistico in Italia* (Bologna: Il Mulino, 1992), p.114.
7. An extensive list of websites of the European teams and their supporters, official and unofficial, has been compiled by Mariella Grimaldi and is to be found in Colombo and De Luca (eds.), *Fanatics*, pp.186–210.
8. *Supertifo* is the magazine of the *'tifoso organizzato'*, a term often used to refer to the *ultras*.
9. Roversi, *Calcio, tifo e violenza*, p.89.
10. D. Colombo and D. De Luca, 'Gemellaggi, rivalità e razzismo', in idem (eds.), *Fanatics*, pp.94–112.
11. D. Purkiss, *The Witch in History* (London: Routledge, 1996); A. Llewellyn Barstow, *Witchcraze: A New History of the European Witch Hunts* (San Francisco: Harper, 1995).
12. K.A. Henderson and S.M. Shaw, 'Research on Women and Leisure: Past, Present, and Future Research', in L.A. Barnett (ed.), *Research About Leisure: Past, Present and Future* (Champaign, IL: Sagamore, 1995).
13. R. Giulianotti, *Football: A Sociology of the Global Game* (Cambridge: Polity Press, 1999), p.159.
14. This data refers to 1995.
15. As noted above, the *curve* 'belongs' to them.
16. V. Marchi, *Stile Maschio Violento: I demoni di fine millennio* (Genova: Costa and Nolan, 1994), p.4.
17. V. Marchi, 'Ultrà, uno stile di vita', in Colombo and De Luca (eds.), *Fanatics*, p.24.
18. See Roversi, *Calcio, tifo e violenza*; C. Podaliri and C. Balestri, 'The Ultràs, Racism and Football Culture in Italy', in A. Brown (ed.), *Fanatics! Power, Identity and Fandom in Football* (London: Routledge, 1998); F. Bruni, 'Storia del movimento Ultrà in Italia', in V. Marchi (ed.), *Ultrà: Le sottoculture giovanili negli stadi d'Europa* (Roma: Koiné, 1994).
19. Podaliri and Balestri, 'The Ultràs, Racism and Football Culture in Italy', p.90. The spelling of 'Fedayn' and 'Tupamaros' are as used in Italy. The literal meaning of *'Folgore'* is 'lightning', however, within right-wing Italian circles this is normally used in reference to the Parachute Corps *'La Folgore'* (renowned for its fascist tendencies), whose symbol is a lightning bolt.
20. A. Dal Lago and R. De Biasi, 'Italian Football Fans: Culture and Organization', in R. Giulianotti, N. Bonney and M. Hepworth (eds.), *Football, Violence and Social Identity* (London: Routledge, 1994), p.79.
21. Podaliri and Balestri, 'The Ultràs, Racism and Football Culture in Italy', pp.88–100.

22. P. Ginsborg, *Storia d'Italia dal dopoguerra a oggi: Società e politica 1943–1988* (Torino: Einaudi, 1989), pp.404–68.

23. Ibid., pp.465–6. Ginsborg has outlined the main failure of the reforms of the various centre-left coalitions as being unable to reform the Italian state, especially the fiscal organization (it is during this time that the national debt started growing at an alarming rate) and its over-bureaucratic structure (the complete and utter failure to reform the public administration).

24. Podaliri and Balestri, 'The Ultràs, Racism and Football Culture in Italy', p.90.

25. Ibid.

26. M. Grispigni, *Il settantasette* (Milano: Il Saggiatore, 1997), pp.23–4.

27. Podaliri and Balestri, 'The Ultràs, Racism and Football Culture in Italy', p.91.

28. Ibid., pp.92–3.

29. Ibid., pp.94–5.

30. I. Diamanti, *La Lega: Geografia, storia e sociologia di un nuovo soggetto politico* (Roma: Donzelli Editore, 1993), p.3.

31. R. Cere, 'Media Access and New Political Formations in Italy: "*Lega Nord*" and "*Forza Italia*"', Paper presented at the European Film and Television Studies Conference, London, 1994.

32. This is a distorted term used to describe citizens from other countries and continents who have arrived in Italy in recent years. The absence of positive words to describe immigrants says a great deal about Italian racist practices. The word '*extracomunitari*' (external to the European community) uncritically and automatically defines the Italians as part of the nation and the new communities as 'extra', outsiders and external. For a sustained argument about racism in Italy, see L. Balbo and L. Manconi, *I razzismi possibili* (Milano: Feltrinelli, 1990); and idem, *I razzismi reali* (Milano: Feltrinelli, 1992).

33. *Alleanza Nazionale* is a party recently reconstituted from the former MSI (*Movimento Sociale Italiano*), which in turn was born out of the ashes of the Fascist Party.

34. Rusconi has defined the politics of such parties as Forza Italia as 'Democratic ethnocentrism ... a soft surrogate of racism'. See G.E. Rusconi, *Se cessiamo di essere una nazione: Tra etnodemocrazie regionali e cittadinanza europea* (Bologna: Il Mulino, 1993), p.11.

35. Roversi, *Calcio, tifo e violenza*, p.138.

36. Podaliri and Balestri, 'The Ultràs, Racism and Football Culture in Italy', pp.97–9.

37. Ibid., p.98.

38. Bruni, 'Storia del movimento Ultrà in Italia', pp.230–31.

39. Ibid., p.234. For a detailed description of the '*curve in nero*', see pp.234–40.

40. The 'Progetto Ultrà', whose present co-ordinator is Carlo Balestri, was established in 1995 with the aim of eradicating racism and intolerance on the *curve*. In the process they have set up a kind of 'popular centre for football', which comprises an archive on football support around Europe. Recent projects have included the creation and organization of an annual anti-racist championship. The first of which was Montecchio, Reggio Emilia, 29 June–2 July 2000.

41. Podaliri and Balestri, 'The Ultràs, Racism and Football Culture in Italy', p.98.

42. Bruni, 'Storia del movimento Ultrà in Italia', p.233.

43. S. Redhead, *Post-Fandom and the Millennial Blues: The Transformation of Soccer Culture* (London: Routledge, 1997), p.24.

44. R. Boyle and R. Haynes, *Power Play: Sport, the Media and Popular Culture* (Edinburgh: Longman, 1999), pp.187–205.

45. Redhead, *Post-Fandom and the Millennial Blues*, p.24.

46. 'Non prendo calciatori neri gli ultrà non li vogliono', *La Repubblica*, 30 Jan. 2001, p.13; E. Milanesi, 'I tifosi non vogliono negri: Sconcertante dichiarazione del presidente del Verona sul calciomercato', *Il Manifesto*, 30 Jan. 2001.

47. 'If any country is the epicenter of racial abuse in soccer, it is Italy' – R. Hughes, 'The "Ugly Face" of Racism Bedevils Soccer', *International Herald Tribune*, 28 Feb. 2001.

48. 'And Italy's Project *Ultra*, based in Bologna, has created an annual anti-racist championship that this June will involve 800 participants in 96 teams – male, female and mixed from around

Europe and from immigrant communities' – R. Hughes, 'Rallying Behind the "Beautiful Game"', *International Herald Tribune*, 28 Feb. 2001.

49. Cannizzaro *et al.*, 'Tutte in curva, girls', 42–5.
50. Ibid., 43.
51. Ibid., 44.
52. Ibid., 45.
53. D. Segre, *Ragazzi di stadio* (Milano: Mazzotta, 1979).
54. Ibid., p.26.
55. Colombo and De Luca (eds.), *Fanatics*.
56. Ibid., p.83.
57. Ibid., pp.97–8.
58. Law 45/1995, which goes under the name of Decreto Maroni, then Home Office Minister of the Berlusconi Government. Maroni is a member of the Lega Nord, which had entered in coalition for government with Berlusconi's party Forza Italia and the so-called post-Fascist party Alleanza Nazionale, all mentioned above. The law is very controversial as it tends to criminalize the *ultrà* activities beyond the question of violence.
59. Colombo and De Luca (eds.), *Fanatics*, p.142.
60. G. Tassistro, 'Considerazioni criminologiche sul fenomeno hooligan nella realtà sportiva di Genova' (Unpublished thesis, Università di Genova, 1989).
61. Ibid., 176.
62. A. Dal Lago and R. Moscati, *Regalateci un sogno: miti e realtà del tifo calcistico in Italia* (Milano: Bompiani, 1992).
63. Ibid., p.41.
64. Roversi, *Calcio, tifo e violenza*, pp.67–99.
65. A map is currently being drawn of the presence of female-only *ultrà* groups for the Italian teams in Serie A, B and C.
66. Roversi, *Calcio, tifo e violenza*, p.70.
67. Ibid., p.86.
68. Ibid., p.124.
69. A. Francia, 'I sostenitori del Pisa S.C. Ricerca sulle caratteristiche socioculturali di 100 ultras rilevate mediante questionario' (Unpublished thesis, Università di Pisa, 1990), cited in Roversi, *Calcio, tifo e violenza*, pp.75–6.
70. In order of importance and circulation: *La Gazzetta dello Sport*, *TuttoSport* and *Corriere dello Sport*.
71. For an account of women in football media in Britain, see L. Crolley, 'Women and the Football Media', in V. Duke and L. Crolley, *Football, Nationality, and the State* (New York: Longman, 1996), pp.141–4.
72. Cannizzaro *et al.*, 'Tutte in curva, girls', 44.
73. Roversi, *Calcio, tifo e violenza*, op.cit., p.128.
74. Marchi, cited by Cannizzaro *et al.*, 'Tutte in curva, girls', 45.
75. Hughes, 'The "Ugly Face" of Racism Bedevils Soccer'.
76. Also cited in M. Chiusano, 'Calcio, l'Europeo del razzismo: "E l'Italia guida la classifica"', *La Republica*, 1 March 2001, p.58.
77. The *striscione* in 1998 bore the following anti-Semitic message: 'Auschwitz la vostra patria, i forni le vostre case' [Auschwitz your nation, the crematoriums your homes].
78. The *striscione* in 2001 bore the following anti-Semitic message: 'Squadra di negri, curva di ebrei' – I have Italianized the words as they were actually written in Roman dialect – [Team of Negroes, *curva* full of Jews]. See 'Lazio, per questo striscione rischia la squalifica', *La Repubblica*, 30 April 2001, p.38.
79. Roversi, *Calcio, tifo e violenza*, p.28.
80. Marchi in Colombo and De Luca (eds.), *Fanatics*, p.24.
81. Stuart Hall, 'The Treatment of "Football Hooliganism" in the Press', in R. Ingham, S. Hall, J. Clarke, P. Marsh and J. Donovan (eds.), *'Football Hooliganism': The Wider Context* (London: Inter-Action, 1978).

82. Tassistro, 'Considerazioni criminologiche'.
83. Ibid., 102.
84. Ibid., 97.
85. Segre, *Ragazzi di stadio*, p.25.
86. Bruni, 'Storia del movimento Ultrà in Italia', p.219.
87. Roversi, *Calcio, tifo e violenza*, p.70.
88. A process that is especially true of Italy, where nearly half of the media is still in the hands of the now Prime Minister Silvio Berlusconi, previously known as one of the first European moguls.
89. Neil Blain and Rinella Cere, 'Dangerous Television: The *tv a luci rosse* Phenomenon', *Media, Culture and Society*, 17, 3 (1995), 495.

9

'We Got Next':
Images of Women in Television
Commercials during the
Inaugural WNBA Season

STANLEY T. WEARDEN
and PAMELA J. CREEDON

Much of sport sociology centres on two themes: sport is an expression of the societal and cultural system in which it occurs and sports mirror the rituals and values of the societies in which they are developed. Feminist scholars suggest two additional themes: sport 'perpetuates patriarchal ideology by making men's power over women seem "natural"'[1] and images of women in sport reinforce traditional stereotypical images of femininity and gender roles.[2]

In corporate America product-related sports marketing and advertising is big business. Over the past decade, the number of females participating in sports in high school and college has risen from 1.99 million to 2.64 million.[3] A recent study by the Women's Sports Foundation found that women are spending around $21 billion a year on athletic apparel and shoes for themselves and their families.[4]

The athlete or sport with the 'right' or marketable image is the key. Feminist scholars point to the huge disparity in endorsement revenue between male and female athletes as evidence of a male hierarchy in sport. For example, male tennis player Michael Chang (last on the list of the Top Ten Male Endorsers in Sport) was paid $9.5 million in endorsement contracts in 1997, yet the top female endorser, tennis player Monica Seles, earned only $6 million in endorsements.[5]

The gender hierarchy argument holds that female athletes are both 'other than' and 'less than' their male counterparts.[6] Moreover, researchers have found a sex-appropriate ranking scheme in sport that suggests individual sports (that is, tennis, figure skating, golf and gymnastics) are more appropriate for women than team sports.[7] A 1997 study by the National Sporting Goods Association reported that US females led participation in 12 of 56 sports activities studied including: step aerobics, aerobic exercising, gymnastics, traditional roller skating, walking, exercising with equipment and callisthenics, ice/figure skating, horse riding, badminton, swimming and volleyball – apart from volleyball, these are all predominantly individual sports.[8] The percentage of US females age seven or older who participated in basketball more than once stood at 32.8 per cent. Overall, females represented 10.9 per cent of total participation in basketball, which ranked basketball fortieth out of 56 sports in terms of female participation, below darts and soccer. Not surprisingly then, all Top Ten Female Endorsers played sex-appropriate or individual sports, not team sports. However, three National Basketball Association (NBA) players were on the Top Ten Male list.

Faced with these realities, the NBA realized that audience interest would be the key to ensuring success for the team sport of women's basketball in attracting advertising revenue and corporate sponsorships. The launch of the Women's National Basketball Association (WNBA) was preceded by what could be characterized as global marketing research by the NBA and its marketing arm, USA Basketball. In 1995, they provided an unprecedented $3 million budget to what would become the US Women's Olympic basketball team.[9] Each team member was paid $50,000 and USA Basketball won corporate sponsors including Sears, State Farm, Tampax, Champion and Nike.[10]

According to one account, NBA commissioner David Stern told Olympic Coach Tara VanDerveer that 'the immediate future of women's basketball – and the new women's professional league that he had been secretly planning – depended on the success of the U.S. team'.[11] VanDerveer, who took a year's leave from her job as Stanford University's women's basketball coach to look after the 1996 Olympic team, knew Stern meant success was winning games, drawing crowds and winning the Olympic Gold.[12] Her team won 52 games in front of record crowds in the US, China, Australia and Russia. By the time the team reached the Atlanta Olympics in August, the stage was set. Dubbed 'the Real Dream Team' by fans, they won eight straight games in the Olympics and the gold medal in front of more than 30,000 fans, the largest crowd ever to watch women's basketball.[13]

'WE GOT NEXT': THE WNBA LEAGUE

On 22 October 1996, Sheryl Swoopes, a high-profile member of the Olympic Gold Medal basketball team and Texas Tech star, signed the first WNBA player contract.[14] Next, the WNBA launched its $15 million, high-profile 'We Got Next' campaign,[15] bolstered by five-year television contracts from NBC, ESPN and Lifetime television.

The WNBA marketing strategy was to have the women's league play in the summer 'when the sports calendar was less crowded'[16] so games could be televised at consistent times – Saturday afternoons on NBC, Monday or Tuesday nights on ESPN and Friday nights on Lifetime Television.[17] The marketing squad selected a logo design, team names, uniforms and the ball[18] and the NBA publicized the start-up of the league during games including the 1996 NBA All-Star Game, the playoffs and the finals.

In its first season, 33 WNBA games were televised nationally and average attendance was just over 9,000. In October 1997, the WNBA announced two expansion franchises in Detroit and Washington DC. However, while the amount of coverage rose, many of the ratings dropped. In its first year, the WNBA drew average ratings of 2.0 on NBC, 0.9 on ESPN and 0.5 on Lifetime.[19] In the 1998 season, including the playoffs, it averaged only 1.6 on NBC, 0.7 on ESPN and 0.5 on Lifetime.[20] One rating point is worth approximately 980,000 households. In comparison, Lifetime averages about 1,764,000 million households for a movie (a 1.8 rating) compared with 500,000 for WNBA basketball. However, Lifetime spokesman Brett Henne reportedly claimed, 'Our demographics show that we drew in a younger audience, and that's what we wanted'.[21]

Several recent studies have suggested that the quality of televised coverage of women's sports is improving. Unlike earlier studies, which found that television commentators trivialized and subordinated women athletes through overt references to physical beauty, use of diminutives and reference to stereotypically feminine traits, a 1996 study of the language used to describe men's and women's National Collegiate Athletic Association (NCAA) basketball games found no statistically significant differences in sports announcers' descriptions of male or female participants.[22] A subsequent study of NBC Olympic broadcasts of 40 events, representing ten sports (including basketball) involving 109 women and 100 men, found no significant difference in the way that announcers described the personal appearance or athleticism of male or female athletes in competition.[23] These studies may indicate that sports announcers are moving away from traditional stereotypes and focusing instead on athleticism and skill, regardless of gender.

When the WNBA began broadcasting its first games in the summer of 1997, it offered not only the opportunity for highly skilled women basketball players to be paid to showcase their athletic talent on national television, it also offered viewers a rare glimpse of a different image of women – as powerful, aggressive, competitive, muscular and capable. It showed women succeeding at a high level without the stereotypical dependence on conventional beauty or sexuality. It showed women succeeding in a heretofore exclusively male domain – and succeeding with every bit as much ability as that displayed by men at the same level in sports. In short, the WNBA offered a new and compelling role model for American girls and women, devoid of the sexual and occupational stereotypes of the past.

However, the success of televised WNBA games in bringing this new role model to America depended in part on the images of women in commercials during the games. The commercials could either reinforce the non-traditional images of women seen during the games or they could contradict and undermine them. Indeed, past research (see below) has shown highly stereotypical portrayals of women in commercials and in advertising in general. This essay seeks to examine the extent to which stereotypes were used in commercials during the WNBA's first season (1997).

LITERATURE REVIEW

As Lazier and Kendrick pointed out in 1993, one of the benchmark studies on the use of stereotypes in advertising was conducted by Pingree *et al.* in 1976.[24] That study used the Consciousness Scale of Sexism, a modified form of which is used here. The scale was initially developed by Butler-Paisley and Paisley-Butler[25] but refined and applied to advertising in the Pingree *et al.* study. The idea was to create an ordinal scale that showed how much sexism exists in a given presentation. The scale ranged from women depicted in roles completely limited by stereotypes to women depicted in roles free from all stereotypes. The scale has five Consciousness levels:

1. Put Her Down – 'Presentations of women at this level include the dumb blonde, the sex object, and the whimpering victim. The woman is portrayed as being less than a person, a two-dimensional image.'[26]

2. Keep Her in Her Place – 'Traditional strengths and capacities of women are acknowledged, but tradition also dictates "womanly" roles. Women are shown functioning well as wives, mothers, secretaries, clerks, teachers and nurses [but] ... struggling with roles that are "beyond them".'[27]

3. Give Her Two Places – 'The woman can be a lawyer or architect as long as she has dinner on the table for her husband at six. ... It is the career that is often viewed as the "something extra". Housework and mothering come first. The image is that women may sometimes work outside the home professionally, but always work in the home.'[28]

4. Acknowledge that She is Fully Equal – 'There is no mention of her private life, her favorite recipes, or how she cleans the house. ... Level IV images do not remind us that housework and mothering are non-negotiably the woman's work'.[29]

5. Non-stereotypical – 'Individual women and men are viewed as superior to each other in some respects, inferior in other respects. ... Individuals are not judged by their sex.'[30]

Pingree and her colleagues found varying levels of sexism in adverts from *Playboy*, *Time*, *Newsweek* and *Ms.* magazines. Overall, however, they found that over half the adverts in all the magazines (including *Ms.*) showed women at the two lowest positions on the consciousness scale.[31]

Several other studies since 1976 have further developed this theme. Also noted by Lazier and Kendrick, Erving Goffman's *Gender Advertisements* concluded that women's images in advertising are minimized in six ways:

1. Relative size – smaller relative to men;
2. Feminine touch – constantly touching selves;
3. Function ranking – lower-ranking occupations;
4. Family scenes, ritualization of subordination – bashfulness, coyness, flirtiness; and
5. Licensed withdrawal – blank, far-off gazes.[32]

In 1979, Schneider and Schneider examined trends in sex roles in television commercials. They examined the portrayal of age, occupational category, setting (private residence, business, outdoors and so on), marital status and number of children, among other categories. They found little change over time in the portrayal of women as younger than men, in the portrayal of men as more likely than women to be employed (although women were more likely to be portrayed in white-collar occupations), or in more frequent portrayal of women than men in domestic settings (spouse/parent, but apparently not otherwise employed).[33]

Gilly compared sex roles in American, Australian and Mexican television commercials aired in 1985. Her results were similar to those of Schneider and Schneider, but there were differences from country to country. Although sex-role stereotypes existed in the commercials from all three countries, they were manifested in different ways. In terms of similar use of stereotypes, Gilly found that:

> Male voices are much more likely than female voices to be used in voiceovers, women are portrayed as young more often than men, and men are more likely to be portrayed in independent roles whereas women are portrayed in roles relative to others.[34]

In terms of differences between countries, Australian commercials exhibited the fewest differences between male and female roles. In American and Mexican commercials, women were more likely to appear in promotions for men's products than vice versa, men were more likely than women to be portrayed as employed and men were more likely to be portrayed as product authorities (with women portrayed as product users). In American commercials, women were more likely to be shown in the home.[35]

In another study of advertising outside the United States, Livingstone and Green analyzed British television commercials and found that the 'portrayal of men and women conformed closely to traditional gender roles'.[36] Males were used more for voiceovers, shown more often as credible authorities and portrayed more frequently as autonomous. A 1989 study of Italian television commercials found a similar pattern of sex-role stereotypes in that country.[37]

Rak and McMullen examined sex-role stereotyping in television commercials aired in the United States during daytime and primetime between October 1983 and January 1984. Although they found more sex-role stereotypes in daytime than in primetime, they concluded that,

'On the whole, the results indicate that sex-role stereotyping still exists in television commercials and that it is present at subtle as well as obvious levels of analysis.'[38] In an examination of MTV commercials, Signorielli, McLeod and Healy found that 'female characters appeared less frequently, had more beautiful bodies, were more physically attractive, wore more sexy and skimpy clothing, and were more often the object of another's gaze than their male counterparts'.[39]

Finally, to emphasize the importance of studying the phenomenon of sex-role stereotypes in television commercials, Lafky *et al.* found that even brief exposure to stereotypical images in television commercials 'plays a role in reinforcing stereotypes about gender roles'.[40] These authors also found that the differential socialization of males and females ('the lens of gender') leads to differences in the ways that males and females cognitively process the visual images they see in television commercials. In other words, 'the process of learning about gender-appropriate behavior and observing the gendered nature of social life may lead to the development of gender-specific heuristics – or seeing the world through gendered lenses'.[41] For example, while both males and females who viewed a role-neutral image were likely to say that the woman in the image performed most of the household chores:

> this effect was not as strong for the females as it was for the males. The young men ... may have more at stake ... in preserving such stereotypical images. ... Deeply embedded cultural values and beliefs about the proper division of labor between men and women may also play a part.[42]

RESEARCH QUESTIONS

The purpose of this essay is to use the Consciousness Scale of Sexism to examine television commercials during WNBA games in 1997. Specifically, we attempted to address the following research questions:

1. What is the overall level of sexism in commercials aired during 1997 WNBA games?
2. Does the level of sexism vary by sponsor or by product/service category?
3. Does the level of sexism vary by network?
4. Does the level of sexism vary over the course of the season (from June to August)?

We also were interested in the physical appearance of women depicted in these commercials and developed a coding scheme accordingly (see description in the section below). We also composed several research questions related to this:

1. Does depiction of age or beauty vary by sponsor or by product/ service category?
2. Does depiction of age or beauty vary by network?
3. Does depiction of age or beauty vary over the course of the season?
4. Does depiction of age or beauty vary by level of sexism portrayed as defined by the Consciousness Scale of Sexism used in this study?

RESEARCH METHOD

Nineteen WNBA games were videotaped over the course of the inaugural 1997 season. Most of these were taped from broadcasts by NBC or Lifetime (in simulcasts with ESPN). One game was also taped directly from ESPN, for purposes of comparison, and one game was taped from the Madison Square Garden Network (MSG) also for purposes of comparison.[43]

Content analysis was performed by one primary graduate assistant and several intercoder reliability checks were performed by four additional graduate assistants. The unit of analysis was each woman portrayed in each commercial. Portrayals were coded using a modified version of Pingree *et al.*'s Consciousness Scale of Sexism. The modifications included the addition of a 'Mixed' category in an attempt to measure portrayals that seemed to exist at more than one level on the scale and the coding of each separate appearance of a woman in a commercial (up to four total appearances) in an attempt to measure possible changes in level of sexism for a given woman over the course of the commercial. Ultimately, neither modification proved useful. Coders rarely used the 'Mixed' category and when they did it was clearly the case that the dominant level was Level 1 (Put Her Down), so the few cases coded as 'Mixed' were re-coded as Level 1. Cross tabulation showed no change whatsoever in the portrayal of a woman from appearance to appearance during a commercial. That is, if the first portrayal was at Level 1 on the scale, so were the second and subsequent appearances. Of the 1,632 women coded in this study, only 21 – one per cent of the total – showed any changes in level of role portrayed from one appearance the to next in a commercial. Therefore, the results are based on each woman's first appearance in each commercial.

Women appearing in commercials were also coded for appearance in two ways so as to test the second set of research questions listed above. First, coders assessed the estimated age of the woman in three broad categories: young (late teens to 20s), mature (30s to 50s) or elderly (60s or older). Second, coders rated each woman as either conventionally beautiful (looking like a typical fashion or swimsuit model – thin, heavily made-up, sexily dressed) or not conventionally beautiful (women in this category may be beautiful, but not in the sense of the fashion-model convention mentioned above). Clearly, this coding involved some subjective judgement, which might have been further affected by the gender and ethnicity of coders. While it is important to be sensitive to the complexity of such coding, it also is useful to note that intercoder reliability scores on these items were relatively high. Coders agreed on the age and beauty categories nearly 80 per cent of the time (see below). Finally, the network, date and sponsor of the commercial also were coded. Intercoder reliability ranged from a high of 100 for items such as sponsor and network, to a low of 78 per cent for estimated age. Average intercoder reliability across all categories was 92 per cent.

RESULTS AND DISCUSSION

In all, 1,632 images of women were analyzed from 591 commercials. For purposes of comparison, the WNBA's 'We Got Next' image advertisements were eliminated from the study and the analysis focused on female images in product advertising.

There were 71 different commercial sponsors, but the primary sponsors in terms of frequency of showing images of women were Sears, Champion (sporting goods), Nike, Bud Light and Lee. Together, these five sponsors accounted for 858 images of women, or 52.7 per cent of all the images of women seen during the 19 WNBA games. Also, for purposes of comparison, these five sponsors were the only ones treated individually in the analysis. All other sponsors were re-coded into one of six categories: Other Sports-Related Products, Health and Beauty, Furniture and Appliances, Automobile Related (cars, car repair, car insurance), Services (banking, credit cards, insurance, phone services, etc.) and Food.

In terms of the first research question:

- 22.1 per cent of the roles portrayed in the commercials fell into the Put Her Down (Level 1) category;
- Seven per cent were coded as Keep Her in Her Place (Level 2);
- 0.8 per cent were coded as Give Her Two Places (Level 3);
- 1.7 per cent were coded as acknowledging equality (Level 4); and
- 59.7 per cent were coded as non-stereotypical.

This seemingly astonishing statistic needs to be examined closely, however, before one concludes that commercials aired during WNBA games have undergone a dramatic change from those examined in previous studies. Because of the small numbers in Levels 2, 3 and 4, the categories were collapsed. Levels 2 and 3 were combined, as were Levels 4 and 5. Before examining this table further, it should be noted that the small numbers in Levels 2, 3 and 4 were not due to inherent problems with Pingree *et al.*'s scale, rather this phenomenon reflects the very different nature of commercials aired during WNBA games. They seemed primarily to fall at one extreme or the other of the scale, with very few in the mid-range. Images were either extraordinarily traditional and stereotypical, or completely void of stereotype.

As Table 1 illustrates, Nike, Sears, Champion and Other Sports Related accounted for the large majority of equal or non-stereotypical portrayals of women. These types of portrayals tended to show women in active, competitive roles wherein gender largely was irrelevant. Women in these commercials were shown perspiring; they were muscular; they were psychologically intense; and they were powerful and competitive. Together these sports-related sponsors also accounted for 46 per cent of the portrayals of women but only 33 per cent of the commercials. In other words, while a majority of the images of women in commercials during WNBA games appeared in egalitarian or non-sexist roles, a majority of the commercials contained conventionally sexist images of women. Since the unit of analysis in this study is the individual woman in each commercial, the results are skewed by the interesting fact that the least sexist commercials, which were actually in the minority, contained an overwhelmingly larger number of women (more women per commercial than in the more sexist commercials). For example, the completely non-sexist Champion commercials accounted for only 3.7 per cent of all commercials coded, but since they averaged

TABLE 1
GENDER ROLE CATEGORIES BY PRODUCT CATEGORIES

Role	Nike	Sears	Lee	Bud Light	Champion	Other Sports Related	Health/ Beauty	Furniture/ Appliances	Auto Related	Services	Food
Put Her Down	1.50%	11.20%	39.20%	37.60%	0%	0%	79.80%	41.80%	46.10%	54.90%	56.50%
Put Her in Her Place/ Give Her Two Places	0.00%	3.10%	7.80%	5.50%	0%	0%	9.20%	50.90%	17.60%	7.60%	13.60%
Equality/ Non-Stereotypical	98.50%	85.70%	52.90%	56.90%	100%	100%	11%	7.30%	36.30%	37.50%	29.90%
Total n (women)	134	294	102	109	210	104	109	55	204	144	147
Percentage of Women	8.30%	18.20%	6.30%	6.80%	13.00%	6.50%	6.80%	3.40%	12.70%	8.90%	9.10%
Number of Commercials	34	53	65	27	22	85	72	41	52	80	60
Percentage of Commercials	5.80%	9%	1.70%	4.00%	3.70%	14.40%	12.20%	6.90%	8.80%	13.50%	10.20%
Women per Commercial	4.1	5.6	1.7	4	9.6	1.2	1.5	1.4	3.9	1.9	2.5

Chi Square (20 df) = 811, p<.000009.

9.6 images of women per commercial, they accounted for 13 per cent of the total images of women coded in the study. Health and Beauty commercials, on the other hand, were the most sexist of all. This category accounted for 12.2 per cent of the total commercials but, at only 1.5 women's images per commercial, the category accounted for only 6.8 per cent of the total images of women.

Thus the findings regarding the first two research questions are somewhat mixed. In terms simply of individual women appearing in commercials during WNBA games, the data are encouraging. The majority of images were coded as being in equal or non-sexist roles. However, 51.6 per cent of the commercials (Health and Beauty, Furniture and Appliances, Auto Related, Services and Food) portrayed the majority of their female characters in traditionally sexist roles. These portrayals involved either conventionally beautiful women (slender, heavily made-up fashion models) shown as objects of sexual desire or women in traditional domestic roles. The least sexist commercials were for sporting goods. They typically showed either WNBA players or other accomplished female athletes in non-gender-related roles. Sears commercials were also relatively low in sexist roles, although some Sears products (like paint) were still promoted in fairly traditional ways (housewives using the products). Lee and Bud Light commercials seemed torn between traditional women-as-sex-object portrayals and equal or non-stereotypical portrayals. Often this ambivalence was evident within the text of a single commercial, with some of the women appearing as strong and independent and others depicted as passive, sexually available and dependent upon men.

When portrayals of conventional or non-conventional beauty are broken down by product categories, an identical pattern emerges. Table 2 shows that the sporting goods commercials, followed by Sears commercials, were the least likely to use conventionally beautiful models. While there was an emphasis on youth in the sporting goods commercials, the women were shown in gender-neutral roles as accomplished athletes. Health and Beauty products were the most likely to use conventionally beautiful models, followed by Furniture and Appliances, Auto Related, Services and Food (all of which used a majority of conventionally beautiful models – that is, passive, carefully made-up slender women whose sexuality was emphasized). Again, Lee and Bud Light fell in between. As with Table 1, although a majority of the images were not of conventionally beautiful models, a majority of the

TABLE 2

PORTRAYAL OF CONVENTIONAL BEAUTY BY PRODUCT CATEGORIES

Appearance	Nike	Sears	Lee	Bud Light	Champion	Other Sports Related	Health/ Beauty	Furniture/ Appliances	Auto Related	Services	Food
Conventionally Beautiful	3.60%	13.90%	44.90%	43.10%	0%	0%	96.30%	70.20%	69.10%	68.50%	63.30%
Not Conventionally Beautiful	96.40%	86.10%	55.10%	56.90%	100%	100%	3.70%	29.80%	30.90%	31.50%	36.70%
Total n (women)	134	294	102	109	210	104	109	55	204	144	147
Percentage of Women	8.30%	18.20%	6.30%	6.80%	13.00%	6.50%	6.80%	3.40%	12.70%	8.90%	9.10%
Number of Commercials	34	53	65	27	22	85	72	41	52	80	60
Percentage of Commercials	5.80%	9%	1.70%	4.00%	3.70%	14.40%	12.20%	6.90%	8.80%	13.50%	10.20%
Women per Commercial	4.1	5.6	1.7	4	9.6	1.2	1.5	1.4	3.9	1.9	2.5

Chi Square (10 df) = 700.53, p<.000009.

TABLE 3

ESTIMATED AGE CATEGORIES BY PRODUCT CATEGORIES

Age Range	Nike	Sears	Lee	Bud Light	Champion	Other Sports Related	Health/ Beauty	Furniture/ Appliances	Auto Related	Services	Food
Young (Late teens–20s)	98.60%	98.30%	90.70%	95.40%	99%	100%	84.40%	52.60%	76.50%	77.90%	69.40%
Mature (30s–50s)	0.00%	1.70%	4.70%	0.00%	1%	0%	14.70%	43.90%	19.10%	12.80%	14.30%
Elderly (60s or older)	1.40%	0.00%	4.70%	4.60%	1%	0%	1%	3.50%	4.40%	9.40%	16.30%
Total n (women)	134	294	102	109	210	104	109	55	204	144	147
Percentage of Women	8.30%	18.20%	6.30%	6.80%	13.00%	6.50%	6.80%	3.40%	12.70%	8.90%	9.10%
Number of Commercials	34	53	65	27	22	85	72	41	52	80	60
Percentage of Commercials	5.80%	9%	1.70%	4.00%	3.70%	14.40%	12.20%	6.90%	8.80%	13.50%	10.20%
Women per Commercials	4.1	5.6	1.7	4	9.6	1.2	1.5	1.4	3.9	1.9	2.5

Chi Square (20 df) = 322.07, p<.000009.

commercials contained images of predominantly conventionally beautiful models. To reiterate, this occurred because the least sexist commercials had a dramatically larger number of discrete images of women (some of the sporting goods commercials contained images of as many as ten different women in 30 seconds) while the most sexist commercials contained only one or two images of women.

The analysis of product category also indicates the way in which sponsors affect the content of their commercials. Commercials for more traditionally gendered products (health and beauty, beer, clothing, automobiles and so on) are more likely to perpetuate 'comfortable' stereotypes that have long been used to sell those products. However, in the case of 'new' products, or at least products being promoted to a 'new' market (such as sporting goods for women), sponsors seem to have been forced to examine their market in new ways and they appear to have determined that traditional stereotypes will not work in promoting products that challenge traditionally male-gendered activities.

In terms of age range, the most striking finding is that young women are in the majority in commercials in every product category. This is not entirely surprising, however, as advertisers develop images to connect with the audience of a television programme. Professional basketball is a sport played by young women and watched by young women. It is likely that sporting goods are sold more to young women or to women trying to preserve youthful health and vigour. Youth is somewhat less dominant in Health and Beauty, Furniture and Appliances, Auto Related, Services and Food commercials, but young women still are in the majority in each of these categories. Furniture and Appliance commercials use far more women in their 30s to 50s than any other category does; Food commercials use more women in their 60s or older than any other category.

Table 4 breaks down gender role portrayals by network. Commercials on NBC tended to be more non-sexist than did those on Lifetime, self-described as 'television for women'. However, it is important to remember that the Lifetime broadcasts were often simulcast with ESPN. While those taped from Lifetime were slightly more non-sexist than those taped from ESPN, there is little difference between the two, perhaps reflecting the fact that the sponsors of the simulcast games may have been more the traditional ESPN programming sponsors than the traditional Lifetime programming sponsors (see above on the effect of sponsors on the content of commercials). MSG was similar to NBC in the level of non-sexist portrayals. Again, however, it is important to note that while the majority of women's images on these three networks were egalitarian or non-sexist, the majority of commercials on all three networks still contained predominantly sexist images of women (see above).

Table 5 examines age range by gender role. Not surprisingly, the majority of Put Her Down images were of young women. On the other hand, so were the majority of Equality/Non-Stereotypical images. These images appeared in Health and Beauty commercials and sporting goods commercials, respectively. In both cases, advertisers likely define the market for the products as youthful or youth-orientated (trying to look or feel young). The largest age category for Put Her in Her Place/Give Her Two Places images was women in their 30s to 50s. They were mainly depicted as middle-aged housewives or career women still primarily responsible for domestic work.

When we examined conventional beauty by gender role stereotypes, the results were not surprising. The vast majority of Level 1 portrayals were of conventionally beautiful women. Portrayals of women as sex objects obviously use the conventional physical attributes that define the stereotype. Level 4 and Level 5 portrayals were predominantly of women in the Not Conventionally Beautiful category. These were mostly female athletes in the sporting goods commercials – beautiful,

TABLE 4
GENDER ROLE CATEGORIES BY NETWORK

Role	NBC	Lifetime	ESPN	MSG*
Put Her Down	27.60%	31.10%	35.40%	32.10%
Put Her in Her Place/ Give Her Two Places	6.90%	9.20%	10.80%	3.60%
Equality/ Non-Stereotypical	65.60%	59.70%	53.80%	64.30%
Total n (women)	686	688	130	112
Percentage of Women	42.50%	42.60%	8.00%	6.90%

Chi Square (6 df) = 12.89, p<.045.

Note: *Madison Square Garden Network.

TABLE 5
ESTIMATED AGE CATEGORIES BY GENDER ROLE CATEGORIES

Age Range	Put Her Down	Put Her In Her Place/ Give Her Two Places	Equality/ Non-Stereotypical
Young (late teens–20s)	92.60%	37.50%	92.30%
Mature (30s–50s)	5.80%	41.40%	4.90%
Elderly (60s or older)	1.60%	21.10%	2.80%
Total n (women)	485	128	1,003
Percentage of Women	30.00%	7.90%	62.10%

Chi Square (4 df) = 337.67, p<.001.

but not fashion models. They were powerful, often sweating, mentally focused and aggressive. Level 2 and Level 3 gender role portrayals were fairly evenly split between conventional and non-conventional beauty. Again, these were often housewives and working mothers, where the emphasis was not so much on their beauty as their role. As previously noted, the coding of appearance clearly involved subjective decision-making and readers should be aware of the potential bias inherent in this set of categories. On the other hand, the coders agreed 78 per cent of the time in their assessment of appearance, so the authors have some confidence that these are conceptually useful categories. There was no change in portrayals of gender roles, conventional beauty or estimated age of women in commercials over the course of the WNBA season.

TABLE 6
PORTRAYAL OF CONVENTIONAL BEAUTY BY GENDER ROLE CATEGORIES

Appearance	Put Her Down	Put Her In Her Place/ Give Her Two Places	Equality/ Non-Stereotypical
Conventionally Beautiful	99.18%	46.69%	6.78%
Not Conventionally Beautiful	0.82%	53.31%	93.22%
Total n (women)	485	128	1,003
Percentage of Women	30.00%	7.90%	62.10%

Chi Square (2 df) = 1,196.77, p<.0001.

The WNBA Revisited

Although we did not perform a systematic analysis, we examined three WNBA games during the 2000 season to see if change was apparent three years after the initial study was performed. The games were broadcast by NBC and ESPN. To a large degree, we found very similar commercials with very similar portrayals to those shown during the 1997 broadcasts. Sporting goods commercials continue to have dramatically more images than commercials for other products and these images continue to depict non-stereotypical views of women as muscular, powerful, skilled and intense. Likewise, commercials for household products and automobiles are still showing women in domestic roles and commercials for health and beauty products continue to show conventionally beautiful, young models. However, we did find that at least in the three games examined, there were more commercials with non-stereotypical portrayals than in 1997. In addition to the sporting goods commercials, the 2000 season brought commercials for credit companies, medical care, dot-com companies and the Army, all of which showed women in equal or non-stereotypical roles. There seemed to be fewer commercials during these three games for beauty products, beer, jeans and automobiles than there had been in 1997. Although the sample was small and the analysis was not systematic, the commercials during the 2000 season may indicate a slow shift away from traditional stereotypes in commercials airing during women's sporting events, but further scientific analysis will be necessary to confirm this.

CONCLUSION

As Lafky *et al.* and others have found, portrayal of gender roles during television commercials makes a difference to the socialization of American viewers. This study suggests that viewers of WNBA games during the summer of 1997 received a strangely mixed message. The majority of individual images of women, while still focused primarily on youth, were surprisingly non-sexist in terms of the sexist level of the portrayals, coded using the Consciousness Scale of Sexism, and in terms of portrayals of conventional, model-like beauty. On the other hand, the majority of commercials contained mostly sexist images at Levels 1 and 2 on the Consciousness Scale of Sexism and in terms of showing women as conventionally beautiful. How this mixed message might be received by viewers is the subject for future research.

This study also shows that the sporting goods companies – Nike, Champion and Other (Spalding, Reebok, Lady Foot Locker, Powerade) – seem to have the clearest sense of WNBA viewers as a new kind of audience receptive to a new kind of appeal. These sponsors showed the least sexist images overall, followed by Sears. Future research might focus on audience receptivity to these commercials versus the more traditionally sexist approach used by Health and Beauty, Furniture and Appliances, Auto Related, Services and Food sponsors. If advertisers see that their audience is not identifying with the images shown, there is a greater likelihood that they will change their images.

Overall, we must conclude that commercials aired during WNBA games in 1997 represent a change from commercials examined in earlier studies. There appears to be movement toward a more non-sexist image of women in some product categories. However, the fact that the majority of commercials contained sexist images of women illustrates that even television focused on powerful, non-traditional women athletes may serve, ultimately, as a socializing agent for the *status quo*. In fact, given that most of the non-sexist imagery in commercials occurred in adverts for sporting goods, it might be argued that a new form of ghettoization of women is developing. Beyond the recognition that women purchase sporting goods in large quantities, the message of such commercials, combined with the images seen during the games, may suggest that it's acceptable for women to be powerful and aggressive, as long as they limit that behaviour to sports. In all other areas of life, the commercials may be saying, women are expected to maintain the *status quo*. On the other hand, the brief and non-systematic examination of commercials during the 2000 season suggests that change in the portrayal of women in commercials during WNBA games may be occurring at an incremental but real pace.

The WNBA represents a substantive change in the types of role models available to girls and adolescents, but to the degree that the commercials aired during these games represent traditional sexist images, they may undermine the message of strength and independence implicit in the images of powerful, accomplished female athletes. Is change occurring over time in these commercials and will that change eventually spread to commercials in other forms of television programming? These would seem to be important questions for future scholarly investigation.

NOTES

The authors wish to gratefully acknowledge the assistance of their primary coder, Kent State University graduate student Didi Tang, as well as assistance from graduate students Jennifer English, Kathryn Spearman, Wang Ying, Brian Dodez and Zhao Aiwu.

1. L.M. Weidman, 'In the Olympic Tradition: Sportscasters' Language and Female Athleticism', Paper presented at the annual meeting of the Association for Education in Journalism and Mass Communication, Baltimore, MD August 1998, 2.

2. M.J. Kane and S. Greendorfer, 'The Media's Role in Accommodation and Resisting Stereotypical Images of Women in Sport', in P. Creedon (ed.), *Women, Media and Sport: Challenging Gender Values* (Thousand Oaks, CA: Sage, 1994), pp.28–44.

3. Women's Sports Foundation, *Participation Statistics Packet* (East Meadow, NY: Women's Sports Foundation, June 1998).

4. D. Lopiano, 'Women Athletes Deserve Respect from the Media', *USA Today*, 124, 610, 74–6.

5. M. Fish, 'Sponsors stuck with Reece's Looks, not Skills', *Atlanta Constitution*, 25 Sept. 1998, D14.

6. Kane and Greendorfer, 'The Media's Role in Accommodation and Resisting Stereotypical Images of Women in Sport'.

7. A. Colley, J. Nash, L. O'Donnell and L. Restorick, 'Attitudes to the Female Sex Role and Sex-Typing of Physical Activities', *International Journal of Sport Psychology*, 18 (1987), 19–29.

8. *Females Lead Participation in 12 Sports Activities* (Mt. Prospect, IL: National Sporting Goods Association, June 1997).

9. S. Smith, 'Not Quite the Game Intended', in L. Smith (ed.), *Nike is a Goddess* (New York: Atlantic Monthly Press, 1998), pp.293–314. The NBA had considered starting a league in 1992, but the US women's Olympic team had 'only' won a bronze medal so it was decided that the timing was not right. See K. Whiteside, *A Celebration: Commemorating the Birth of a League* (New York: Harper Horizon, 1998).

10. Smith, 'Not Quite the Game Intended'.

11. Ibid., p.308. A team of Silicon Valley investors announced the start-up of a nine-team Associated Basketball League (ABL) in September 1995 and nine members of the US Olympic team announced that they had signed with them. At press conferences, Olympic team players who had signed with the ABL appeared wearing ABL T-shirts and hats. When one athlete was questioned about possible competitive plans for an NBA-sponsored league she replied, 'We don't want to be a sideshow to the men, playing in the summer, during the off season'. See S. Corbett, *Venus to the Hoop* (New York: Doubleday, 1997), p.296. Conflict arose because the NBA's marketing arm, USA Basketball, was sponsoring much of the ABL team's tour. When several of the Olympic players draped ABL jackets over their chairs before a practice, USA Basketball's Lynn Barry reportedly turned the chairs around to obscure them. See ibid., p.296. Within a month of the conclusion of the Olympics, training camp started for the ABL and one later the NBA Board of Governor's officially announced the formation of the eight-team WNBA. The NBA announcement caused ESPN and sponsor Nike to back away from a television deal with the ABL. Sheryl Swoopes, who originally had agreed to play with the ABL, announced that she would sign with the WNBA. However, the ABL found corporate sponsors in Nissan, Lady Foot Locker and the Phoenix Insurance Group and went ahead with its plans. The ABL spent about $1.5 million on marketing its first season in 1996 with the slogan, 'It's a Whole New Ballgame'. Attendance averaged around 3,000 per game (see Smith, *Nike is a Goddess*). In its second season, SportsChannel and Black Entertainment Television provided television packages. However, the ABL folded midway through its third season.

12. Corbett, *Venus to the Hoop*.

13. Smith, 'Not Quite the Game Intended', p.309.
14. Whiteside, *A Celebration*.
15. It means, 'We get the court next. It's our turn.'
16. Of course, the television schedule could be consistent and arenas were less crowded in the summer because the NBA was not playing.
17. Whiteside, *A Celebration*, p.56.
18. Tom O'Grady, NBA Vice President and Creative Director, looked at more than 50 logo designs and suggested that the final choice, a dribbling basketball player on a red and blue background 'went through more trims and tucks than an aging Hollywood starlet'. If possible, names and colours of teams were required to be close the NBA. For example, the NBA Charlotte Hornets have a WNBA counterpart know as the Charlotte Stings and the NBA Houston Rockets have a WNBA counterpart known as the Houston Comets. Uniform proposals included leotards, jumpers, skirts and even dresses, but the designs selected were 'two shorts silhouettes and three jerseys, designed to fit a woman's body'. It worked and the NBA's chief marketing officer Rick Welts and WNBA President Val Ackerman were honoured by *Brandweek* magazine as the 1997 Marketeers of the Year. See ibid., p.61.
19. J. Schultz, 'TV Exposure on the Upswing: But Ratings Slow to Follow', *Atlanta Constitution*, 28 Sept. 1998, G11.
20. Ibid.
21. Ibid.
22. L.M. Weidman, 'They Called a Game: The Language Television Sportscasters use to Describe Men's and Women's NCAA Basketball Games', *Journal of Sport and Social Issues*, forthcoming.
23. Weidman, 'In the Olympic Tradition'.
24. L. Lazier and A.G. Kendrick, 'Women in Advertisements: Sizing up the Images, Roles and Functions', in P. Creedon (ed.), *Women in Mass Communication* (Newbury Park, CA: Sage, 2nd Edn. 1993), pp.199–219.
25. M. Butler-Paisley and W.J. Paisley-Butler, 'Sexism in the Media: Frameworks for Research', Paper presented at the annual meeting of the Association for Education in Journalism, San Diego, CA, August 1974.
26. S. Pingree, R.P. Hawkins, M. Butler and W. Paisley, 'A Scale for Sexism', *Journal of Communication*, 26 (1976), 194.
27. Ibid.
28. Ibid., 194–5.
29. Ibid., 195.
30. Ibid.
31. Ibid.
32. E. Goffman, *Gender Advertisements* (New York: Colophon, 1979).
33. K.C. Schneider and S.B. Schneider, 'Trends in Sex Roles in television Commercials', *Journal of Marketing*, 43 (1979), 79–84.
34. M.C. Gilly, 'Sex Roles in Advertising: A Comparison of Television Advertisements in Australia, Mexico, and the United States', *Journal of Marketing*, 52 (1988), 83.
35. Ibid., 75–85.
36. S. Livingstone and G. Green, 'Television Advertisements and the Portrayal of Gender', *British Journal of Social Psychology*, 25 (1986), 149.
37. A. Furnham and V. Voli, 'Gender Stereotypes in Italian Television Advertisements', *Journal of Broadcasting and Electronic Media*, 33 (1989), 175–85.
38. D.S. Rak and L.M. McMullen, 'Sex-Role Stereotyping in Television Commercials: A Verbal Response Mode and Content Analysis', *Canadian Journal of Behavioral Science*, 19 (1987), 25.
39. N. Signorielli, D. McLeod and E. Healy, 'Gender Stereotypes in MTV Commercials: The Beat Goes On', *Journal of Broadcasting and Electronic Media*, 38 (1994), 91.

40. S. Lafky, M. Duffy, M. Steinmaus and D. Berkowitz, 'Looking Through Gendered Lenses: Female Stereotyping in Advertisements and Gender Role Expectations', *J&MC Quarterly*, 73 (1996), 379.

41. Ibid., 386.

42. Ibid.

43. MSG Network aired the games of the New York Liberty on cable channels when the team played at home.

10

Fitba Crazy?
Saturday Super Scoreboard and the
Dialectics of Political Debate

HUGH O'DONNELL

Radio sport, certainly when compared to television sport, is a somewhat neglected object of study. It can at times be a quite invisible object of study: thus the publisher's flyer for a recent book on radio announced that it would cover 'all principal radio genres', listing these as 'short stories, plays, documentaries/drama documentaries, talks and features, adaptations/dramatizations, poems and advertisements'[1] – sport merited no mention at all. It is likewise almost entirely absent from *Understanding Radio*, despite this book having an entire section dedicated to phone-ins, a key element of radio sport reporting.[2] There are of course exceptions – Peter Dahlén's comprehensive study of sport radio in Sweden from its inception until the mid-1990s is a major contribution to the field[3] and there have been useful studies analyzing the link between sport on radio and broader nation-building processes.[4] Even so, academic interest in the phenomenon of radio sport seems to lie some distance behind its actual social importance.

The programme on which this essay is based – Radio Clyde's *Saturday Super Scoreboard* – is one of the most listened-to radio programmes in the west of Scotland. According to RAJAR figures for 18 Sept. 2000 to 25 March 2001 it regularly achieves audiences of over 300,000, a figure that represents around 14 per cent of the population aged four and over in that area (independent local radio having always been stronger in Scotland than elsewhere in the UK[5]) and that reflects an audience pull many television programmes would be envious of. This situation is by no means restricted to Scotland. So great is radio sports coverage in certain parts of Catalonia, for example, that radio sport there has been termed a 'macrogenre'.[6] The language situation of *Saturday Super Scoreboard* is rather complex, in that many of the exchanges in its phone-in are carried out at least partly in west of Scotland dialect (see below). This explains some of the rather unusual forms appearing in a number of the quotes given below, which will no doubt appear somewhat unexpected to those unfamiliar with this particular mode of speech.

THE FORMAT

Saturday Super Scoreboard was launched in 1978 and although there have been personnel changes its basic format has changed little over the intervening period. It goes out every Saturday during the football season and lasts four hours in all. It starts at two o'clock in the afternoon and the first hour is given over to a pre-match studio discussion on the state of play in the Scottish Premier League, on-going stories about individual players and managers, comments on previous games, predictions about the games that are about to start and so on. Since Radio Clyde is a commercial radio station, this discussion is frequently punctuated by commercial breaks (usually immediately preceded by a phrase like 'don't touch the dial'), the adverts tending to presuppose a male (though not necessarily young) listener. At three o'clock attention switches to the featured game, though goals and highlights from other games in the Premier League are also covered as news of them comes in. Each featured game has two commentators, one of whom is a former footballer, and adverts are suspended for the duration of the match, except for the half-time break. When the game ends at quarter to five there are interviews with players and managers, which last until the classified results (for both Scotland and England) at five o'clock. The remaining 50 minutes or so are taken up with what this essay will concentrate on in particular: the phone-in or 'Openline'.

The majority of callers to the phone-in are male, although most weeks perhaps two or three women callers are also heard. Given Radio Clyde's physical location in Glasgow, it is perhaps not surprising that the bulk of callers also come from the west of Scotland and that the majority of calls relate to Glasgow's two leading clubs, Celtic and Rangers. (This distinguishes the programme substantially from its rival *On the Ball*, broadcast by Radio Scotland, that though enjoying much smaller audience figures, attracts callers from all over Scotland.) Occasionally, however, listeners do call in from places that would probably appear rather remote to most Glasgow listeners at least, places such as Ayrshire or Dumfries – culturally very 'distant' despite a physical distance of between 40 and 70 miles. (In fact, these callers participate in the Openline as it is relayed live to this part of Scotland by Radio Clyde's sister station West Sound). Despite this, west-of-Scotlandness is an important feature of *Saturday Super Scoreboard*'s relationship with its audience and often takes the form of anti-Edinburgh humour. A traditional west-of-Scotland stereotype of Edinburghers presents them as mean, summed up in the classic phrase, 'You'll have had your tea' (implying that if you visit someone in Edinburgh, they will pre-empt the need to offer you anything to eat or drink by insisting from the outset that you have already eaten). Given that the traditional consumption at half-time in Scottish football matches is a meat pie (indeed there have been competitions to determine which ground offers the best fare from this point of view), on one occasion two commentators who had travelled to Edinburgh (all of 35 miles from Glasgow) to cover a match there were informed by their colleagues in the Glasgow studio 'You'll have had your meat pies'. The world of *Saturday Super Scoreboard* is, in some respects at least, a highly localized one.

An interesting feature of the phone-in is also a noticeable level of 'intermediality'. Since more or less the launch of the programme in the 1970s, it has been quite common for one or more of the studio panel also to be active as a journalist. At the time of writing both ex-Celtic footballer Davie Provan and match commentator Hugh Keevins have highly popular columns in Scottish tabloids (these being, pro rata, among the most read newspapers in the world[7]). It is not only quite common, but to some extent expected within the programme format that listeners will call in to take issue with one or other of these columnists about comments they have made in their articles during the week and these debates have at times been fairly robust.

DEFINING FEATURES

A major feature of *Saturday Super Scoreboard* is its indefatigable sense of humour. In the run-up to the 1998 season, an advert on Radio Clyde for *Saturday Super Scoreboard* consisted of approximately one minute of the various members of the panel laughing uproariously with no voice-over at all. Much of the humour is provided by the extremely quick-witted ex-Rangers footballer Derek Johnston (who also has a highly successful alternative career as an after-dinner speaker). For example, someone complaining that a particular player cannot cross the ball will be met with the rejoinder, 'Him? He couldnae cross a cheque', while Celtic's proposed signing of a Brazilian defender whose surname was Scheidt was the cause of endless mirth. Particularly impressive flashes of wit are accompanied by a hotel-reception style bell being made to ring by programme co-ordinator (and Managing Director of Radio Clyde) Paul Cooney. Absolutely everyone takes part. So well established is the expectation for wit and humour that managers and players interviewed after matches will also join in, often at the panel's expense, and callers also frequently contribute to this aspect of the programme.

A second defining feature of the programme, particularly of the phone-in, is its extremely youthful mode of address. Despite the ages of the panel members – probably none of them is under 40 – Paul Cooney constantly refers to them as 'the gang', 'the lads', 'the guys'. 'Hello, John, you're through to the lads' is a common way of introducing a new caller, while the most frequent opening statement by callers on the line is 'How's it gaun, guys?' or 'How's it gaun, panel?'. Indeed, this mode of address is sustained through implicit agreement with the callers since – at least in so far as one can deduce from the timbre of their voices and their at times elephantine memories of footballing history – they would not appear (as also suggested by the adverts, as mentioned earlier) to be a necessarily youthful group either. Male callers in particular are frequently addressed as 'mate' and exchanges between the panel and callers are (with remarkably few exceptions, see below) strictly on a first-name basis. Even this somewhat artificial youthfulness can be the subject of humour; when Derek Johnston celebrated a birthday on the show in the 1999 season he was mockingly referred to by the others as 'faither' ('father'). It goes without saying that the panel enjoy a range of fairly obvious institutional advantages over the fans.[8] They can, for example, and sometimes will, simply cut off an unwelcome caller in mid-sentence,[9] as Hutchby puts it:

> Given the host's institutional siting as organizational 'hub' of the broadcast, as processing agent both accessing callers to the air and removing them from the air, it is in a very basic sense the host's task not only to 'open' calls ... but also to 'close' them.[10]

Despite this imbalance, the youthful atmosphere of *Saturday Super Scoreboard* is overwhelmingly democratic and egalitarian. If it is true that 'Radio is much more democratic than the rest of the media. At least talk radio is',[11] this programme is surely at the forefront of this particular phenomenon.

A further ubiquitous element is the all-embracing mutual courtesy.

Callers will always follow requests to speak to a particular panel member with 'please' ('Can I speak tae Davie, please') and panel members' views, even if the caller does not necessarily agree with them, will always be acknowledged with 'thanks'. Anyone tempted to stray beyond the programme's unstated but nonetheless quite clear limits of decency will apologize either in advance or after having allowed themselves whatever peccadillo they think they can get away with (in many years of listening to this programme I have never heard a gross breach of these unstated rules by a caller). For example, a caller with a relatively poor view of a former Celtic chairman suggested that a new manager had been brought in to compensate 'us fur aw the crap we went through wi McCann, if ye'll excuse the French'.

Panel members themselves do not necessarily always speak with one voice and there are often robust and lively exchanges of views, but courtesy is the order of the day and particularly intense differences of opinion will often by defused by an unexpected flash of humour accompanied by the inevitable ringing of the bell. The most spectacular failure of mutual respect took place in 1998 when a bitter argument erupted between Davie Provan and commentator Gerry McNee (author of well-known football column, 'The Voice of Football') about issues relating to the Scottish national football team. Though Provan attempted to keep the debate civilized, McNee adopted a sneering and dismissive manner that was well beyond the pale of *Saturday Super Scoreboard*'s unspoken mores. An attempt was made to patch things up the following Saturday, but McNee (for reasons which have never been made public) vanished from the programme shortly afterwards and did not make a reappearance until almost two years later.

A particularly strong taboo maintained by the programme relates to anything that the panel suspects of being driven by unstated sectarian purposes. Though somewhat diminished in recent times as a result of changes affecting not only west-of-Scotland society in general, but also elite-level professional football in particular, the problem of sectarianism remains,[12] with Celtic continuing to attract a large Catholic following and Rangers a broadly Protestant one (both teams' management have been actively involved in recent years in attempts to break or at the very least reduce these inherited patterns). Sectarianism is a vigorously defended no-go area for the programme and anyone attempting to sidle into this minefield will suddenly find the first name terms abandoned, their identity being reduced to that of 'caller'.

When Celtic recently won the League after a long period of Rangers domination, a caller suggesting that Celtic did not deserve to be 'in Europe' was roundly informed that, in the opinion of the panel, he belonged to 'the narrow-minded minority in Scotland'. Others attempting to broach this subject no matter by how circuitous a route will be told to 'Get a life' or 'Wake up and smell the coffee' and will be dismissed with no further opportunity to develop their argument. Another strong taboo relates to any comments suspected of being motivated by racist prejudice, no matter what their origin. For example, when Rangers player Lorenzo Amoruso was caught on camera calling an African Borussia Dortmund player a 'black bastard' during a European Championship qualifying match (an incident that was widely debated in the Scottish sporting press), he was openly criticized by the panel for his actions, but praised the following week after issuing an apology.

LANGUAGE, DIALECT AND IDENTITY

A particularly striking feature of *Saturday Super Scoreboard* is the unquestioned availability of Scottish dialect (mostly west-of-Scotland urban dialects, though occasionally Ayrshire rural dialects are also heard) as a means of communication. Whether these dialects constitute a language in their own right – as opposed to being part of the dialectical continuum of contemporary English – is very much a live issue in certain academic circles in Scotland, though the debate is too wide-ranging to be addressed within the confines of this essay.

The linguistic situation of Scotland from this point of view has been and continues to be rather complex. Standard English – historically the dialect of the English court – is, and has been for a very long time, the language of education in Scotland. Until very recently (when there was something of a revival of interest in Scottish dialects, collectively known as Scots), Standard English was the only variety of English taught in Scottish schools and indeed in the not too distant past, say 30 or 40 years ago, the use of Scottish dialect by pupils was met on occasions with physical force. As a result, Standard English is also the language of 'the educated', many of whom often adopt extremely censorious and even discriminatory attitudes towards the use of the various dialectical variants of Scots, despite the fact that these are the preferred means of everyday communication among a sizeable majority of the population. For people located outside this axiological system, it is difficult to imagine the hostility aroused among Scottish educated elites by non-standard forms such as 'I seen', 'I done', 'I've came', 'I've went' that, although absolutely dominant 'on the streets', have become shibboleths not just for a lack of education, but even for crass ignorance and stupidity. Indeed, these non-standard forms are frontier markers in that linguistic division into 'the articulate and the barbarians' that has been around in British culture since at least the beginning of the twentieth century.[13]

Given the relationship between educated elites and the media in general, it goes without saying that Standard English has also traditionally been the language (or more precisely dialect) of the media in Scotland. Scottish dialect is, with very few exceptions (these being certain cartoons), virtually non-existent in the press, even the local press,[14] and remains under-represented on television as a whole. There has been a slow process of change since perhaps the mid-1980s on, with the gradual emergence of Scots into certain forms of mainstream television in particular. For example, the long-running detective series *Taggart*, filmed and set in Glasgow but broadcast throughout the UK, often featured various elements of Glasgow dialect, but always watered-down to a strength suitable for the non-Scottish audience.

A trail-blazer in the use of Scots was the 1990s comedy television programme *Rab C Nesbit*, whose central character, known throughout Scotland simply as 'Rab C', spoke an uncompromising Glasgow dialect of such strength that comprehension was genuinely difficult when the series was screened in England. More recently the television comedy series *Chewing the Fat* has continued the use of (and even allowed itself a certain amount of fun at the expense of) west-of-Scotland dialects, with some of its most classic phrases (for example, 'gonnae no dae that') entering into popular speech. However, despite this slow colonization of certain areas of television – mostly in the field of comedy – Scots remains virtually absent from the bulk of television (certainly anyone taking part in an official capacity in a television programme would be expected to speak Standard English) and, with two main exceptions, from radio.

These two exceptions are the two Saturday afternoon sports programmes, *Saturday Super Scoreboard* and *On the Ball*, but there is an important difference between the two. One of *On the Ball*'s two-man team is well-known Scottish comic Tam Cowan who speaks *only* west-of-Scotland urban dialect for the entire duration of the programme (as he does also on his television programme *Off Side*), while the other, Stuart Cosgrove (also Head of Programmes at Channel 4), keeps by and large to

Standard English. Despite Radio Clyde's more demotic persona when compared with Radio Scotland (a branch of the BBC), *Saturday Super Scoreboard*'s presenters use only (or with very few exceptions) Standard English when talking to each other or to callers. However, it is taken as axiomatic by all concerned that callers can use whatever dialect of English they like (including regional English dialects) with no value judgements of any kind being passed. As a result, a whole range of individuals who would normally be excluded from any kind of participation in the media are offered a space where not only is their chosen mode of speech not criticized in any way, but where their contribution, providing certain basic rules are observed, is invariably welcome. In this way *Saturday Super Scoreboard* continues what is now a long-standing tradition of Radio Clyde. As Bill Williams put it:

> Radio Clyde captured the articulacy of the West of Scotland in a way BBC Scotland and the ITV companies had never managed to do. It scooped Glasgow patter out of the street and the public bar and got it on the air.[15]

A few examples of west-of-Scotland urban Scots from recent programmes by way of illustration:

> Why's it no workin the noo?
> [Why is it not working now?]

> They've got money noo, noo that a player's oot.
> [They've got money now, now that a player is out.]

> We'd maist ae the play.
> [We had most of the play.]

> He's got tae go wi his ain thinking, insteid ae aw this clamour fur his heid.
> [He's got to go with his own thinking, instead of all this clamour for his head.]

> The papers should lay aff him fur a bit.
> [The papers should lay off him for a while.]

Needless to say, forms such as 'I seen', 'I've went' and the like are a commonplace among the callers, evoking no reaction from the panel of any kind.

However, while the availability of contemporary varieties of Scots, whether urban or rural, is taken for granted by everyone involved, the kind of artificial, antiquated Scots which *is* by and large acceptable within certain restricted areas of the educational system, and which belongs to a discourse constructing Scotland as a quaint and nostalgically rustic land, is quite clearly rejected. Outside education, a major media outlet for this kind of Scots is the Sunday newspaper the *Sunday Post*, whose cartoons 'Oor Wullie' and 'The Broons' have been reproducing this kind of unchanging, folksy Scots for decades. For *Saturday Super Scoreboard* this kind of 'kailyard' Scots is invariably the object of laughter.[16] In one episode commentator Dougie MacDonald became the butt of incessant mockery when he described a particular warm-up routine before a match as 'hunch cuddy hunch' – the name for an old Scottish game similar to leap-frog. None of the other panel members had ever heard this word and, amidst their recurring merriment, they eventually decided that it was 'an old Scottish word like "jings", "crivvens" or "help ma boab"'. This is an amusing counter-attack by the panel against the opponents of contemporary Scots since 'jings', 'crivvens' and so on are precisely the kinds of word used by educated elites to denigrate this particular mode of speech, despite the fact that such terms have no real place in it. Things that are seen as old-fashioned stereotypes invariably evoke mirth. On one occasion there was undisguised hilarity when a caller let it be known that his name was actually William Wallace, whereupon he was invited, in the midst of guffaws, to 'address the nation'. Not only does *Saturday Super Scoreboard* come out against these 'couthie' discourses of Scottishness, it constantly underlines its own modernity, repeatedly reminding its listeners to consult its website or to communicate with the panel via email.[17]

Diglossia – the simultaneous availability of two linguistic codes within the same speech community – is, of course, an extremely common occurrence and has been the object of much study, whether the two codes in question are two different languages, as in the case of Catalan and Castilian in Catalonia, two versions of the same language enjoying (at least in theory) equal status, such as bokmål and nynorsk in Norway, or two versions of the same language one of which is considered 'high' and the other 'low', as with katharevousa and demotiki in Greece.[18] However, two areas of this broad field of study have remained to some extent relatively under-explored.

The first of these is the question of standard versus dialect in relation to notions of collective identity, whether these be national, regional, or indeed class identities.[19] All language communities are characterized by high levels of dialectal variation and indeed the variation can be so great that speakers of different varieties of the same language can at times have difficulty understanding each other. Yet while much attention has been paid to the question of language and national identity,[20] particularly in the case of (actual or so-called) minority languages,[21] rather less work has been done on the relationship between dialect (rather than language) and national or regional identity,[22] particularly where these dialects are what is known technically as 'heteronomous',[23] in other words where they are dialects of a language whose main power base, so to speak, is a different country. Scots English is not the only example; others include the dialects of German spoken in Austria, Belgium, Switzerland, Luxembourg or Alto Adige, the dialects of Dutch spoken in Flanders and even the dialects of Catalan spoken in Valencia.

A second and closely related area is the different discursive dimension energized by each of the linguistic codes available in a situation of diglossia. If we take the case of Catalonia, for example, precisely the same factual information can be conveyed in either Castilian or Catalan indiscriminately (and over 60 per cent of the population are fluent speakers of both), but this does not imply that the same sentence uttered in both languages necessarily *means* the same thing. On the contrary, choosing Catalan, for example, energizes a discursive dimension that is simply not available in Castilian and the same is also true in reverse. The use of Catalan implies a distance not only from the symbolic and political construct 'Spain', but also from what are seen as many key elements of its history including, crucially, the repression of Catalan during the Franco regime (1939–75).

Catalan speakers are well aware of this distinction and a small example will suffice to illustrate this point. In its issue of 28 February 1994, the Catalan-language magazine *El Temps* used its front cover to call attention to the continued presence in Catalonia and Valencia of people who had been guilty of torture during the Franco regime. The first line of its title, in smallish letters, proclaimed in Catalan: 'Members of Franco's Political Police are still in command.' The second line continued in medium-sized letters, also in Catalan: 'The Same Old Torturers.' Beneath this in very large letters stood the Castilian word: 'Present!' On the written level, the difference between the Catalan and the Castilian for 'present' is a single 'e' ('presents' as opposed to 'presentes'), but that 'e' is sufficient to open up an entire discursive dimension associating torture with a Spanish army of occupation and casting Catalonia as the victim of foreign oppression.

In an earlier study of the Lillehammer Winter Olympics,[24] I argued that the fact that the Olympic hymn was sung by Norwegian soprano Sissel Kyrkjebø in nynorsk rather than in bokmål would have been an important element in its 'meaning' for Norwegian listeners, due to the very different discursive dimensions associated with these two varieties of Norwegian. Here I argue that the highly exceptional availability of varieties of Scots in *Saturday Super Scoreboard* (and indeed in *On the Ball*) is sufficient to energize a shared field of meaning between panel and callers. This field of meaning is structured around a set of values that are widely viewed in Scotland as being in some sense typically 'Scottish' – a distrust of hierarchies, a refusal to be impressed, impatience with circumlocution, every man's (or woman's) right to speak his or her mind. In fact, the defence of this demotically re-inscribed set of social democratic values has become 'the touchstone of "authentic" national identity in Scotland'.[25]

This refusal to bow to the 'endodiglossia'[26] of the elites – in other words the refusal to accept the value judgements they apply to different dialects – is essential to the overall operation (and no doubt to the enduring appeal) of the programme. The use of Scots by the callers – echoed by the strong Scottish accents of the presenters, even if they speak Standard English – is a key element in its strongly democratic feel, in the complete absence of any kind of 'talking down' or pulling rank and in the callers' taken-for-granted conviction that they have the right to tackle the panel on any issue that comes within the agreed ambit of the discussion.

SPORT AND POLITICS

The basic philosophy of *Saturday Super Scoreboard* could be summed up as follows:

1. The programme is about football ('fitba' in Scots);
2. It is about Scottish fitba in particular; and
3. Whatever the pattern of ownership of clubs as businesses might be, at the end of the day fitba belongs to the fans. In fact, this last point is *the* fundamental bedrock position of everyone involved.

Since football belongs to the fans, they are of course, within the philosophy of the programme, free to criticize any and every aspect of it. Callers frequently express considerable hostility against ruling bodies such as the Scottish Football Association or FIFA and UEFA for what are seen as intolerable acts of appropriation taking no account of the wishes of the fans. More recently, television companies such as Sky have been the butt of much animosity for changing the timing of matches to suit their television schedules irrespective of the wishes of the paying fan – and fans are well aware that their presence on the terraces is essential if the game is to provide an appealing televisual spectacle. No one is excluded so long as the basic philosophy of the programme is respected. In a recent broadcast an English woman calling to complain about the rising cost of purchasing team strips for her children was given vocal support by the panel. Towards the end of the same programme there was serious debate as to whether the financial health of a club was more important than on-the-park success. However, anyone attempting to move the basic focus away from football will be given short shrift: a caller trying to attribute Celtic's financial problems to dark moves by 'power brokers' was met with impatience and considerable terseness from the panel, was encouraged to 'get to the point' and was eventually dropped when it became clear that he would be unable to bring his argument back to a central location within football.

So long as some convincing relationship to football can be found, a vast range of topics can be raised. Many of these are issues that are currently in the news. Examples of topics raised in the course of recent seasons (covered, it is true, in varying degrees of depth) include:

- The changing economics of football, in particular the growing importance of the 'bottom line';
- The advantages and disadvantages of share-issues for football clubs and fans;
- The increasing cost of season tickets and the problems this poses for low-income fans;
- The lack of training for youth teams as pitches are sold off for office space;
- The increasing cost of season tickets;
- Issues relating to the policing of games;
- The role of the media in modern society (with open recognition of today's listeners as 'media-savvy'), in particular the ability of television stations to dictate the timing of games; and

- The increasingly large salaries earned by the top players as compared with the wages earned by the average fan (for some time now the panel have been trying to justify these using a 'they've got families to feed' discourse, which is cutting no ice with the callers whatsoever).

It is easy to see that, though these issues are initiated into *Saturday Super Scoreboard*'s debate through their central relationship with 'fitba', at their outer edges they merge with questions of much broader social, economic and political significance. In fact, on occasions quite explicitly political issues will be raised, such as the then Scottish First Minister's problems resulting from the sacking of his main adviser (raised in relation

FIGURE 1
FOOTBALL ISSUES AND POLITICAL ISSUES

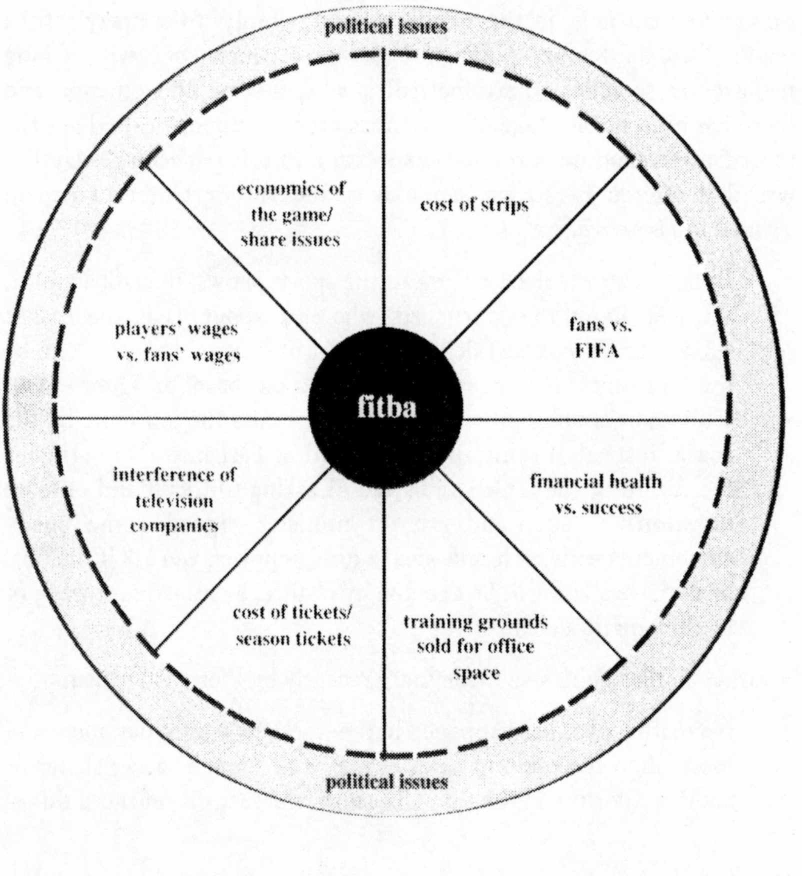

to the sacking of a manager) and Australia's relationship with the Queen (raised in relation to an Australian player then playing for Rangers). Both fans and panel are more than aware of the political dimension of many of the issues raised and will at times pursue their argument to the point of criticizing government policies and priorities, whether in relation to the Scottish Executive or the British Government in London. The relationship between football-centred issues and more political debates is graphically expressed in the (appropriately shaped) Figure 1, where the line between the football-related issues and broader political issues has been deliberately made 'porous' to indicate the ways in which these, at first sight, apparently quite narrowly-focused questions seep into a much broader political debate.

CONCLUSION

So are football fans, in the words of song, simply 'fitba crazy', 'fitba mad'? This derogatory point of view is, of course, one with a long pedigree in societies where football is a significant phenomenon and there has been no shortage of academics keen to support it. Perhaps the most famous (and most quoted) expression of this particular prejudice was that offered by Italian semiologist and author Umberto Eco in *Travels in Hyperreality*:

> In fact ... sports debate (I mean the sports shows, the talk about it, the talk about the journalists who talk about it) is the easiest substitute for political debate. Instead of judging the job done by the minister of finance (for which you have to know about economics, among other things), you discuss the job done by the coach; instead of criticizing the record of Parliament you criticize the record of the athletes; instead of asking (difficult and obscure question) if such-and-such a minister signed some shady agreements with such-and-such a foreign power, you ask if the final or decisive game will be decided by chance, by athletic prowess, or by diplomatic alchemy.[27]

A rather similar point was made more recently by Pierre Bourdieu:

> No matter what has happened in the world on a given day, more and more often the evening news begins with French soccer scores or another sporting highlight ... In short, the focus is on those things

which are apt to arouse curiosity but require no analysis, especially in the political sphere.[28]

It is not my intention to suggest that all issues raised on *Saturday Super Scoreboard* invariably develop a political dimension. On the contrary, many fans will call in to discuss a particular player's form, or a manager's decision to substitute this player or that. However, the political tone of the debate in relation to numerous issues is unmistakable and the active involvement of the fans in this debate shows that sport does not operate only as a top-down process in which fans are co-opted, to one degree or another, into others' nation-building or nation-strengthening projects.

I hope to have shown in this essay that the (ultimately very damaging) view of sport represented above by Umberto Eco is a short-sighted and fundamentally uncomprehending one. Leaving aside the (inherently elitist) question of whether it really is necessary to know about economics in order to criticize the performance of the minister of finance, as far as *Saturday Super Scoreboard* is concerned it is not a question of discussing *either* sport *or* politics, with sport as the 'bread and circuses' of the uneducated while the elites get on with the serious business of real political debate. Programmes such as *Saturday Super Scoreboard* show not only that it is perfectly possible to discuss political issues *through* sport, but that this is in fact something which the fans take for granted. *Saturday Super Scoreboard* is thus a media space where the media-culturally disenfranchised can have their say on a remarkable range of issues. Their voices may not be educated or 'Standard English', but this does not mean that they have nothing interesting or worthwhile to say.

NOTES

I would like to thank Craig McVittie, Planning Manager at Scottish Radio Holdings, for the audience figures given at the beginning of this essay.

1. V. McInerney, *Writing for Radio* (Manchester: Manchester University Press, 2001).
2. A. Crisell, *Understanding Radio* (London: Routledge, 1986).
3. P. Dahlén, *Från Vasaloppet till Sportextra: Radiosportens etablering och förgrening 1925–1995* (Värnamo: Stiftelsen Etermedierna i Sverige, 1999).
4. For example, Raymond Boyle, 'From Our Gaelic Fields: Radio, Sport and Nation in Post-Partition Ireland', *Media, Culture and Society*, 14 (1992).
5. N. Blain and D. Hutchison, 'The Limits of Union: Broadcasting in Scotland', in S. Harvey and K. Robins (eds.), *The Regions, the Nations and the BBC* (London: British Film Institute, 1993), p.54.

6. R. González, 'Les Retransmissions Esportives', in J. Julià i Muné (ed.), *Llengua i ràdio* (Barcelona: Publicacions de l'Abadia de Montserrat, 2000), p.117.

7. See H. O'Donnell, 'Yes, We Love This Land That Looms: The Lillehammer Winter Olympics in the Scottish Press', in R. Puijk (ed.), *Global Spotlights on Lillehammer* (Luton: University of Luton Press, 1997).

8. For an analysis of the conversational strategies involved in these unequal power relations, see I. Hutchby, 'Power in Discourse: The Case of Arguments on a British Talk Radio Show', *Discourse & Society*, 7, 4 (1996).

9. M. Shingler and C. Wieringa, *On Air: Methods and Meanings of Radio* (London: Arnold, 1998), p.118.

10. I. Hutchby, 'The Organistion of Talk on Talk Radio', in P. Scannell (ed.), *Broadcast Talk* (London: Sage, 1991), p.132.

11. B. Hayes, 'The Role of the Public Voice in Present-day Radio', in A.M. Hargrave (ed.), *Annual Review 1994: Radio & Audience Attitudes* (London: Broadcasting Standards Council, 1994), p.40.

12. W.J. Murray, *The Old Firm: Sectarianism, Sport, and Society in Scotland* (Edinburgh: J. Donald, 1984); T.M. Devine (ed.), *Scotland's Shame? Bigotry and Sectarianism in Modern Scotland* (Edinburgh: Mainstream, 2000).

13. T. Crowley, *The Politics of Discourse: The Standard Language Question in British Cultural Studies* (London: Macmillan, 1989), p.214.

14. R. Smith, 'The Local Press: What's In It For You', in C. Macafee (ed.), *Speak Scotch or Whustle* (Aberdeen: Elphinstone Press, 1998).

15. B. Williams, 'Broadcasting', in D. Hutchison (ed.), *Headlines: The Media in Scotland* (Edinburgh: ESPB, 1978), p.70.

16. D. McCrone, *Understanding Scotland: The Sociology of a Stateless Nation* (London: Routledge, 1992), pp.177–80.

17. www.superscoreboard.net.

18. See, for example, G. Kremnitz, *Gesellschaftliche Mehrsprachigkeit* (Vienna: Wilhelm Braumüller, 1990); J. Fishman, *Reversing Language Shift* (Clevedon: Multilingual Matters, 1991).

19. However, for a number of studies in this area, see D. Graddol, D. Leith and J. Swann, *English: History, Diversity and Change* (London: Routledge, 1966); W.B. Gudykunst (ed.), *Language and Ethnic Identity* (Clevedon: Multilingual Matters, 1988).

20. See, for example, W. Petersen, 'On the Subnations of Western Europe', in N. Glazer and D. Moynihan, *Ethnicity: Theory and Experience* (Cambridge: Harvard University Press, 1975); J. Edwards, *Language, Society and Identity* (London: Blackwell, 1985); A.D. Smith, *National Identity* (London: Penguin Books, 1991); T.K. Oomen, *Citizenship, Nationality and Ethnicity* (Cambridge: Polity Press, 1997).

21. See, for example, M. Viladot, *Identitat i vitalitat lingüística dels Catalans* (Barcelona: Edicions Columna, 1993); D. Atkinson, 'Minoritisation, Identity and Ethnolinguistic Vitality in Catalonia', *Journal of Multilingual and Multicultural Development*, 21, 3 (2000).

22. Though, following W. Labov's seminal study *Language in the Inner City* (Philadelphia: University of Pennsylvania Press, 1976), their relationship with class identities has been much more fully explored.

23. P. Trudgill, *Sociolinguistics: An Introduction to Language and Society* (London: Penguin, 1988), p.16.

24. H. O'Donnell and R. Boyle, 'Playing the Game: The Lillehammer Winter Olympics on British Television and in the UK Press', in R. Puijk (ed.), *Global Spotlights on Lillehammer* (Luton: University of Luton Press, 1997).

25. A. Law, 'Near and Far: Banal National Identity and the Press in Scotland', *Media, Culture and Society*, 23, 3 (2001), 307.

26. B. Navarro and X. Rull, 'Estàndard, dialecte, endodiglòssia: la llengua que tots volem', in I. Creus, J. Julià and S. Romero (eds.), *Llengua i mitjans de comunicació* (Lleida: Pagès Editors, 2000), p.272.

27. U. Eco, *Travels in Hyperreality* (London: Picador, 1986), pp.170–71.

28. P. Bourdieu, *On Television and Journalism* (London: Pluto, 1998), p.51.

Beyond 'Media Culture':
Sport as Dispersed Symbolic Activity

NEIL BLAIN

Since the 1980s it has been a commonplace that the media, especially television, have altered culture to such a marked degree that it has become inadequate to discuss this transformation as merely an occupation of more and more cultural space by the media. Rather, it has increasingly seemed that very considerable areas of culture have been remade in their substance by interaction with the media.

Of course there has existed a clear spatial aspect to the expansion of media culture. Activities such as cooking and gardening have become subjects for media spectatorship, with implications for a variety of spaces, not least of consumption. Food programmes can fill or depopulate spaces like shops, restaurants and domestic kitchens. The media have long exerted considerable influence not just on who watches which sports where, but even over the nature of sports and over their growth and decline. However, something more fundamental has been taking place at the sub-atomic level of culture for around 40 years or more, whereby the fusion of culture and media culture has produced structural alteration right through the body of the cultural system (a process made visible by artists like Eduardo Paolozzi and Richard Hamilton as early as the 1950s).

Indeed, like sports programmes, food programmes represent a significant if demographically selective transformation of cultural activity, which can be argued negatively as a shift from cooking to television viewing; or positively as a trend from fast-food consumption to the production of new aesthetic interests and capabilities. In sport a parallel set of arguments balances the award of new choices in television spectatorship against stadium attendance, or participation and performance.

Evaluative judgements over increased media presence in society have been a feature of serious commentary on the media in one form or another since the arrival of cinema at the end of the nineteenth century. They have usually been pessimistic in tone. The attribution of damaging consequences to media expansion in society has appeared in many contexts, such as that of long-running debates, sometimes strident, fuelled by social scientists, censorship campaigners and libertarians about the possible effects of the media in fostering anti-social attitudes and behaviour. It has been encountered also in pessimistic accounts from literary artists and critics especially in the post-war period, about the cultural inferiority of media products, not least when compared to 'literature' or other more 'valuable' or 'authentic' forms of culture. This attribution was central to some of the political concerns of the Frankfurt School who feared the growth not just of cultural degeneration, but of new technologies of ideological domination.

However, by the 1990s, when this language of criticism itself depressingly became that of its supposed object of critique – 'dumbing down' – social and economic processes had occurred which had greatly changed the nature of 'culture' as understood in the work of often pessimistic commentators like Eliot, Adorno or Leavis; changed it greatly even since Steiner's work of the 1960s.[1] By the 1980s there was already evident the sense in much writing about society and culture of a momentous change in the relationship between individuals and society on the one hand, and the media and culture on the other. From a variety of sources emerged the conviction that the unparalleled growth in the production of symbolic activity, which is associated with the media in developed societies, had precipitated a crisis for its comprehension. This is variously referred to as a crisis in representation, or the loss of reality or authenticity.

In Baudrillard's perspectives of the early 1980s[2] and those of Enzensberger and others, the media transform society and culture by damaging 'real' symbolic activity, or even replacing it with pseudosymbolic or post-symbolic forms which are really only commodities for buying and selling. In Enzensberger's formulation television becomes the 'zero medium', in other words, a nullity.[3] These perspectives are part of a chorus of grieving accounts of society and culture which follow the imagined death of the modern world. By the time that John Thompson spoke of the 'mediazation' (now 'mediatization') of culture in 1990 – that is to say its transformation into media culture – the concept could be understood by many readers as part of that much larger development of economics, society, culture, psychology and politics that we call post-modernization.[4]

Despite its celebrants there has been a critical mass of anxiety in academic accounts of the post-modern world, in which the media often figure. Forms of culture that do not depend on the media for their reception and transmission are becoming more and more to resemble curiosities. This is partly the result of the relentless search by television producers to fill the empty steppes of multi-channel space with serviceable content, which in turn produces an assumption of general familiarity with the various forms and genres of popular television and the expectation that new television product will be generated – like *Big Brother*, for example – from within the medium itself and not as the result of discoveries of 'unknown' forms outside media culture.

The media system is increasingly astonished when it discovers cultural material with which it is unfamiliar and rushes to transform it, should it demonstrate potential for supplying momentary sensationism or more lasting advantage. When the Great Britain women's curling team unexpectedly won gold at the Salt Lake City Olympics in 2002, actuality television, including the news, began actively and rather amusedly 'discovering' curling, dispatching correspondents to distant Scotland for an explanation of the sport's provenance and nature. In fact curling had appeared on television screens before, but it seems that in the particular circumstances of this competition it was more appealing to present it as an undiscovered treasure. Thereby, curling – despite its local social and cultural identity and its distinct material history – becomes identified precisely by its 'novelty' within the perceptual system of media producers.

SPORT AS 'FLEXIBLE ACCUMULATION'

By 1973 the world economic system was reeling from the impact of various setbacks, some new and some – such as over-production in certain sectors of manufacture – suffered for longer. Thereafter what David Harvey terms 'flexible accumulation' increasingly characterizes the global economic system. Whereas the 'Fordist', that is to say 'mass production' system, inaugurated early in the twentieth century and greatly influential after 1945, was characterized by 'rigidity', the new landscape of the mid-1970s favours 'flexibility'. 'Flexible accumulation' is 'characterized by the emergence of entirely new sectors of production, new ways of providing financial services, new markets, and, above all, greatly intensified rates of commercial, technological, and organizational innovation'.[5]

Harvey further notes that 'the half-life of a typical Fordist product was from five to seven years',[6] but that by the end of the 1980s the half-life of 'thoughtware' industries products such as video games and computer software programmes dipped below 18 months. In other words, vast new ranges of goods and services were developed from the early 1970s, a number of these products and services being characterized by very short-term marketability. When applied to sport, this economic perspective sheds light on the arrival and departure of new televisual sports forms as well as the continuing transformation of others. (It likewise gives us some theoretical purchase on that most typical mode of recent media activity, celebrity – to which this argument will return in the context of sport.)

Of the concomitants of this new round of economic activity, 'mediatization' is probably itself an instance. Despite rapid growth in the colonization of culture by media culture even by the 1960s, both the range and intensification of the process took larger steps from the 1970s and especially against the backdrop of a shift from the production of goods to services.

Modelling schematically the features of this new economic world after 1973, we can say that alongside more 'flexible accumulation', necessitated by severe recession partly caused by system rigidity (in other words the incapacity of production systems to change the nature of their output), there develops:

• More culture, more of which is
• Media culture, which helps to lead to
• New growths of aesthetic awareness and activity and sensation-seeking, all of which lead to
• More consumption.

It is against this background that we require to comprehend media sport theoretically.

Where sport appears as 'new culture', for example, on what is sometimes in various domains of society referred to as 'the street', in other words as 'spontaneous culture', it is often quickly appropriated by the media system. Sometimes however new sport is best understood as new media sport from its inception. The inter-penetration of new forms of aesthetic activity with both sport and the media, and the demands of 'flexible accumulation', have long been evidenced by marketing initiatives that simultaneously sell clothing, sports personalities and sports lifestyles, alongside a variety of identities variously defined by ethnicity, gender, social class, age and locality. In the case, for example, of new extreme sports it sometimes seems likely that from their inception they are designed to contain elements friendly to media construction and product marketing.

Some challenging analytical and theoretical questions emerge from this nexus of causes and effects. For example, to determine objectively the circumstances in which any new fashion of sport has emerged becomes difficult if the intention behind the development of the sport is precisely recognition by television. As in a number of areas of contemporary culture, it becomes difficult to disentangle the operation of the lure of media celebrity, and material reward, from interests and activities which are valued 'in themselves' as attractions, in this case sports performance or participation. In the age of confessional television, where every private experience is also potentially a televisual product, disentangling media influence from the rest of culture is very difficult indeed now, as an analytical proposition. This is all the more so because the process identified by Thompson and others at the end of the 1980s has reached a new stage.

Put simply, we should no longer note 'mediatization' with any sense of discovery. The phase during which a variety of commentators identified the media as a transformative influence on culture, including sports culture,[7] has been left behind. Culture generally has absorbed so much media culture that we are clearly in a phase beyond 'mediatization'. Much of our culture is now predefined by the cultural hegemony of the media. This has produced in writers about sports culture formulations such as 'mediasport',[8] but sport is still too important a socio-economic and politico-cultural category for us to discard the advantages of retaining it analytically. Though most certainly often closely related to the nature and purposes of the mass media, sport is a distinct sphere of practices. The relationships that sport bears to culture, society, economics, politics, institutions, technology, discourse and the media themselves are both too many and too important to be occluded.

Sport, as Elias pointed out, does not produce finished forms.[9] Television sport has already passed from accessible terrestrial television forms to more exclusive cable and satellite delivery and is appearing in still-developing incarnations on the internet. A term such as 'mediasport' suggests both a transformation which has far from completely occurred and at the same time commits errors of simplification, and reification, in representing what are actually complex and dynamic processes. Moreover, this compound term blurs the variety of relationships different sports have with media culture itself, which are in fact highly differentiated, involving different forms like radio, television, the press and the internet and addressing a great variety of audiences, targeted with careful attention to demographics.

That qualification over, we must recognize the fact of an intense relationship between sport and the media, which has the capacity to impact on very large areas of sport culture, as well as vice versa. What was so remarkable about the British women who won the curling gold at Salt Lake City was that their cultural activity as sportswomen appeared to have a previous unmediated and lively existence of its own.

They belong to what may be understood as a lingering remnant of an era when sport could demonstrate autonomy as a cultural activity much more clearly than now (and even remain relatively 'hidden'). Truly, for the delighted producers and reporters of the media who stumbled upon them, curlers were like a lost tribe. Then, for a time, we all knew who the British 'ladies' team were. Their play, and likewise their contributions to interviews, were self-contained and dignified. The BBC commentator Dougie Donnelly, himself a Scot, remarked approvingly that we would not see any 'high fives' from this team. (His remark was occasioned by some unexpectedly American behaviour from the Swiss in the final, who may conceivably have been role-playing.)

Time will tell if curling will resume its secret life in Britain. However, we might note that the response of the British women – succinct, a polite but minimal gesture to the demands of television – can be seen every week in many of those brief interviews with footballers and even coaches after league matches, in which the participants signal their haste to return to the dressing room both verbally and non-verbally. Most footballers are not instantly transformed into media personalities or celebrities. These interviews hint at a balance between the reality of sport as an activity in itself and sport as a televisual product. 'Cultural autonomy' is not necessarily a relic where sport is concerned. This question becomes yet more interesting when we consider how meanings attached to sport often become more important, in many contexts, than either the sport itself or its practitioners.

Sport's symbolic functioning often usurps the directly-connected network of meaning attaching to the original activity. Sport's symbolic importance for categories such as collective identity is well established. However, sport as a symbolic resource has been more and more important in society generally and for a broadening and perhaps even deepening range of cultural functions. Now that observers are well past the stage of being struck by the transformation of culture into media culture, as has been suggested, we can contemplate a new phase in the interaction between culture and the media, which is in part the normalization of media culture as culture.

THREE DAVID BECKHAMS AND THEIR FOOT

To illustrate this process of normalization we may turn to the most celebrated footballer of the turn of the century in Britain. Ominously, we discover not one David Beckham, but several. There is Beckham the footballer (category: real life) and Beckham the husband of Posh Spice, a spectacular consumer, fashion icon and post-modern parent (category: media and consumer culture). Yet a third Beckham has emerged beyond media culture: a Beckham of Everyday Life. This is neither exclusively nor even most pertinently a 'sport' Beckham, a 'media' Beckham, or yet a 'media sport' Beckham (even if in this Everyday Beckham's genealogy, such ancestry is clearly discerned).

This third Beckham has passed from sport culture via media culture into a generalized cultural life where he becomes a sinuous symbolic resource liberated from the mechanics of mere spot-kicking – good though he is at that! Whether discussed in relation to philosophical questions surrounding his intellect, his putative operation as a 'gay icon', or referenced by a bottle of the German beer Becks, on British supermarket posters the length and breadth of the islands, Beckham becomes a renewable semiological resource.[10]

It will be objected: 'Is this not merely the media Beckham (Beckham No.2), writ very large?' The answer is no; this is an advanced stage of generalization of media culture. It is part of a recent pattern in which media culture turns into culture in general on an immense scale and it is a large and complex process in which celebrity, though only one element, is a very important influence. When *Hello!* magazine was launched in May 1988 it was one of a number of signs which marked such an advance in the colonization of culture by media culture that a decade or so later, when Diana, Princess of Wales met her death in Paris, the public reaction suggested the need to think fundamentally about how to separate analytically the notion of 'culture' from 'media culture'. One of the problems was to separate what the public reaction really was, as distinct from the 'public reaction' constructed by the media.[11] Certainly by this point it seemed inadequate to understand culture as a large space in the process of being partially colonized by the media.

In the period after Diana's death, the difficulty in Britain seemed to be rather that of discerning any cultural reality beyond media construction, of knowing how even to imagine a 'cultural' response that was theoretically separable from a response to media coverage. Such was the power of the media account that individuals found themselves querying their own emotional responses, unsure of which strands in their reaction were psychologically 'authentic'. It is in this sense that we need to acknowledge as our starting point for any contemporary analysis of the culture/media culture distinction that the inter-penetration of these two domains is so far advanced that to speak of one as distinct from the other is a hazardous task.

In a joke recounted on Radio 2, David Beckham walks into a library and orders, 'Two cod and chips please'; when told it is a library he lowers his voice and says in a whisper, 'Sorry, two cod and chips please'. The joke is told with a degree of 'sympathy' – there is nothing deprecating in the manner of its delivery and it is accompanied by a laugh, both warm and also designed to be a little 'weary'. In other words, it is at least a performance of sympathy. For its impact it is dependent on an advanced stage of Beckham's generalized recognition in the culture. Since it is not intended unpleasantly it assumes a consensus in which Beckham's supposed intellectual limitations are known to be compensated by his intriguing cultural persona (more interesting and more sympathetic than his failings) and by his decency and of course his acknowledged strengths as a footballer – after Manchester United's 5–3 defeat of West Ham, George Best observed: 'he works his socks off and is a wonderful example of how to play the game for youngsters'.[12] Of course the 'sympathy' operates upon an imagined Beckham, but the narrative nonetheless depends on an advanced stage of its assimilation.

This Everyday Beckham is understood as important even when his influence fails to live up to expectations: the question was raised at the end of the 1990s as to why more children were not being named Brooklyn (after his first child). The Everyday Beckham is part of a symbolic apparatus posing questions about a number of aspects of identity, not only gender, for example, but also the British class system: his expensive residence is ironically dubbed 'Beckingham Palace' and his wife Victoria, in a wordplay upon the late Diana's self-description, the 'Queen of Herts'.

Certainly, this cultural life has its origins in an expansion of the media in culture. 'The hero was distinguished by his achievement; the celebrity by his image or trademark. The hero created himself; the celebrity is created by the media. The hero was a big man; the celebrity is a big name.'[13]

History may look back on David Beckham mainly as an excellent footballer justly respected by opposing sides, a committed and talented player and captain, but (in Boorstin's terms) his 'achievement' is swamped by his celebrity – to an extent that even Boorstin would have found it difficult to predict 40 years ago. Celebrity has become a thing in itself. In Boorstin's perspective, if it matters to us, we can distinguish between celebrities of whom it can be said that achievement precedes celebrity, and celebrities of the sort defined in timeless fashion, who are known for being well-known. In the end, the economic imperatives of celebrity, coupled with the strengthening grasp of media culture over the rest of culture, make of celebrity currently the primary virtue obtainable in British culture, achieving its full force when coupled with wealth.

But though this celebrity is created by the media, it can transcend it. To frame it as 'media culture' imposes artificial limitations on its comprehension. In this process and in this instance, sport, which began as culture, ends as culture. Although Beckham's life in culture has become something in itself it is still associated with sport. Had Beckham been a celebrity hairdresser rather than a footballer his symbolic resonances would be quite different. We cannot take sport out of the symbolic framework even though it has travelled into areas of culture far beyond its habitat. In fact this is precisely what sport does in a number of its dimensions, as when the English tabloid press obsessively negotiates questions of national character during periods of soccer conflict with Germany. If that example suggests a different symbolic route from sport to culture than the trajectory of personal celebrity, both examples, nonetheless, suggest a sport–culture relationship in which the media, though at the heart of the exchange, may cede a degree of autonomy to broader cultural processes.

Can we reclaim the category of sport from the media? Let us suppose that media culture has indeed colonized large areas of culture in general. One process through which sport may transcend 'media culture' is by being transformed thereby into something sufficiently substantial to become partially independent of it, even while being nourished by it. For example, at a certain phase of development, the thermodynamic equation binding a celebrity and a culture no longer needs the continuous media input of energy required at earlier stages. Aberrant features can appear (as in the saga of Diana). Swollen by an excess of energy, Beckham's relationship with the media spawned an anatomical-symbolic offshoot, Beckham's Foot, when he broke the second metatarsal in his left foot during a match with Deportivo La Coruna in early April 2002. His Foot's ubiquitous media presence, the day after, created the strong sense that it had been launched on a celebrity trajectory of its own.

Its appearance on broadsheet front pages drew criticism. Yet alongside the Foot's post-modern character was another dimension corresponding to the modern world that sport still inhabits (a dual modern/post-modern nature shared with culture generally and explored below). That the media were actually responding to a degree of sensible national concern over the Foot was not implausible.

It will be suggested toward the end of this argument, in more detail than presently, that sport's representative function, in speaking about life generally, has some special qualities. The specifically indexical aspect of sport as a cultural trope – in other words the manner in which we read sport as associated with real life – is explored in some detail below. Meanwhile we should note that this celebrated injury was perhaps quite correctly judged by many as a potential threat to aspects of English identity. The real psycho-cultural importance of Beckham's injury – an apparent threat to England's understanding of itself, consequent on the representative functions of team performances at the World Cup – may have been rightly recognized.

Whatever this Foot signified (the Queen herself was quoted in the media giving advice on the matter[14]) its existence, like its owner, transcended media culture while being unimaginable without it.

And there is another fashion in which sport may be independent of media culture. So far this discussion has been taking the transformation of culture into media culture for granted. It may be that 'mediatization' has always, despite its rapid growth, had some limitations.

CULTURAL HYBRIDITY AND SPORT

Part of the long transformation of the modern world since the 1950s has involved the putative growth of *hybridity* as evidence of post-modernization. By 'hybridity' in this context is intended new combinations of cultural activity, often conditioned by the demands of 'flexible accumulation', which may appear as new services or products. The two television 'lifestyle programming' examples mentioned at the start of this analysis, cooking and gardening, function inter-penetratively in the burgeoning of patio products like heaters and ceramic ovens, in the growth of an arcane aesthetics of the barbecue, in cults of kitchen gardening and herbal window boxes. Likewise sport appears in many combinative forms both as commodity (goods and services), symbol and ideology.

In the world of global capitalism critiqued by Klein[15] and others there is observed in the products of Nike and other large companies a complex mix of commodity functioning, symbolic process and ideological operation in which, for example, it becomes very difficult to separate the practical utility of a pair of running shoes from a variety of signifiers of personal development and collective identity. Of course this plurality is not uncommon in the world of marketing, but sport has a flexibility of symbolic operation that makes it a very distinct case. The sovereignty of consumer culture produces hybrid cultural-economic domains – for example, sport and sportswear, or sport and fashionwear, or sport and nutrition products – which suggest that sport is best understood as subject to the same post-modernizing influences as other social processes.

Yet the readiness merely to dub sport 'post-modern' is as analytically unsatisfactory as to invent compound concepts like 'mediasport'. It has been argued in more detail elsewhere that sport, like the rest of culture, is best seen as exhibiting *both* modern and post-modern characteristics.[16] In an adaptation of the theoretical work of Charles Jencks,[17] it has been suggested that post-modernity is best seen as *the continuation of modernity and its transcendence*. This is to suggest that we should retain our sense of the nature of sport as modern and argue about its concurrent post-modern traits from that point.

One of the analytical devices widely used to discuss the distinction between modern and post-modern elements in culture has been the list of antinomies, wherein oppositional qualities are constructed, for example, the modern world being seen as having connected and closed forms, the post-modern world as disconnected and open forms. If viable, these distinctions have to hold good for different areas of culture, for example, architecture, music, dance and literature. An influential table of opposites by Hassan suggests a variety of qualities by which modern culture can be recognized.[18] He lists characteristics of modern culture, such as form (conjunctive, closed), purpose, design, hierarchy, mastery/logos, creation, centring, genre/boundary, selection, master code, type and determinacy. Their post-modern equivalents include antiform (disjunctive, open), play, chance, anarchy, exhaustion/silence, decreation, dispersal, intertext, combination, idiolect, mutant and indeterminacy. Many such lists and groupings of opposites have been produced as a way of trying to understand post-modern culture, but their general propositions have been similar.

If we apply Hassan's categories to sport and then to sport in media culture, or sport in culture generally, we get different results. The 'modern' set of characteristics works well for the design and implementation of sports practice, with clear and distinct forms, select purposes, hierarchical groupings, closure and other traits. When we look at the post-modern list (disjunctiveness, play, chance, decreation, dispersal, combination, mutation), we can also clearly apply these tendencies to sport, but in this instance they fit only when we consider sport as part of media culture or as dispersed more widely across culture.

If we take 'disjunctiveness', 'play' and chance' as examples, we might note the manner in which television sport can be interrupted by advertisements, placed in trailers and cross-product advertising beside other television forms like drama. A European Championship match, for example, is the first part of an 'evening of drama' also involving a Hollywood feature film. Sports quizzes also work as both celebrity and comedy programming. 'Chance' in this perspective implies all the contingent factors that will determine whether a match is covered, when it is scheduled for television, how it is framed by commentators and which highlights are covered afterward.

The post-modern 'play' – here contrasted with the modern 'purpose' – has many potential referents, including the replacement of traditionally-understood fan support with new forms of television connoisseurship, for example, the supporting by British 'fans' of continental teams, made visible by programmes offering Italian or Spanish football. Needless to say if we take a very clear case of post-modern culture – a Nike sport product advertisement, for example – the post-modern traits (dispersal, intertext, combination, mutation) are yet more clearly visible.

What appears to be the case here is that sport, in relation to Hassan's list, leads a double life. On its own, as it were, it seems to exhibit traits consistent with the continuation of modernity, but it is seldom left alone – as we have seen in the case of curling. It often enjoys in practice, as far as the performance of the sport goes, and even, up to a point, as far as interaction between fans and performance is concerned, a 'modern' existence.

However, the terms of its wider reception in culture are more complex and as soon as we look at the phenomenon as a media product we find that the second, 'post-modern' set of characteristics starts to apply. Yet that second group of traits is plainly not the whole story. There is an element of the phenomenon that still conforms to modern characteristics. When athletes train for the Olympics or for European Athletic Championships it may well be that they lead an extended life as product sponsors, media commentators, even eventually as media celebrities or movie stars, but in the discipline of training and in the particulars of strategy and performance, there is nothing especially 'post-modern' about the process. The engagement of the spectators with the spectacle of performance and ceremony has a history very much older than either modernity or post-modernity. All too easily do academic commentators see something 'post-modern' in the old attraction of spectacle.[19]

When we pay necessary attention to the way the world has changed by using post-modernism theory to understand sport, we require to use it subtly enough to avoid blanket formulations. The Olympic Games and the soccer World Cup are no more satisfactorily described as 'post-modern' than their innocent little sibling, the curling finals. They have a modern life too. (Obviously in the case of the Olympics, but more generally, there are also pre-modern traditions to be considered.) They belong both to the age of media culture and to an age before its hegemony. The next section re-engages the question as to whether they also have a life 'after' media culture.

'MEDIA CULTURE' AS CULTURE

When football became a satellite product as well as a terrestrial product, it was noted that terrestrial ideologies – not very surprisingly – continued to accompany it in its new delivery mode.[20] There has often tended to be an assumption, which follows the general trend of pessimistic interpretations of post-modernization, that 'media culture' is a mere denatured copy of culture. Yet when sport, like any other part of culture, becomes a constituent of media culture, we would do well to remember something not always realized in talk of 'mediatization', which is that media culture is perforce the offspring of culture. Mediatized sport culture cannot reasonably be seen as engendering a 'loss' of sport culture even where it transforms it. Media producers and presenters and their discourses, including those in the sport departments, can come from nowhere other than culture and so there is another set of arguments with which we can reinstate sport in place of media sport.

In the proliferation of late-night television chat programmes about football in the UK, it is as much as anything a visible love of the game that animates discussion (and likewise audience participation), which is to say that there is relatively little sense of a fabricated media product, but rather a report, from participants, of their aesthetic, psychological and political reactions to watching sport. Of course in these activities there is always present that sense identified by Umberto Eco and others of 'performance' in post-modern life, of life in inverted commas,[21] but if we insist on seeing that everywhere then there will be more obvious places to look than these modest talk shows.

In these instances there is a persuasive alternative argument, in fact, in favour of seeing television at least in part as a conduit of cultural activity, not a replacement. For those of us who love these soccer discussions (and are not prepared to accept that we are merely performing the act of loving them), the key lies in the fact that the rhetorical apparatus of television in this instance is minimal. These programmes are, of course, very cheap to make and belong to the extended category of television that is radio with pictures. If producers do deploy artifice beyond the capacity of radio (which can amount to little more than matters of lighting, dress code and interpersonal style) it is scarcely obtrusive. The only factors that might alienate an audience from this form of television, apart from any minor infelicities of presentation, would be the opinions of participants, a discordance to which the mediated element of the exchange is peripheral.

This form of television is close, in other words, to a fairly simple cultural exchange between football specialists and an interested audience. To frame this form of 'media culture' in terms of its distance from, or replacement of, culture itself is not a convincing approach. It is much more persuasive when understood as a form of culture extended into late-night television. It is a natural extension of conversations in pubs and bars, or during pauses in the workplace. Naturally the restrictions that operate amidst the rather one-sided nature of people's interaction with television still apply, despite the possibility of emailing (producers find emails safer and cheaper than phone calls) and we should not exaggerate the lack of artifice in this television form, for example, the deployment of a suitable persona by the presenter or guests. Nonetheless there are more arguments in favour of representing this kind of television as more or less an extension of culture than there are for interpreting it as the replacement of culture.

If we can successfully argue a case for one kind of sports programming as culture, then the possibility opens up of reclaiming other forms of sports broadcasting or indeed journalism of any kind as culture and of putting 'media culture' in a better perspective than it has often enjoyed. In a later section of this argument we will examine how sport 'media culture' interacts with cultural questions about identities.

However, before the argument moves in that direction, it is worth considering another television instance, that of the 'big match', whether national or international. Here, the rhetorical apparatus of television is much more heavily engaged. Expensive graphics, music and celebrity presenters add to a rich mix of production values in an offering that is at least at face value much more of the media than of general culture. Much of the professional television knowledge that is in abeyance during a late-night chat programme is flaunted. The time and space of soccer are reshaped by television technology in an increasing variety of dimensions so that while, for example, certain special instances (goals, most obviously) have become multiple performances in the time of television, space is also increasingly colonized by marking or colouring the screened pitch, for example, to indicate the distance and angle of free kicks.

Yet any single moment of athletic brilliance can eclipse the medium – or so it seems. Denis Bergkamp, his back to goal, takes possession of the ball, flicks it to chest height, turns and, tranquilly, giving the appearance of having stopped time while he considers his choices, chips it over the goalkeeper – at such moments television becomes a conduit for an act of extraordinary artistry and athleticism on the pitch. At these moments television is characterized, to put this another way, more by its transparency than by its opacity. It is not the medium that is the object of attention. That metaphor often used naively of news and current affairs broadcasting – television as a 'window on the world' – applies well enough when sport asserts itself as the prime element, as a general rule, in fact, whenever events whether human or natural emphasize their presence strongly in front of the cameras.

'Essentialist' arguments – about whether a particular instance is 'essentially' sporting or televisual – are usually difficult and sometimes pointless, but that does not mean that we can allow ourselves vague generalizations about the 'mediated', 'mediatized' or 'post-modernized' nature of media sport. The growing inter-penetration of culture and media culture characteristic of the last half of the twentieth century and beyond is best seen both as a partial process and as one in which hybrid forms are produced which neither owe sovereignty to the media nor are yet separable from them. For example, while it is true that Bergkamp's moment of brilliance is received within a tradition of appreciation of athletic control and skill that long predates the media age, its portrayal, from a variety of camera angles, in slow motion and within a syntax of editing still historically quite recent, nonetheless raises a serious question about what sort of hybrid cultural product is being admired here. If watched on television, it has no unadulterated existence either as sport or as television, but we underestimate the importance of the realm of sport to comprehend such a moment as primarily televisual. Likewise, it is an exaggeration to insist that this moment is now a complete fusion in which we are unable to apportion analytically that which belongs to the realm of sport and that which belongs to the realm of media.

What really seems to be happening is that production and reception of sport and television events develop amidst other broad influences, such as the growth of aesthetic consciousness and new forms of talking about aesthetic matters, and also the emergence of novel forms of consumerism, to produce new hybrid cultural forms. These are not merely 'media forms'. The ability to attract an audience for a football chat show late at night, for example, has required the growth of novel forms of connoisseurship dependent on a variety of social and cultural shifts ranging from multiple television ownership and new forms of domestic space to more privatistic leisure practices (and even conceivably on growing stress levels – football chat is relaxing).

The relationship between sport and television is also interestingly problematized when it does not work well, or when it fails entirely. The penultimate section of this essay considers economic failure, but there are a variety of disjunctive moments between television and sport. Far from Denis Bergkamp's world, in the damp undergrowth of Scottish Premier League football, when Kilmarnock insist on playing Hearts and when the cameras yet more mysteriously insist on being present, television cannot sustain the attention to its apparatus thrown back by the unremitting lack of spectacle on the pitch. These are raw events for real fans. They illustrate the uneven development of post-modernization in advanced societies. Warnings of reality crisis from Université de Paris X-Nanterre 30 years ago were distinctly premature for parts of Ayrshire.[22] It is true that Kilmarnock began to enter the post-modern world when its meat pies became the stuff of Scottish media legend (and beyond), but Kilmarnock's pies are only fully comprehensible within the aesthetic-consumerist continuum of post-modern culture generally.[23] (They are not media pies.)

During these encounters television increases in opacity and the small bands of viewers begin to concentrate on the inanity of the commentary or other inconsequential features of the apparatus. Another reaction is to assert sovereignty over the medium by ignoring its intended offering and concentrating yet more forlornly on entirely ancillary features, perhaps the emptiness of the stands.

On one occasion (never explained, but which must have been the result of some awful mishap, which also involved a silencing of the commentary) Scottish Television broadcast the end of the Glasgow Marathon with one distant and immobile camera in a shot within which the exhausted contestants were partly blocked by a sponsorship hoarding and were in any case almost indistinguishably tiny. After a few minutes this minimalist coverage started to produce a sense of profound tragedy and acquired something of the dignity of an avant-garde experiment. While revealing (by its absence) the importance of the constructedness of mediated sport, it also reminded the viewer of the often superordinate nature of the sport event itself: the tragic sense was unachievable without the awareness that these almost obscured little figures had just run 26 miles.

FEAR AND DIGITIZATION: ECONOMICS, CULTURE AND IDENTITY

The first quarter of 2002 saw the long predicted consequences of over-investment in the English soccer game. This happens in many service-orientated industries prone to uncertain fashion. In the 1960s Hollywood spent heavily on blockbuster films, largely after the huge financial success of *The Sound of Music* – the film that Alfred Hitchcock blamed for the subsequent financial disasters and near extinction of the movie capital – persuaded many producers that expensive production values guaranteed box office success. At the turn of the century, so-called dot.com companies spelled heavy losses for investors. The over-investment at the heart of the digital television crisis early in 2002 was both by clubs in expensive players and by Britain's main commercial broadcaster ITV in football as a media product. The two processes were linked, in that the clubs were spending money which the owners of ITV Digital, Granada and Carlton, did not have and the broadcasters were in turn trying to sell a media product dependent for its attractiveness on the ability to showcase star players that the clubs could not afford. They were all engaging in wishful thinking. As it happens the difficulties being experienced by the broadcasters went well beyond sport and well beyond ITV Digital because this period saw a growing caution, for a number of reasons, over predictions about the growth of digital television provision in Britain. Some analysts began to suggest that government plans to switch off the analogue signal in 2010 were premature and the most cautious estimates revised substantially downwards the proportion of the population likely to avail themselves of digital services in the foreseeable future.[24]

Not unexpectedly the apparent crisis for the English League in 2002 was interpreted largely in terms of football's dependence on television money. The relationship between sport and television has been one of interdependence, as it has been between sport and the media generally.[25] The changing nature of the British press, especially during the 1990s, incorporated much more attention to sport, with separate sport sections becoming a feature of broadsheet provision. Sport became a prime product in the search for marketable content. This is easily argued as a stage in the developing process of 'flexible accumulation'. Paul Gascoigne, for example, in his heyday, was a frequent presence in quality newspapers, billed on the front pages of weekend editions with figures from what was once understood as 'high' culture or with politicians or prominent entrepreneurs.

Widespread acceptance of football and other sports into previously restricted cultural discourses appears, from the 1980s onward, as something of the equivalent of the enfranchisement of popular music in the 1960s, when songwriters Lennon and McCartney found themselves spoken of in the company of composers from the classical canon. After Pop Art first prominently marked the beginning of the end of high/popular culture distinctions (the first major Pop Art exhibition was in 1962), it is unsurprising that sport may have been enfranchized later than some other elements of popular culture. The 'popular' element in sport long appeared more persuasive than the 'cultural', in the days when the latter term tended to be used in a restricted sense. This was true despite the deployment, over a longer time period, of a language of 'artistic' appreciation for virtuoso footballers like Pele, Eusebio and George Best.

Few domains of popular culture remain beneath the gaze of media gatekeepers, even if some are treated only with irony. There has been an element of distanciation in the performative aspects on television of certain sports such as darts and the medium still has some difficulty in avoiding a dubious demographic framing of a variety of sports. Sometimes it more or less ignores demographic variants such as women's football leagues whose existence is acknowledged only in the reporting of scores on far-flung television text pages. Mainstream media sport acquires a medium-specific or media-specific identity (that is, typical of the general media framing of a sport, or else of one medium such as radio in particular).

Sport sometimes leads where television has difficulty in following. Though the English Premiership was only indirectly threatened by the digital crisis of 2002, the flagship of that national game which was causing so much apprehension had already radically altered its identity in pursuit of economic goals. It was clear by the turn of the century that the Gallic tones of a Wenger or a Houllier, respectively the Arsenal and Liverpool coaches, were as intrinsic to the new English game as the Midlands vowels of 'Big Ron' Atkinson (or the accents of its many Irish- and Scotsmen). London's Arsenal had become one of the finest showcases for French talent in Europe and could face up to rivals Chelsea with scarcely an Englishman on the field. In Scotland there was widespread surprise and disappointment at Rangers' apparent solecism in 2001, when they appointed an indigenous coach. Intriguing questions arose from proposals for an 'Atlantic League' involving countries like Scotland and the Netherlands, a potential (if unlikely) development, driven by economics, which suggested possible new identity formations, as did indications that Celtic and Rangers might want to play in England.

A number of questions raised for the local dimensions of collective identity by the globalization of some aspects of sport have been well rehearsed, but the pace of change requires constant reappraisal. In some domains television has not always seemed ready to catch up with change, even if in others it appears to set the pace. On football chat shows or among studio specialists during big football matches there is a preference for ex-footballers with British regional or national accents (disproportionately Scottish and usually working class, as though to affirm the search for a 'default identity' within the soccer brand). Given the availability of European and other specialists who are occasionally visible in soccer coverage, but still restricted within UK presentation, this choice is not so tightly conditioned by the demographics of the British game as it might seem. There has been less cross-fertilization between mainstream television soccer provision and connoisseur offerings like UK Channel 4's cosmopolitan *Football Italia* than might have been expected (even in the latter instance the default tones often provide expert summarization).

There is an entire history of tension, as yet not fully mapped, between the economic imperatives of service industries on the one hand and, on the other, considerations of local rights and local democracy. The conundrum facing Scottish football in 2002 was intensified by an aspect of legitimacy surrounding claims of rights both by its two global 'Old Firm' brands in Glasgow to develop on a European scale and also, equally, on the part of the other clubs and their fans in Scotland to keep Scottish football alive locally. In addition, of course, there was the right of some English interests to keep English football English (or at least English and Welsh). These phenomena are, in a different perspective, a function both of capitalism in general and globalization in its most recent and voracious phase.

IDENTITY: CULTURE VS. SOCIETY

> At certain periods of history, when the masses are no longer interacting with those in government ... the political universe dies and sociality takes over. Furthermore, I believe that this movement is a swing of the pendulum, proceeding by saturation: on the one hand, direct or indirect participation predominates: on the other hand, there is an increased emphasis on everyday values. In the latter case, one can say that sociality preserves energies which in the political reign tend to take place in public.[26]

In this discussion so far, the category of the 'social' has been present only tacitly. Fredric Jameson has noted that 'everything in our social life – from economic value and state power to practices and to the very structure of the psyche itself – can be said to have become "cultural" in some original and yet untheorized sense'.[27] This involves a process through which more and more of our lives become 'cultural' ('culturalization'), usually imagined as a growth of cultural development within the pre-existent and pre-determinate category of the 'social'. Academic fields, particularly cultural studies and often media studies, have in recent times privileged the term 'culture' over 'society', while in the older field of sociology the relationship between the social and cultural has been debated with new emphases.

Michel Maffesoli notes that 'even if one feels alienated from the distant economic-political order, one can assert sovereignty over one's near existence'.[28] *The Time of the Tribes* explores a tendency in post-modern culture for social fragmentation to be offset by novel forms of collective identity. Apparently insubstantial, coalescing as they do around the products of consumer culture, Maffesoli's 'tribes' nonetheless offer an intriguing and subtle alternative to a dystopian model of linear political disengagement. He quotes Durkheim on 'the social nature of sentiments':

> 'We are indignant together', he writes, referring to the proximity of the neighbourhood and its mysterious, formative 'force of attraction'. It is within this framework that passion is expressed,

common beliefs are developed and the search for 'those who *feel and think as we do*' takes place [Maffesoli's emphasis].[29]

Participation in sport or congregation in sports stadia constitute circumstances in which 'passion', 'common beliefs' and the search for 'those who feel and think as we do' have, as attributions, some application, even when expressed adversarially. The relatively untrammelled march of market forces across Britain since the 1970s has produced still greater fractures and quantities of space, within traditional structures of collective identity, than in Maffesoli's France or in some other European societies, but it is plausible to understand the growth of domestic and international sport as linked to crises in society and politics.

What is less clear is where our proper emphasis should be when it comes to balancing the social with the cultural in our account. Maffesoli refers to present social tendencies as indicating an 'empathetic period'. His interest in the nature of spatial relationships in society (often termed 'proxemics') – given both the nature of physical congregations at sports events and also the virtual contiguities of the sports media – is fruitful when theorizing sport in electronic societies. Apply growth in the cultural centrality of sport as a plausibility test for this 'empathetic period' and we find a mixture of signals. The prominence of the symbolic apparatus of sport in society is neither of a unitary nature nor an even reach.

Forms of 'sociality' that may be available in sport beyond the field and the stadium, and even within, are difficult to address because of their complicity with, or their subjection to, consumer culture, which is in at least some respects a 'post-social' concept. Maffesoli's 'tribes', since they coalesce around consumer culture, present an ambiguous dimension. Purchasing a specific type of fashionable trainers and sports top may only constitute further evidence of wider wants in sociality; may in fact signal at best a fleeting and tenuous self-subjection to nothing other than a momentary style. Likewise it is possible to apply that critique in slightly different terms to apparent instances of 'team-work' or other characterizations of collective activity, which seem quite successfully at least to mimic social cohesion.

However, the forms of collective identity produced by sport can, in other circumstances, demonstrate characteristics of depth and longevity, which are often closely linked to relatively stable demographic factors such as social class and rural living. There is a golfing way of life, which groups a number of dimensions including socio-economic position, domestic location, age and often ideological disposition. If we preserve that persuasive metaphor through which these relatively stable *social* factors are in some sense seen as 'underlying' *cultural* developments of more recent appearance, we may conclude that there are aspects of the signifying power of sport whose dynamics are more clearly 'social' than 'cultural'. That is true even if both qualities must always apply (not least because the social and cultural domains overlap and interact).

What applies to sport in society also applies to Maffesoli's general ideas about collective identity. If it is true that consumption is the driver for new forms of collectivity, and if this happens during the partial suspension of other modes of thinking and feeling, our judgement as to the positive or negative features of this state of affairs will hinge on Maffesoli's phrase, 'an increased emphasis on everyday values'.

In a media-saturated society it has become very difficult to know what everyday values are and who produces them. It has become precisely a point of argument as to whether the media, in filling their pages with the imagined love affairs of football coaches or the bruises on Beckham's Foot, are imposing an ideological or marketing agenda of their own (or both); or playing back to us, for our gratification, our own concerns. When some sets of values in society are replaced by others, which are then in turn read as 'everyday values', the question of whose interests they represent is a crucial one. Our evaluation of new normative developments will depend in part on how central the forces of consumption are, as drivers of new forms of identity. The post-modernist dismissiveness of authenticity in social and cultural forms, assuming as it does a mere mimicry of qualities such as cohesiveness in new socio-cultural formations, takes for granted a central or even exclusive role for consumption in these processes.

But one of the grounds on which we are required to challenge this judgement in the domain of sport is precisely the particular manner in which sport is implicated in the domain of the real. When we speak of the 'symbolic' functioning of sport we do so loosely. In its tropic function sport is often not, in its main effects, 'symbolic' at all. We may approach this question traditionally through the literary terminology of 'metaphor' and 'metonym', or through the semiological vocabulary of 'symbol' and 'index'. In truth the distinction is not especially complicated, but it is very important.

BEYOND SYMBOLISM

The (primarily) literary distinction between metaphor and metonym has long been widely understood. The realm of semiotics includes the former within its category of 'symbols' and the latter in its category of 'indexes'.[30] The form of trope termed index or metonym makes a specific kind of reality claim. An index takes the form of a sign that (as smoke is a sign of fire) works because it has a real-life connection with its referent, unlike a symbol. In the alternative case of a symbol – as in the processes of metaphor and simile – two equivalents are posed, which have no connection in real life. For example, the line by Robert Burns, 'o my luve's like a red, red rose' is plainly in more than one sense very suspect as a reality claim (the reality to which it alludes is one of perceptual or emotional experience). Sport can work metaphorically, but often what begins as symbolic then moves toward the domain of the metonymic/indexical. To compare German football teams (when they are successful) to military units initially appears to be a metaphor, but this comparison, for example in the British media, works differently, indicating that the appropriate interpretative frame of this linguistic approach is indexical.

Previous research has argued that there are national variations in the nature and extent of inter-penetration between sport and culture,[31] but at its most forceful, sport becomes interpreted as a form of real life – actually it transcends its existence as a 'symbolic' medium.[32] It is in this light that we may understand the readiness, say, of much of the continental press to read German football as *indexical* of the German character. Efficiency, organization or even military character in German football teams are not 'equivalents' of the German character in general life. The traits visible on the football field are held to be continuous with traits in German culture and society, rather as Cameroon football players, as we saw above, can be presented as 'childlike' or 'innocent'; or French and Italians seen as possessing 'flair', but inconsistently and without northern 'character' (despite evidence to the contrary and despite these latter countries having 'northern' regions).

It is therefore appropriate to speak only loosely of sport's 'symbolic' activity. In fact the authors of its narratives often makes claims about other areas of life 'indexically' by holding it to be true that characteristics in sport are actually linked with the world in which it takes place. These reality claims are coupled with the immense power of sport to push its way into the news agenda, as has been seen; a formidable combination.

Much attention has been paid to the symbolic importance of mediated sport in its processing, in particular, of discourses of collective identity. Manuel Vázquez Montalbán describes Barça as 'the unarmed army of the Catalans',[33] but Montalbán, writing at the beginning of the 1990s, was already gloomily aware that the clarity with which Barça might signify the distinctness of Catalan culture was becoming muddied in post-modern Barcelona. The South End of the Nou Camp contains the *boixos nois* ('rough boys') who will wave any flag that is not red or Spanish. Asked why they carry Union Jacks, they respond: '"Per tocar els collons" ("To get up people's arses")'.[34] One contemporary response has been to read this kind of phenomenon as a post-modern breakdown in communication, variously described as 'post-symbolic' and also 'post-ideological'.

We could alternatively argue, however, that everything signifies something and that the brandishing of the British flag by the 'rough boys' at the Nou Camp expresses at the very least new forms of disaffection among Catalan youth. Symbolic realignments of this kind can be found in innumerable instances in sport. (If Glasgow Rangers are ever to play in the English League or Premiership, what will their supporters' Union Jacks, or their England strips, mean when displayed every fortnight in England? As signs, they are already quite complex in the Scottish context, but their functioning as forms of dissent, connected with real perceptions and attitudes, is not in doubt.)

In fact what we find, much of the time, in mediated sport and beyond mediated sport, is the assumption that sport is strongly connected with real life. It is understood not as an equivalent of real life, but as continuous with real life. This is more 'indexical' than 'symbolic'.

There are many losses to be faced in the contemporary world; of peace, of security, of habitats, of species, of beliefs in progress – most certainly of the utopian intuition, all but vanished – and of the sense of place. For many cultures this loss extends to the security of settled family life, of permanent paid work, of religion. How sport now functions and how it can be understood ontologically are rapidly shifting questions. Sport has become a highly developed symbolic universe and the media have been a central influence in its growth, but finally that is only a statement of the obvious, a recognition of the interdependence and connectedness of contemporary society and culture. The symbolic narrative structure thus created is larger than the sum of its parts.

Neither is it clear that this growth is that of an 'alternative world', with compensatory features of shared values and stability to turn to, in the difficult conditions of the real world. It is just as persuasive to understand sport as a domain of the real, which withstands the vicarious drift of electronic media, including the internet. Sport contains an impulse to experience the real. Even in its stereotyping of identities it often tends toward the real world of politics, its misrepresentations notwithstanding.

Likewise, the meanings implicit in its economic development are ambiguous. Shortfalls in the audience for digital sport can be read as produced by an exaggerated estimate of its popularity, but precisely the trend emphasized by digitization in television is the move toward demographic fracture which contrary impulses in mass-audience analogue television have always resisted. This opens up a choice of interpretations over the pace of digital development. In a single moment we can find an apparent mixture of signals – large stadia attendances, a plateau in media audiences, accelerating expenditure on sports consumer products – which caution us to be careful in our evaluation. There is much more, not least by empirical procedure, which needs to be done to understand the function of sport in its followers' lives and in culture generally.

This has been, in part, a plea in favour of keeping all the components in that process – 'culture', 'society', 'sport', 'media', 'economics', 'technology', 'ideology' and, implicitly at some stage in the investigation, 'self' – as strong terms in the inquiry. Yet more than that it has been, in particular, an argument about the need to treat the sport-media relationship with subtlety and not to let it obscure sport's especially interesting relationship with real life.

NOTES

1. G. Steiner, *In Bluebeard's Castle: Some Notes Towards the Redefinition of Culture* (New Haven, CT: Yale University Press, 1971).
2. J. Baudrillard, *Simulacra and Simulations* (New York: Sémiotext[e], 1983).
3. H.M. Enzensberger, 'The Zero Medium or Why All Complaints About Television Are Pointless', in idem, *Mediocrity and Delusion: Collected Diversions* (London: Verso, 1992).
4. J. Thompson, *Ideology and Modern Culture* (Cambridge: Polity, 1990), pp.12–20, 163–271.
5. D. Harvey, *The Condition of Postmodernity* (Oxford: Blackwell, 1990), p.147.
6. Ibid., p.156.
7. G. Whannel, *Fields in Vision* (London: Routledge, 1992).
8. L.A. Wenner, *MediaSport* (London: Routledge, 1998).
9. N. Elias and E. Dunning, *Quest for Excitement: Sport and Leisure in the Civilizing Process* (Oxford: Blackwell, 1986), p.156.
10. G. Whannel, *Media Sports Stars: Masculinities and Moralities* (London: Routledge, 2001).
11. N. Blain and H. O'Donnell, *Media, Monarchy and Power* (Bristol: Intellect, 2002).
12. www.skysports.com, 17 March 2002.
13. D. Boorstin *The Image: A Guide to Pseudo-Events in America* (New York: Harper Colophon, 1961), p.61.
14. 'Queen Elizabeth Steps into National Debate About State of Beck's Foot', www.hellomagazine.com, 26 April 2002.
15. N. Klein, *No Logo* (New York: Picador, 1999).
16. N. Blain and H. O'Donnell, 'Living Without the *Sun*: European Sports Journalism and its Readers During Euro '96', in M. Roche (ed.), *Sport, Popular Culture and Identity* (Aachen: Meyer and Meyer, 1998), pp.37–56; H. O'Donnell and N. Blain, 'Performing the Carmagnole: Negotiating French National Identity During France 98', *Journal of European Area Studies*, 7, 2 (1999), 211–25; N. Blain and H. O'Donnell, 'Current Trends in Media Sport and the Politics of Local Identities: A "Postmodern" Debate?', *Culture, Sport, Society*, 3, 2 (2000), 1–22.
17. C. Jencks, *What is Post-Modernism?* (London: Academy Editions, 1989), p.10; idem, *The Language of Postmodern Architecture* (London: Academy Editions, 1991), p.12.
18. I. Hassan, 'The Culture of Postmodernism', *Theory, Culture and Society*, 2, 3 (1985), 123–4.
19. O'Donnell and Blain, 'Performing the Carmagnole'.
20. N. Blain, R. Boyle and H. O'Donnell, *Sport and National Identity in the European Media* (Leicester: Leicester University Press, 1993), pp.18–36.
21. U. Eco, *Reflections on the Name of the Rose* (London: Secker and Warburg, 1985).
22. Where Baudrillard began to teach sociology in 1966: J. Baudrillard, *Symbolic Exchange and Death* (London: Sage, 1993), originally published as *L'exchange symbolique et la mort* (Paris: Gallimard, 1976).
23. After Kilmarnock pies lost their top status in a national competition in 1998, the commercial director of the club, Jim McSherry, noted that:
   Real men don't eat quiche and Killie fans will continue to eat meat pies at the game. This was some chicken and mushroom thing that won, but we still sell the top meat pies in British football. This isn't sour grapes or sour pies, but meat pies traditionally go with football. Are we really getting so far away from our roots that we're not eating meat pies at half-time? Nothing else goes as well with your Bovril'. (S. Breen, 'Pie Throwing Starts as Killie Loses Snack Crown', *Scotsman*, 7 Feb. 1998.)
   In fact much doubt has been cast over the uniqueness of the pie, also allegedly supplied to other clubs.
24. O. Gibson, 'Further Doubt Cast on Switchover Plans', *Guardian*, 3 May 2002.
25. R. Boyle and R. Haynes, *Power Play: Sport, the Media and Popular Culture* (London: Longman, 1999).
26. M. Maffesoli, *The Time of the Tribes* (London: Sage, 1996), p.46.

27. F. Jameson, *Postmodernism, or, the Cultural Logic of Late Capitalism* (London: Verso, 1991), p.48.
28. Maffesoli, *The Time of the Tribes*, p.44.
29. Ibid., pp.12–13.
30. P. Guiraud, *Semiology* (London: Routledge Kegan Paul, 1975).
31. Blain and O'Donnell, 'Living Without the *Sun*'.
32. N. Blain and R. Boyle, 'Sport As Real Life: Media, Sport And Culture', in A. Briggs and P. Cobley (eds.), *The Media: An Introduction* (London: Longman, 2nd Edn. 2002), pp.415–26.
33. M. Vázquez Montalbán, *Barcelonas* (London: Verso, 1992), p.40.
34. Ibid., pp.189–90.

Notes on Contributors

Alina Bernstein is a lecturer at the Film and Television Department, Tel Aviv University, Israel. Her main area of research is media and sport. Among her recent publications is the 'Representation, Identity and the Media' section in *The Media Book* (2002).

Neil Blain is Professor of Media and Culture at the University of Paisley. He has published widely on cultural and political dimensions of collective identity. A co-author of *Sport and National Identity in the European Media* (1993), his most recent work is *Media, Monarchy and Power* (2002, with Hugh O'Donnell).

Raymond Boyle is a member of the Stirling Media Research Institute at Stirling University, Scotland and of the editorial board of *Media, Culture and Society*. He is the co-author (with Richard Haynes) of *Power Play: Sport, the Media and Popular Culture* (2000).

Rinella Cere lectures in Media and Cultural Studies at Sheffield Hallam University. She has written articles on Italian media culture and representations of women and, more recently, on the internet and new social movements, including feminism and women's liberation.

Pamela J. Creedon began her interest in sports research while directing the Public Information and Sports Information Office at Mount Union College in Alliance, Ohio. Editor of *Women, Media and Sport* (1994), she served as a faculty member at the Ohio State University from 1984–94, director of the School of Journalism and Mass Communication at Kent State University in Ohio from 1994–2002 and is now director of the School of Journalism and Mass Communications at the University of Iowa.

Richard Haynes is a member of the Stirling Media Research Institute at Stirling University, Scotland. His publications include *The Football Imagination: The Rise of Football Fanzine Culture* (1995) and *Power Play: Sport, the Media and Popular Culture* (2000, with Raymond Boyle).

Mirko Marr is a lecturer and Ph.D. candidate in communication science at the Institute of Mass Communication and Media Research at the University of Zurich. His research interests include computer-mediated communication, journalism and media sport.

Hugh O'Donnell is Professor of Language and Popular Culture at Glasgow Caledonian University. He specializes in comparative analyses of popular cultural products on a pan-European level and has published widely on sport, soap opera and representations of monarchy. He is currently working on a comparative analysis of situation comedies.

Nancy Rivenburgh is an associate professor in the Department of Communication at the University of Washington. She is the co-author of *Television in the Olympics* (1995) and has conducted research on the Seoul, Barcelona, Atlanta and Sydney Games. She was named International Professor of Olympism for 1997–98 by the Centre for Olympic Studies (Barcelona) and International Olympic Committee.

Amir Saeed is a lecturer in Media and Cultural Studies at the University of Sunderland. He holds a Ph.D. in national identity and British Muslims from Glasgow Caledonian University and his current research interests are in the field of race and ethnic studies.

Hans-Joerg Stiehler has been Professor for Empirical Media Research at the Institute for Communication and Media Science, University of Leipzig since 1993. His research interests include media and sport, the use of the media in East Germany and the history of television in the German Democratic Republic.

Stanley T. Wearden is Associate Professor of Journalism and Mass Communication at Kent State University, where he has worked since 1984. He holds a Ph.D. in mass communication research from the University of North Carolina at Chapel Hill. His research interests include images of women in mass media, accuracy in television news, user perceptions of website credibility and user perceptions of the utility and navigability of electronic publications.

Garry Whannel is Professor of Media Cultures and director of the Centre for International Media Analysis at the University of Luton. His publications include *Media Sport Stars: Masculinities and Moralities* (2001) and *Fields in Vision: Television Sport and Cultural Transformation* (1992).

Index

Danish model of (*Roligans*), 166
football, 15, 24, 82, 85, 109–11, 121, 131,
  142, 159, 166–84, 214, 221–5, 239, 243,
  246
international types in football, 166
Italian model of, 166
Italian women *ultrà*, in alternative media,
  176–9
of Bologna, 170, 175, 180–81, 184
of Genoa, 179, 180, 183
organizing committee (*direttivo*) in Italy,
  167, 172, 184
politics, of *ultrà* support (Italy), 170–76
South American model of (*bailado*), 166
twinning (*gemellaggi*) between in Italy,
  167–8, 179
fanzines, *ultrà* fans in Italy, 167
female athletes, media portrayal of, 7–9,
  189–208
feminist critique of sport, 6–9
Figo, L., 108
'flexible accumulation' and sport, 229–33
Foot, of David Beckham, 233–7
football
  and national identity, 15–16, 84–6,
    139–63, 220, 235–6, 246–7, 250–51
  and race and ethnicity, 18–19, 216
  English Premier League, 75, 103–8, 111,
    245, 251
  FA Cup, 75, 77, 83, 84
  German media coverage, 140–44, 148–63
  international fan types, 166
  international support, 166
  Israeli Premiership League, 130
  Italian fans, 166–84
  Italian *ultrà* fans in media, 173, 176–9,
    181–3
  League Cup, England, 88, 89
  League Cup, Scotland, 109
  Scottish Premier League, 212, 243
  World Cup, 13–15, 18, 22, 23, 24, 34, 38,
    74, 75, 83, 90, 120, 132–3, 135, 139–63,
    236, 239
Ford, G., 63
Fordism and sport, 229–30
Foreman, G., 12, 63
Forza Italia, 173
Franco, F., 220
Frankfurt School, 228

Gardell, M., 56
Garvey, M., 56
Gascoigne, P., 245
Gay Olympics, 11
gemellaggi (twinning) among *ultrà* fans, 167–8,
  179

Gender Advertisements (Goffman), 193–4
gender
  and collective identity, 5–12, 73–92,
    166–84, 189–208
  in media and sport research, 5–12
  stereotyping, 8, 176, 183, 192–5, 198,
    203–6
  terminological questions, 5–6, 8–9, 10–12
gendered products, commercials for, 203
Genoa supporters, 179, 180, 183
German
  'character', accounts of, 140, 159, 250
  media coverage (football), 140–44, 148–63
  national side (football), Austrian and
    Swiss attitudes to, 151
  national side in European Championship
    (football), 139–43, 149–63
  national side, in World Cup (football),
    139–43, 149–63
  national side, indigenous attitudes toward,
    139–63
Germany vs.
  Bulgaria (football), 1994, reporting of,
    140–44, 149–63
  Croatia (football), 1998, reporting of,
    140–44, 149–63
  Czech Republic (football), 1996, reporting
    of, 140–44, 149–63
  Portugal (football), 2000, reporting of,
    151–4, 160
Gilady, A., 2, 5, 24
  biography of, 116–17
Gilly, M.C., 194
Ginsborg, P., 170
global reach of sport, 17, 31–48, 51, 66, 70, 74,
  95–113, 119–22, 246
globalization, 1, 4, 12, 21, 31–48, 65, 116,
  246–7
  as research topic, 21–4
Goffman, E., 193
gratification and media sport, 161–3
Great Britain women's curling team, Salt Lake
  City, 229, 232, 239
Guevara, C., 172

Haley, A., 66
Hall, S., 64, 183
Hamilton, R., 227
Harris, J., 9
Harvey, D., 229–30
Harvey, J. *et al.*, 22
Hassan, I., 238–9
hegemony and gender relations, 6, 8–9
Heider, F., 144–5
Hello! magazine, 76, 78, 233
Hendry, S., 99

BRUNEL UNIVERSITY LIBRARY

Bannerman Centre,
Uxbridge Middlesex,
UB8 3 PH

Renewals: www.brunel.ac.uk/renew
OR
01895 266141

OVERNIGHT LOAN

ONE RENEWAL ONLY

Printed in the United Kingdom
by Lightning Source
103344UKS00001B/

60 4084587 7

9   80714 682617